Dawn Breaks In The East

To dear Ricardo Hernandez
and his family,

May the Lord

direct your steps
to Himself!

Br. Peter Zhou, O.S.B.
周郁蕃 9/26/99

Dawn Breaks In The East

One Spiritual Warrior's Thirty-three Year Struggle In Defense Of The Church

Br. Peter Zhou Bangjiu, O.S.B.

Maria Stein, OH

Copyright ©1992 by Serenity

Editors: Cynthia Clark, Jim Moeller, Fr. Simon O'Donnell, O.S.B.,
        Br. Thomas Babusis,O.S.B., Carolyn Humphreys, O.C.D.S.,
        Ken Moeller

Graphics: Ken Moeller
Cover Photograph: Dennis Frates, " Mt. Rainier at Sunset,"
        Oregon Scenics, Monroe, OR

Published by:
        Serenity,
        8016 Marion Dr.,
        Maria Stein, OH 45860
        (800) 869-1684

Bangjiu, O.S.B., Br. Peter Zhou
        Dawn Breaks In The East

ISBN 1-881614-00-X
Library of Congress Catalog
Card Number: 92-060393

Printed in the United States

10 9 8 7 6 5 4 3 2

978188161400

NOTE BY THE PUBLISHER

In 1988 while watching a local news segment, "Spiritual Warrior," I first heard of Br. Peter's long and arduous battle with the Communists. So impressed was I with his spiritual strength and with the poignancy of his struggle, I contacted him at his Benedictine priory in Valyermo, California. He in turn sent me his first manuscript, which he had been working on since 1985.

I read what he had written and told him the story was powerful, but the work needed to complete it was far beyond the capabilities and finances of my small music label, named **Serenity.**

The project was set aside for a couple of years, but I often read sections of the manuscript to again feel the spiritual strength of Br. Peter.

Finally I shared the manuscript with a friend, Cynthia Clark, my oldest son's English teacher. I asked her for her opinion of the writings. She was impressed with Br. Peter in the same way I was. I then asked her if she would consider becoming the editor for the project, and she agreed.

I called Br. Peter the following day to ask him if he had found a publisher. He said he hadn't, and added that it "must be coincidence" since he had mailed me his updated manuscript the previous day and was going to ask me to reconsider publishing it. The package arrived less than an hour later.

"Coincidence?" I often hear that "coincidence is nothing more than God working anonymously." I don't believe that anything about this project is coincidental.

Since we published the first edition I have had a chance to spend more and more time with Br. Peter. With each visit I feel an increasing sense of peace because "on a lifetime scale" he has done what most of us have trouble doing daily, and that is forgive. With each day he has continued, through prayer, to go deeper inside of himself. He intuitively knows that with each level he will become even closer to God.

Two thank-you's: to Cynthia Clark for accepting the challenge, bringing this story of healing to a world so desperately in need of it; Br. Peter for showing me, and all future readers, a most unusual way to God.

Now read, enjoy, and most important "feel the words" of Br. Peter.

Jim Moeller
Publisher

TABLE OF CONTENTS

Part III First Collection of Poems

FOREWORD BY FATHER PRIOR
TO THE FIRST EDITION

I stood in astonished disbelief one day in 1981 as I read a letter forwarded to me from the People's Republic of China. I felt as if I was receiving a message from the grave. Br. Peter, a vowed member of our community, had disappeared without a trace into the Red Chinese Gulag. We had not heard from him for twenty-five years since the brutal and ruthless Communist regime had arrested him in 1955. He was presumed dead. His miraculous survival and escape from the jaws of death are described in the pages of this book.

Suffering is never a popular subject. People who are not experiencing it, don't want to hear about it. People who are, only want to get rid of it as quickly as possible. After delivering a homily on the theme of personal suffering in union with Christ, I was confronted by a middle-aged woman, obviously offended by the subject. "Have you ever suffered?" she asked. "Probably not," I replied, "but a member of our community has spent twenty-six years in prison under torture for his Faith in Christ." She fell silent, unexpectedly, and asked no further question.

"But doesn't the subject of suffering make a person depressed?" people will wonder. Without the understanding which our Faith in Christ provides, suffering is totally unacceptable and intolerable. It has neither meaning nor purpose. God, in choosing this pathway for His Son, Jesus, gave us a sacred dimension to our suffering such as the world has never dreamed possible. Even as human sin, the mystery of iniquity, is incomprehensible, so also is its consequence, human suffering. In the inspired words of the Apostle Paul, we have the clear expression of the redemptive value of personal suffering: "Even now I find my joy in the suffering I endure for you. In my own flesh I fill up what is lacking in the sufferings of Christ for the sake of his body, the Church." (Col. 1:24)

We might ask, "How does the description of extreme human suffering such as Br. Peter endured provide any help for us ordinary people?" I believe this help comes to us in two ways: First, I think we all too easily lose perspective in our suffering which looms larger than life simply because we feel so alone in our pain. Psychological research now shows that our willing attitude of acceptance of the suffering does the most to mobilize our interior ability to cope as well as releasing physical substances amazingly powerful in counteracting pain. Reading about extreme human suffering reminds us that others have successfully overcome much more, and this lifts us out of our self-pity. Then we come to a more important positive awareness: "God keeps His promise. He will give you a way out of it so that you may be able to endure it." (ICor. 10:13) The lived experience of Br. Peter tends to establish the truth of this assurance of the Apostle Paul to the Corinthians beyond the shadow of a doubt. Jesus, Himself, invites us: "Come to me, all you who are weary and find life burdensome, and I will refresh you . . . Your souls will find rest, for my yoke is easy and my burden light." (Mt. 11:28 - 30).

Fr. Prior John Borgerding, O.S.B.
St. Andrew's Priory
Valyermo, CA

PREFACE BY BROTHER PETER
TO THE FIRST EDITION

On November 27, 1984, I set foot on American soil and rejoined the Priory I had been separated from for more than thirty years. I determined then that rather than studying for the priesthood, the most pressing and important task for me was to put on paper the poems and *The Song of Life* kept in my mind for all these years and to write down my experiences under persecution.

This plan emerged even in those years of incarceration, especially during my solitary confinements. There are many priests in the Church and the Priory, but very few survivors of the Chinese Communist religious persecution who remained loyal to the Lord and yet walked out of the dark prison and passed through the Bamboo Curtain. I firmly believe that the experiences of these survivors can encourage and benefit the Church as well as the rest of the world, and hence are worth recording and publicizing. This is why, for me, the work of writing took precedence to priestly ordination.

Some opinions expressed in this book may differ from those of certain members of the Church. Nonetheless, I believe that they should be expressed all the same. They are personal; but, I suggest, worthy of consideration. In our age the Communist Party has forced dictatorial regimes upon many countries. It has harmed the minds and bodies of millions of people. It has caused wars, tensions, persecutions, massacres, terror and famine. As one of those who has suffered under such a regime, I have, I believe, the right and the responsibility to expose and denounce its crimes, to urge changes for the better and to attempt to attract more attention from the international community. The gall is bitter, as one who has tasted it knows too well! The more afraid we are, the more the Communist Party will bully us. Instead, the more steadfastly we struggle against it, the more vulnerable will its menace be and the more certain of victory and freedom will we be.

Massive student demonstrations for democracy took place in Peking and many other cities in China from April 16 to June 3, 1989. These demonstrations won extensive sympathy and support from the people within and outside the country, and greatly embarrassed the Red regime. In order to maintain their tottering dictatorship and continue to keep the Chinese people in slavery, the Communist hard-liners resorted to military force. They killed thousands of innocent and unarmed people. They have continued their cruel policies, hunting, imprisoning, torturing, and killing the leaders and activists. And up to this moment, the Roman Catholic Church in

China remains forbidden.

The Communists in power still oppress loyal Catholics as witness the savage attack on April 18, 1989, against 1,500 of the faithful in the village of Youtong in Luancheng County, southwest of Peking. More than one hundred clerics and laymen have been arrested since November 1989. The Communist Government continues to make use of and to maintain under strict control the so-called "Patriotic church." They have strengthened the pressure on loyal Catholics to force them to renounce their Faith and to participate in the activities of the official church. According to the *San Francisco Chinese Catholic Newsletter* No. 111 of September 1989, the Chinese Communist Government in Hebei Province issued order No. 26, banning all religious activities of the underground Catholic Church. They attempt in vain to uproot the dissidence, dissatisfaction, indignation and resistance of the people once and for all. They continue to try to close the door of the Mainland to isolate their national territory. Obviously, as long as these circumstances exist, there is no freedom of religion in the Chinese Mainland.

But today is no longer the same as yesterday. Our time is an age of progress, democracy and freedom. The Chinese people have already been awakened. They will never be subjected again to the Communist regime as they once were. Their resistance will never completely be broken, as the great poet, Bai Juyi (772-846), in the Tang Dynasty expressed in one of his poems:

> "Not even a prairie fire
> Can destroy the grass;
> It grows again
> When the spring breeze blows!"

The Communist diehards in power are doomed to failure because people cannot be oppressed forever. Those who live in the free world should do what they can to help their brothers and sisters in Communist China to attain a free political and religious society. In addition to prayers, we should not stop exposing and condemning the Communist rule. We should put constant pressure on them. This book intends, in its small way, to help reach this great goal.

On April 2, 1989, Mrs. Dolores Chavez of San Gabriel, California, visited St. Andrew's Priory, my monastic home here in Valyermo, with her husband Gilbert and their four friends. After a nice talk, I presented her with copies of my manuscripts. On April 13 she called me, telling that she had been deeply touched even to tears while reading my story. Two days later she paid another visit to me with her husband, expressing her deep feelings and offering another donation in thanksgiving. She confided that she had found herself to be closer to the Lord than ever before and to be filled with great confidence and new hope in life. This utterly personal and entirely positive reaction from Dolores' mouth was an inspiration to me and compelled me to continuously strive for the eventual publication of my book, hoping to give others the same opportunity to affect their hearts and spiritual lives.

This writing comes from the hands of a Chinese. The story that it relates took place in the land of China. It therefore goes without saying that Chinese ways of logical thinking and natural expression and a number of new as well as old Chinese proverbs are frequently found here and there in the text. Most of the Chinese typical verses, allusions, proverbs, sayings and idioms in the original text have been preserved in this English version. This is attributed both to the great effort made by Fr. Bernard Hwang Kuo-wei in his translation, and to the active support and guidance given by Dr. Loretta Matulich, Mr. John Desmond, Fr. Denis Molaise Meehan, O.S.B., Mr. Ken Parker, Mr. Joe Duquette, Miss Jean DeBettignies and Mr. Edward Littlejohn in their revision. In a sense, their help has played the role of a link for mutual understanding between East and West in the different ways of expressing and interpreting our thoughts and feelings.

Han Fei, an ancient Chinese philosopher (280-233 B.C.), wrote, "It is impossible to make a sound if one claps, however fast, with one palm." Indeed, without divine favors, without the support of others, I could not have succeeded in recounting the history of my struggle, writing my old and my new poems, and then, especially, completing the process of translating all these Chinese originals into English. Consequently, in thanksgiving for the mercy of God, I have also to express my heartfelt and special gratitude to Fr. Prior John Borgerding, O.S.B., and the whole monastic community at Valyermo for giving me all the time necessary for writing and to many friends for their assistance.

It is impossible for me to thank individually all who have helped me with this book, translating, editing, reviewing, typing, providing pictures, and in many other ways. All my sincere appreciation and constant prayers go to all who have supported and accompanied me throughout the long journey to publication.

With love and respectful obedience,
Brother Peter
Easter Sunday, April 15, 1990

REMARKS

1.   The current Pinyin System is used for the transliteration of all Chinese names in this book, except Peking (Beijing), Canton (Guangzhou), Hong Kong (Xianggang), Kowloon (Jiulong), Sishan (Xishan), and all those of persons living outside the Chinese Mainland and having their own spellings.

2.   All the Biblical quotations are taken from The New American Bible by Catholic Publishers, Inc., 1971, a Division of Thomas Nelson, Inc., Nashville, Camden, New York.

3.   In the translation of the poetry in this text a fundamental effort has been made to keep the meaning, without reproducing the difficult harmonies of the proper rhythms and rhymes of the Chinese characters.

4.   In all sincerity, I have never been good at penmanship, and to write some of the poems of this book in Chinese calligraphy was a tedious job because of the handicap of my right hand. Nevertheless, I have done my best to make the Chinese characters as pleasing as possible not only to the eye but also to the mind of the reader.

5.   The expressions, "accusation meeting", "criticism meeting", "struggle meeting" and "criticism-struggle-meeting", used in this text mean meetings of a small or large crowd of people, more or less wild, to accuse, to criticize or to struggle against the "faults" or "criminal" actions, words, thoughts, articles, literary and artistic works and so forth of a person, a group or an organization. These meetings, lasting from one to several days, or even from one week to one month, or sometimes longer, were used to force the victims to bow down and surrender under the strong pressure of endless shouts, reproaches, insults, beatings and tortures. This had been the most usual, the most extensive and the most constant way applied by Mao Zedong and the followers of his cruel regime to rule, control, oppress and persecute the people, including the common and leading members of his Chinese Communist Party.

獻 詞

—敬獻與榮福童貞聖母瑪利亞

天地皇后，永世童貞，
長助寫作，鳴謝書呈。

烈女元后，助我勝獸；
續援羣孩，戰而凱奏。

中華聖母，垂憫神州！
祈為求得，統一自由！

大能寬仁 救主母親，
促令共黨，領取救恩。

和平之后 憐愛萬民，
和平友愛，望賜紅塵。

DEDICATION

To the Virgin Mary, Our Blessed Mother

Queen of Heaven and Earth,
Ever-Virgin,
You have long helped me write this book.
I present it to you in thanksgiving.

Queen of Martyrs,
With your help
I triumphed over the Beast.
To fight and defeat it,
Come to the assistance of all your children.

Queen of China,
Have pity on the country!
Pray, win for it
Freedom and unity!

Powerful and merciful,
Mother of our Savior,
Please lead the Communists
To receive the grace of salvation.

Queen of Peace,
Gracious to all peoples,
We implore you:
Bring to the world
Peace and charity.

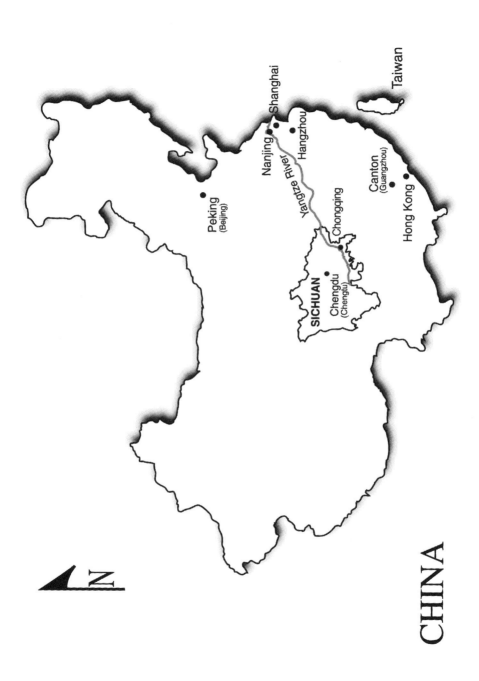

N

Taiwan

Shanghai
Nanjing
Hangzhou
Yangtze River
Canton
(Guangzhou)
Chongqing
Hong Kong
Peking
(Beijing)
SICHUAN
Chengdu
(Chengdu)

CHINA

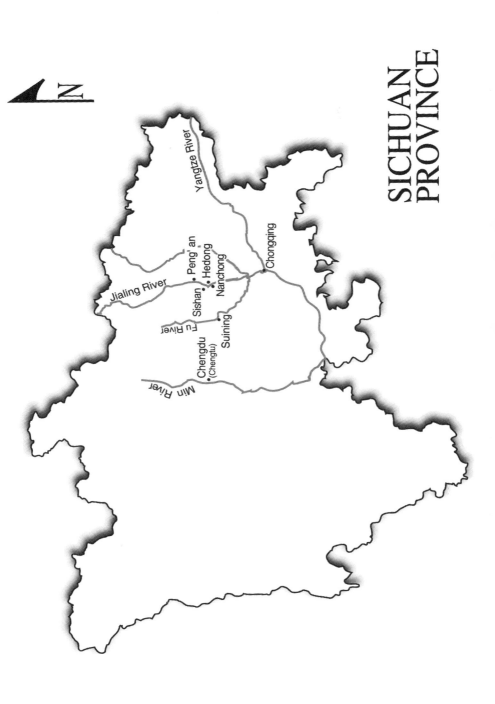

FOREWORD BY FATHER ABBOT
TO THE UPDATED EDITION

Fourteen years ago, Brother Peter returned to his monastic community after 30 years of separation. I was among the younger monks who witnessed his homecoming to an unfamiliar country and to a place he had never seen. It was an overwhelming experience for me to see our brother for whom we had prayed nightly at Compline for many decades. He was here with us alive to resume his Benedictine monastic life. He came to Vespers that first night and to dinner. We had prepared chopsticks for his first meal with us and he pushed them aside to eat with Western silverware--a sign that he was ready to adapt himself to a new culture. After dinner, he wanted to see Father Gaetan privately to go to confession and to receive Holy Communion after so many years without the benefit of these Sacraments. He had indeed waited long enough.

Since our separation from him by the Communist ideology, the vast Pacific Ocean, and by three decades of scientific and social change, the Roman Catholic Church had itself undergone a great self-assessment through the Second Vatican Council. The Church that Brother Peter knew was the same in doctrine and yet changed in form. The Eucharist and the Liturgy of the Hours were said in the vernacular now. We sang several Latin chants at his first Mass with the community so that he would feel at home with some of what we were doing. It was more than touching to see him receive Holy Communion with us that first day and for many months and it put a profound gratitude into our hearts, not only that he had survived but that he was a reminder to us of the privilege of religious freedom that we had heretofore taken for granted.

In those early days, each one of us wanted Brother Peter to feel at home. We made every possible accommodation to him to compensate for the brutality to which he had been subjected. It became apparent that his only need was for the God who had sustained him in prayer. He desired also to live again his cherished monastic vocation and to publicly and solemnly profess those vows he had been faithful to under the most taxing of circumstances.

Brother Peter asked for paper to begin writing. During his years of imprisonment, his soul expressed itself in prayer and in poetry. He committed every verse to memory. He discerned

God calling him to write down everything he had composed. If he had survived, for what purpose? What could God want of him in this newfound freedom?

Brother Peter found within his monastic vocation a new vocation: to encourage many to greater faithfulness to God and to the Church, to cling to the riches of the Sacramental life in the obedience of faith in union with the Vicar of Christ. He suffered persecution; imprisonment and torture not just because he was a Catholic Christian but specifically because he was doggedly faithful to the Pope and could not admit of a Church divided from the authority of the successor of St. Peter.

He saw the effects of Communist brainwashing on many Chinese Catholic priests and laity, which twisted their perspective and seduced them into capitulation to the rhetoric of isolation from the Universal Pastor. Brother Peter was willing to die for the fullness of his Catholic faith and fought against this ideological violence which had broken down so many others around him. In the solitude of his imprisonment, his religious convictions remained intact while his trials were multiplied because he would not affirm the teaching of Mao in any of its atheistic and anti-Catholic perspectives.

The doctrine for which Brother Peter suffered so much was eloquently expressed in the Second Vatican Council's Dogmatic Constitution on the Church, _Lumen Gentium_. "22. Just as, in accordance with the Lord's decree, St. Peter and the rest of the apostles constitute a unique apostolic college, so in like fashion the Roman Pontiff, Peter's successor, and the bishops, the successors of the apostles, are related with and united to one another...*The college or body of bishops has for all that no authority unless united with the Roman Pontiff, Peter's successor, as its head, whose primatial authority,* let it be added, over all, whether pastors or faithful, remains in its integrity. For the Roman Pontiff, by reason of his office as Vicar of Christ, namely, as pastor of the entire Church, has full, supreme and universal power over the whole Church, a power which he can always exercise unhindered. The order of bishops is the successor to the college of the apostles in their role as teachers and pastors, and in it the apostolic college is perpetuated. Together with their head, the Supreme Pontiff, and *never apart from him,* they have supreme and full authority over the universal Church; but *this power cannot be exercised without the agreement of the Roman Pontiff.* The Lord made Peter alone the rock-foundation and the holder of the keys of the Church (Mt.16: 18-19) and constituted him shepherd of his whole flock (cf. Jn. 21: 15 ff)"…"23....The Roman Pontiff, as the successor of Peter, is the *perpetual and visible source and foundation of unity both of the bishops and of the whole company of the faithful."*

His Holiness, Pope John Paul II has had a great longing to see the Church in China fully in communion again with the Supreme Pontiff. He has shown his profound solicitude toward the suffering members of the Underground Church. He has also made every effort to draw under his pastoral care those of the Open Church who have in various ways cooperated with the Communist authorities in maintaining a Catholic Church without open or apparent ties to the Vicar of Christ.

In this regard, many bishops have secretly professed allegiance to the Supreme Pontiff without openly declaring themselves to the Communist Patriotic Association. In the Open Church, the Pope is now prayed for vocally within the Eucharistic Prayers. While the two Churches coexist in a relative peace in some parts of China, the Underground Church meets with terrible persecution and animosity in other areas.

The healing of the two Churches and the future open reunion of all Chinese Catholics under the authority of the universal Pastor are not yet a reality. What Brother Peter suffered for is an absolute fidelity to Christ and His Church through the *perpetual and visible source and foundation of unity.* He is a spokesman for the suffering Underground Church in China. I pray that Brother Peter's sufferings and the sufferings of other Chinese Catholics will make fertile the soil of the People's Republic of China for Catholicism to grow and flourish in that society. And I pray that the minds and hearts of its political leaders will be opened to the people in such a way that their human rights and their religious freedom may once again be respected.

I believe that Brother Peter's life and faith, suffering and witness have not been in vain. May all who read this book be inspired to live courageously the gift of faith and be a leaven of truth and holiness of life for you as he has been for us his monastic community.

Abbot Francis Benedict, O.S.B.
Valyermo, California
July 16, 1999
Feast of Our Lady of Mount Carmel

PREFACE BY BROTHER PETER
TO THE UPDATED EDITION

Seven years ago, just after the appearance of the first edition of the book, the idea for revising it had already come into my mind. Since February 1994, with the help of Mrs. Pat Feller and Miss Jean DeBettignies, and especially since the fall of 1995, under the direction of Br. Thomas Babusis, O.S.B., I undertook the first step. I edited the book while rewriting the Chinese original. Nevertheless, a careful and complete revision could begin only in the fall of 1996, when Mrs. Frederique Barloy of Paris, France, had completed her French translation of the book, which deeply inspired me. In the light of her work, I strongly felt the necessity to do a detailed revision of the first English edition. Without Mrs. Barloy's translation this new edition would never have been born.

Truly, I am very much obliged to render thanks to God for His special favor: to proclaim to many more people the message He would have willed me to proclaim, and thus to let the hearts of my future readers draw profit from my experiences. In January 1996, He gave Mrs. Barloy a desire to translate my book into French. Endowed with high ideals and uncommon zeal, she devoted all her available time to this work and completed the first draft by the following June, a short period of less than half a year. Yet, what was in particular most admirable and less evident was her consent in the fall of 1996 to resume her translation from the beginning as I had suggested. It was precisely from this time that I started to read attentively her translation which contained many excellent alterations worthy of an introduction to the English version.

It was during the summer vacation of 1948 that I had the opportunity to learn French in China. I had less than a half-year for regular study and about two years for self-study. Today, after an interruption of more than forty years, it is natural that my French is much rustier than my English. And accordingly, the revision was really a demanding work for me. At first, I had to read slowly the French translation and simultaneously the English text. Then I evaluated all the French changes, translated most of them into English, and added them to the English text. While doing this I strove to correct errors discovered in words and expressions, to clarify obscure phrases or events, to make the English text more smooth and refined and to supplement new materials whenever necessary. During the entire course of the review, Br. Thomas Babusis, O.S.B., and Fr. Simon O'Donnell, O.S.B., supported me with their precious and indispensable guidance in editing. In late December 1996, the former left Valyermo for Belgium to pursue his study of theology. Then, the latter began generously to undertake this tedious work until the planned publication of the English text in August 1999 and of the French version by the end of the same year. Meanwhile, Mrs. Barloy made a concerted effort on her part with a cooperative spirit and unusual patience. Giving consideration to each one of my suggestions, she did all the necessary changes and additions. We had worked with one heart and achieved together an ideal and satisfactory text both in English and in French.

———————

Seven years have passed since the first edition of the book at the end of July 1992. During this entire period, political, social and religious events, more or less positive, have taken place in the world. It is regrettable to see, however, that the situation of the Catholic Church in Communist China has not known such improvement as has the economy of the country. The Church remains under the same repressed conditions as forty-nine years ago, groaning under the weight of Communist dictatorship and attacked as a main target of their savage opposition and onslaught against God. The current tragic plight of the Church there can be mirrored concretely and unambiguously in an official Chinese Communist governmental document. On October 16, 1997, their State Council Information Office issued a declaration, a so-called "White Paper", under the title of *Freedom Of Religious Belief In China*. Reading the last paragraph of the fourth part, which especially concerns the Catholic Church, you will see how strange and incoherent this declaration appears:

> "The Chinese government has consistently adhered
> to a peaceful foreign policy of independence and
> taking initiative in its own hands, and is willing
> to improve the relations with the Vatican. However,
> such improvement requires two basic conditions:
> First, the Vatican must end its so-called diplomatic
> relations with Taiwan and recognize that the gov-
> ernment of the People's Republic of China is the only

legal government in China and that Taiwan is an inalienable part of China's territory. Second, the Vatican must not interfere in China's internal affairs on the pretext of religious affairs. In the first place, the relationship between China and the Vatican is one between two countries. Therefore, only when the relations between the two countries improve can religious issues be discussed. Whether the relations between China and the Vatican change or not, the Chinese government will, as always, support Chinese Catholicism which holds aloft the banner of patriotism, sticks to the principle of independence and self-management, and stands for selection and ordination of bishops by itself."

From this passage we can see very clearly that the Chinese Communist attitude towards the Vatican and their policy regarding the Catholic Church on the Mainland have not changed one iota since the early fifties when they set off the first terrifying waves of persecution. On the one hand, they stubbornly reject the primacy of the Sovereign Pontiff over the Church, including the appointment of bishops, as is accepted by all other countries of the world. On the other hand, they continue persecuting the underground Catholic Church while entirely controlling and enslaving the official Patriotic church. They call their own domestic interference in, and absolute domination over, religious affairs by the fine-sounding phrases of "fully respecting and legally protecting religious freedom" and of "Chinese religions' principle of independence and self-administration". Without uttering a single word about the real measures of religious restriction and the real act of religious oppression, they have only kept on talking about the articles of the Constitution and laws on religious freedom and protection, putting nothing into practice at all. They have never acknowledged the reality of their persecution of the Catholic Church, but on the contrary, they have always defended themselves by denying their lawless behavior in every possible way. They even have the audacity to brag unblushingly and allege obstinately that their people, as those in all the other countries, have been enjoying the same liberty in all aspects. For almost a half-century they have filled the people within and outside the country with lies both on religious issues and in many other fields. In this, they deserve to be called faithful disciples of the German Nazi Propaganda Minister, Paul Joseph Goebbels (1897-1945), whose notorious adage they practice to the letter: "Repeat a lie a thousand times, and it becomes a truth!"

The Communist document was released to the press on the eve of their leader Jiang Zemin's visit to the United States. Their intention fooled no one. For in reality, the more they sought to hide their course of action, the more obvious was the truth revealed, somewhat like the man in a Chinese folk tale, who put a sign over the place where he had buried the money: "There are not three hundred taels of silver here!" For the people in the know and with a sense of justice, this was simply to offer a velvet glove, to reveal their own guilty conscience and to act like a buffoon! Nevertheless, the facts are all there, and facts speak louder than words! "When there is no freedom of religious belief" can mean nothing except "there is no freedom of religious belief"! All justifications in words or in writing are of no avail and are totally in vain.

This "White Paper" clearly exposes to the view of the good people in China, as well as in the rest of the world, the hideous hegemonical character of the Chinese Communists. Before establishing diplomatic relations with them, they go so far as to command the Vatican to submit to their demands, demands both grave and immoderate. The Vatican has not only a profound concern for the ten million Catholics in their occupied area, but also has had a great care for the salvation of the more than one billion Chinese people, including the Communists themselves. It is just for this reason that the Vatican is inclined to improve relations with them.

In the early fifties, the Chinese Communists had succeeded, by armed force, deceitful propaganda and false promises of democracy, freedom and happiness, in gaining the victory over the National Government and occupying the Mainland. From then on they have never abandoned their plan to conquer the island of Taiwan. They have maintained their arbitrary and groundless position that their dictatorial power is the only legal government in China, and that Taiwan is an inalienable part of their territory. Ironically and tragically, it was right during the most terrible and darkest crisis of the Cultural Revolution that they had actually managed to get their schemes adopted by 76 votes for, 35 against and 17 abstentions during the United

Nations General Assembly on October 25, 1971. Since that date they were authorized to take the place of the Chinese National Government, a founding member who now found itself ousted from the world body. From then onward, they have sought in a thousand and one ways to isolate Taipei in the world community and at the same time, to subject it to the constant menace of armed invasion. They have never diminished their efforts, by granting commercial gains or by assuring economic aid, to rope in countries to recognize them officially. In spite of this, they have benefited the most from favorable balances of trade by exporting large quantities of goods, including antipersonnel firearms, which have not been without creating a certain social unrest, notably in the United States. Otherwise, they resort to pressure, protest and menace to hinder other countries from improving or developing mutual economic exchanges and diplomatic relations with Taiwan. Unfortunately, many statesmen and countries, including the United States of America, have eventually given way under the temptation of the broad promising market on so vast a territory and so large a population, regardless of morality, justice and basic principles of democracy and liberty. They have ended up accepting the prerequisites for establishing diplomatic relations with them by canceling the original ones with Taipei and by admitting that Taiwan is a part of the Communist territorial sovereignty.

Thus, the Chinese Communist rulers have given proof of a real hegemonism on the world stage in all their terrible power by forcing all the nations to deny outrageously the living reality of two Chinas: the Republic of China and the People's Republic of China, or more accurately, a Free China and a Communist China. Nevertheless, how is it possible to disown such an undeniable and indisputable fact in existence for half a century? How should one venture to make concession to the Communist absurd requirement and agree to Sovietize Free China? For the time being, the Chinese people on the Mainland have been deprived of their human rights and religious freedom despite rapid economic development. Yet, the other Chinese people on the precious island have broken the Communist threats, pressure and blockade, and have created a real economic miracle. They march determinedly towards increasing democratization and enjoy at present religious freedom and economic prosperity. In spite of all this, under the pretense of nationalism and of state unity, the Chinese Communist intransigents in authority maintain their ambitious designs, and still manage to force their tyrannical chains on the free Chinese people. They also continue to persecute the Catholic Church under the cover of patriotism, independence, self-management and opposition to all foreign interference. Whatever happens, justice will at long last and without fail prevail over injustice, democracy over autocracy and liberty over tyranny! At the very outset, Christ declared to St. Peter, Prince of the Apostles, "You are 'Rock', and on this rock I will build My Church, and the gates of the underworld shall not prevail against it." (Mt. 16:18). Two thousand years of history have confirmed this solemn declaration of the Lord and history will continue to do so!

The current Chinese Communist persecution of the Catholic Church is shown in two ways. For one thing, by intensifying their oppression of the clandestine Catholic Church, and, for another, by keeping the Patriotic church under strict control and making full use of it as a political propaganda. They do not allow its members to profess publicly their obedience to the Pope and the Pope's primacy, including episcopal appointments; they even urge them to harass loyal Catholics. Under the pretext of nonregistration and illegitimacy, they have been trying to ban and eradicate all sorts of lawful religious activities of loyal Catholics by not returning their former churches, tearing down the newly-built chapels and inflicting various punishments. They persecute the faithful bishops, priests and laity with the same clumsy and cunning trick as that by which they repress the dissident. When world opinion and human rights organizations lodged a strong protest and blame, they were driven to release the prisoners in question to calm down public indignation; yet shortly, even at the same time, they secretly arrested or rearrested someone else. This kind of on-and-off arrest and release has been alternately used and has become a stock trick, bargaining chips in their political deals with the international community. In this unique and effective way, year after year, for the last two decades, they have cynically ridiculed Human Rights and religious freedom in the presence of the whole world.

Facing the Chinese Communist menace and their obstinate moves and challenges, the international Catholic community as well as political leaders are truly acting responsibly by systematically denouncing their persecution of religion and their violation of Human Rights, and by constantly pressing them to change their agenda. We should not shut our eyes, still less abandon our principles to seek some temporary commercial gains. The facts have already shown that with good will in proclaiming the Gospel and working for the unity of the Church, a certain number of Catholic communities and individuals, though having lavished generously their support and financial help to the Patriotic church, have totally failed to bring the Chinese Communists around to make the slightest change for the better or to lessen their persecution. On the contrary, these courses of action have produced pernicious effects, spreading almost everywhere in the world both the wrong image of the Communist-controlled Patriotic church as a true Catholic Church, "passing off fish eyes as pearls," in the Chinese popular expression, and disseminating the false impression that in that area persecution no longer exists and freedom has been totally retrieved.

Moreover, the underground Church has been ignored, forgotten, isolated, abandoned and left helpless and lonely in pain. Her loyal children have been hurt in the depths of their hearts, continuously repressed and subjected to constant pressure to join the official church. Frankly speaking, however, the Chinese Communist Party is nothing other than a paper tiger, outwardly strong but inwardly weak, or rather fierce of mien but faint of heart. Provided that you dare to fight resolutely, you can surely overthrow, defeat and punch holes in it. This is what my own personal experience of a thirty-three year struggle for the Faith against the Communists has taught me.

In the late seventies, the Red Regime, under the stress of circumstances, had no choice but to adopt open-door policies both at home and abroad. At that time, the long-persecuted and crushed Catholic Church on the Mainland unexpectedly revived as if out of her deep silence and out of her sepulchral ruins, and her millions of children as though in one evening miraculously reappeared, working in the open in all sorts of religious activities. This greatly surprised not only the regime itself, but also the rest of the world. One year later, when having suddenly awakened from its old dream, the regime started playing the same old trick by using anew the easily-manipulated Chinese Catholic Patriotic Association and its members to control and destroy the resuscitated Church at long last. Once again, many loyal clergy and laity made their brave choice to remain in the underground Church, to maintain their allegiance to Jesus Christ the Lord and to His Vicar the Pope rather than to participate in the official worship of the Communist-controlled Patriotic church. They celebrate their Masses and recite their prayers in home, in hiding places, in open fields, or even in some newly-built but soon-torn-down chapels (See Note at the end of the Preface), risking each time beatings, fines, arrests, imprisonments, tortures or even murders. Their noble fighting spirit, without fearing to suffer and with generosity to sacrifice their lives for the fullness of the Faith, should serve as an inspiration for us all, for the whole Catholic Church and for the entire world, and surely represents a real hope for the promising future of the Church in China. We do believe that with the intercession and help of Our Lady of China, relying on the love and power of the Lord, they will be able to stand unswervingly in the just struggle to the end and be crowned in the long run with victorious laurels.

In 1997, from October 27 to November 3, the number one Chinese Communist, Jiang Zemin, had a weeklong visit to the United States. It was the occasion for concerned American leaders to voice some frank and pertinent views:

> "You are on the wrong side of history in the denial of Human Rights and basic democratic freedom!" (President Bill Clinton during the joint press conference, October 29, 1997).

> "We do not believe that freedom is limited by geography or by history -- we believe that all men and women should be able to live, work and speak free from governmental interference." (Senate Majority Leader Trent Lott at Capitol Hill breakfast session, October 30, 1997).

> "I believe it was vitally important that we used this opportunity to address the basic lack of freedom -- speech, liberty, assembly, the press -- in China. Had we not done so, we would not only have betrayed our own tradition, we also would have failed to meet our obligations as a friend of China." "I reminded our Chinese guests that you cannot have economic freedom without political freedom, and you cannot have political freedom without religious freedom. You cannot have a system that is half totalitarian and

half free. It will not survive." (House Speaker Newt
Gingrich at Capitol Hill breakfast session, October 30,
1997).

"The great elixir of individual freedom is the best
prescription to accelerate and multiply your success
in achieving your goal of strengthening China."
(California Governor Pete Wilson at the Beverly
Hilton Hotel Luncheon, November 2, 1997).

In the face of these rebukes and other remarks, both sound
and sharp, the Chinese Communist supreme ruler's replies and
retorts seemed ridiculous, untenable and incredible, as witness
the following declarations:

"Democracy and Human Rights are relative,
not absolute concepts, varying in different
countries and different circumstances."
"The most important problem in China is
to help our 1.2 billion people to dress warmly
and to eat their fill." "Without social and
political stability there is no possibility
for the economic reform and development."
"Our historical tradition is that social stability
is much more important than any individual
freedom." "No other country should intervene in
the Chinese policy of Human Rights or in any
other Chinese internal affairs."

Hopefully, this Chinese Communist figure will reflect upon
the remarks of these statesmen of his host country and he should
bear in mind something positive about real democracy and freedom. He and his fellow officials should draw some lessons from
their opposition and give up their own outworn ideas and lame
excuses. They need to be fully aware of the ongoing situation of
the world and get a clear idea of the contemporary direction of
history. They must abandon Marxism-Leninism and replace the
Communist Party with a new party, a democratic party truly and
totally in service of the interests of China and her people. They
must work on essential political reforms, concluding with the
party dictatorship, putting a genuine democratic system in its
place and returning to the Chinese people all their expropriated

human rights and religious freedom. With the demolition of the Berlin Wall in 1989, the local people were able to resume religious freedom and henceforward live and look to the future according to their convictions. It would be in the great interest of the Chinese Communist leaders to destroy their "Berlin Wall," if they truly hope that the Chinese people find prosperity and happiness, and that they find themselves really accepted by the rest of the world. It is not too late to do so!

The Chinese Communist authorities should honestly show and bluntly admit that the key to the problem about the Catholic Church in their domain never laid in the Vatican, but in their rejection of the universally-recognized supremacy of the Pope, in their blunt interference in ecclesiastical affairs, in their control of the official Patriotic church and in their repression of the underground Church. They should not have forgotten the reality of the figures, which, according to an editorial of Kathleen Howley in *Arlington Catholic Herald* of November 16, 1995, "China: A Tale of two Churches", testified that in their Communist kingdom there were 9 million Catholics belonging to the underground Church and only 3 million to the Patriotic church. In the same way, on October 9, 1987, in Taipei, the Blessed Virgin Mary had disclosed in the course of a reunion of the Cenacle of the Marian Movement of Priests of Taiwan (From the book, *To the Priests, Our Lady's Beloved Sons,* chapter 365):

> "I am gazing today with eyes of mercy on this great nation of China, where my Adversary is reigning, the Red Dragon who has set up his kingdom here, enjoining all, by force, to repeat the satanic act of denial and of rebellion against God." (a, p. 575, 17th English Edition). "--Then, with my motherly action, I open your hearts to receive the life of God, which acts within you in a special way, so that there be given Him in secret the adoration and the love which you are prohibited from giving Him with public and external worship. It is in this way that, in silence and in hiddenness, the true religion is again spreading in your midst and sending down roots in the life of many of my children." (f, p.576).

"--Finally I am preparing the day, by
now close at hand, of your liberation, with the
definitive defeat of the Red Dragon of
theoretical and practical atheism, which has
conquered the entire world. The time of your
slavery is about to end. All you nations of the earth,
come out from slavery and darkness and go to meet
Christ who is coming to establish in your midst His
glorious reign of love." (g, p.576).

All these indications show us that the Catholic Church there, far from having been destroyed, is, on the contrary, growing greatly and speedily throughout the long period of their persecution. This also proved that all their repressive methods of state control, systematic espionage, threats, divisions, accusations, criticisms, arrests, imprisonments, expulsions, tortures and murders, could never have obtained the desired results, but only lead to a crushing defeat! In these circumstances, one wonders why the Chinese Communist ruling clique always refuses to wake up to reality and abandon their wishful thinking of persecuting and exterminating the Church. One also wonders why they would not dissolve their three anti-Catholic organizations: the Chinese Catholic Patriotic Association (CCPA), the Chinese Catholic Administrative Commission (CCAC) and the China Catholic Bishops College (CCBC). Why instead will they always keep them and use them? Why should they persist in depriving the Chinese Catholics of their deserved religious freedom? Why do they not listen honestly to the sincere voice of the Holy Father John Paul II issued in his message of the 3rd December 1996?

"The civil authorities of the People's Republic
of China should rest assured: a disciple of Christ
can live his faith in any political system, provided
that there is respect for his right to act according
to the dictates of his own conscience and his own
faith. For this reason I repeat to the governing
authorities, as I have said so often to others, that
they should have no fear of God or of His Church.
Indeed, I respectfully ask them in deference to the
authentic freedom which is the innate right of
every man and woman, to ensure that those also who
believe in Christ may increasingly contribute their

energies and talents to the development of their country. The Chinese Nation has an important role to play in the international community. Catholics can make a notable contribution to this, and they do so with enthusiasm and commitment."

We would persuade and urge our brothers and sisters on the Mainland who have gone astray either a long time ago or more recently, to come back to the truth and to rejoin the real sheep-fold and the real Shepherd. They should distinguish between truth and falsehood, between good and evil, get to the roots of the problem and change their position. Thus, they would depart from the wrong road and bear witness to the true Faith, fearless of Communist persecution. In reality, if most of them would make up their minds to do so, the persecution would probably be shattered and come to an end, and the future of the Church in China would be bright. Now is a good opportunity for them to make a fresh start and to fight for the Lord. We hope that they will not fail to seize this opportunity to work for the glory of the Church! They need to be made aware of the great expectations their kind Shepherd, Pope John Paul II, places on them in his message to the Church in China on December 3, 1996:

"Today too all Chinese Catholics are called to remain loyal to the faith received and passed on, and not to yield to models of a Church which do not correspond to the will of the Lord Jesus, to the Catholic faith, or to the feelings and convictions of the great majority of Chinese Catholics."
"Moreover, with the same conviction, and with the responsibility and the confidence which come to me from the Apostolic mandate which I have received from Christ, I exhort all the Pastors and the faithful of China to express with courage and without fear the true profession of the Catholic faith, thus 'speaking the truth in love' (Eph. 4:15)."

―――――――――

In this updated edition, 42 photographs have been added and

presented in a chronological order. There have been appended as well three pieces from my writings. The first one, my Preface to the French version, may interest the English reader with its new material. The second, my declaration of the 4th November 1951 to the neighborhood assembly of the Yangshi Street Police Station held in the entrance hall of our St. Benedict's Priory in Chengdu, Sichuan, was determinative for the prolonged course of my struggle for the Lord. The third, my appeal of March 8, 1981, to the Peng'an-Labor-Reform Camp, showed the Chinese Communists my persistent Catholic conviction. This appeal unexpectantly marked the coming of a new dawn, put an end to this long night of my captivity and led me to a decisive victory. All the other additions are dispersed here and there. Among them the following three are specially to be mentioned: the terse and forceful Foreword by Fr. Abbot Francis Benedict, O.S.B., to the French version, a concise history of the Church in China and in Sichuan Province included in the Introduction, and a long poem attached to Chapter IX describing my impressions in Peking in the fall of 1984.

Without the will and love of the Lord, neither the French version, nor the English revised edition would have been possible. Without His Providential intervention, without the message from Fr. Werner Papeians de Morchoven, O.S.B., announcing Mrs. Barloy's proposition to translate my book from English into French, without the excellent work of the latter and her total cooperation for more than two years in improving both the English and the French versions, without the precious guidance and editing of Br. Thomas Babusis, O.S.B., and, more especially, of Fr. Simon O'Donnell, O.S.B., without the efforts of the publisher, Mr. Jim Moeller and the editors, Ms. Linda Moeller and Mr. Ken Moeller, and, finally, without the help of all the others, this writing could never have seen the light of day. While rendering thanks to the Lord, I feel indebted to all these friends. And I am glad to be able to present my readers a new edition of the book with substantial content changes as well as important clarifications.

Responding to my request, our Fr. Abbot Francis Benedict, O.S.B., was quite kind to write a Foreword for the new book and to insert a photograph of the whole monastic community. I am much obliged to him for this kindly favor and also to all my monastic confreres for their constant support.

I want to express also my deep gratefulness to Mrs. Mimi H.

Fleischman, a Chinese writer and author of four books, for her calligraphy and the photograph of her family. In the early summer of 1995, when my book of poetry was about to be printed, she had graciously offered her calligraphy for the Chinese title on the front cover and the title page, and sealed these two pages with her personal Chinese seal. Two years afterwards, she renewed this favor on the occasion of this new revised edition of my biography. The unjust ten years' imprisonment she had served during the entire decade of the fifties was just redressed. The Ministry of the National Defense of the Republic of China in Taiwan finally rectified the situation in early May of 1997 when they gave her a retirement decree and pension from military service as a captain. This calligraphy she was so kind to do for my new book, without any doubt, leaves some traces of her enthusiastic and cheerful temperament, as "the thread of a spider's web, or as the trail of a running horse." This was a temperament that she must have shared with Robert, her husband, a retired American who did social work in Asia, Africa and the United States.

I would like to extend my warmest appreciation to all my friends who have helped me by lavishing their financial favors, editing my papers, giving certain information, providing their photographs, or showing kindness in some other ways: Paul and Christina Kim, Marianne C. Papp, Jean DeBettignies, Jaime J. and Audrey B. Abrera, James Mao Yongchang, Martha Benker-Lecomte and her family, Marie-Therese Thoreau, her daughter, Agnes Thoreau and the entire Thoreau family, William F. Hooper and Marie Rosa Martinelli, Agnes Y.H. Kung, Terese Young, Claire Lin, Pat Feller, the late Fr. Gaetan Loriers, O.S.B., Fr. Eleutherius Winance, O.S.B., the late Fr. Felix Tang Tien-shou, O.S.B., Fr. Luke Dysinger, O.S.B., Fr. Paul Pluth, O.S.B., Carolyn Humphreys, O.C.D.S., Cynthia Clark, Deacon Gilbert and Dolores Chavez, Br. Tim Mayworm, F.S.C., Fr. Prior Benedict Chao, O.C.S.O., Fr. Abbot Ambroise Watelet, O.S.B., Dr. John W. and Mary Lou Birsner, Dr. Michel and Pansy Xiao, Shannon MacDonald and her family, Madonna M. Edgar and her family, Professor Rick and Yamilette Chacon, Anna Abderhalden and her family, Fr. Philip Edwards, O.S.B., Fr. Vincent de Paul Martin, O.S.B., Br. Dominic Guillen, O.S.B., Br. Anselmo Taborda, O.S. B., Br. Andrew Hayes, O.S.B., Br. Joseph Iarrobino, O.S.B., Br. Michael Weeks, O.S.B., Br. Carlos Lopez, O.S.B., Br. James Brennan, O.S.B., Dana Peters-Barber, Anna

Huang Ziying, Sr. Marianna So, O.C.D., Sr. Grace Yip Soo-ching, S.D.S.H., Tim and Jeannine M. Veraldi, Isabella Chang Chien-hsi and her mother, Jane Chang Hou Chiu-ke, Lucia Su Dejun, Suky Lee, Michele Rhoden, Delynn Arneson, Sabrina Vincent, Sr. Karen Wilhelmy, C.S.J., Marlene Parks, Sue Pressler, Margie Holman, Tim Benedict, Patrick Bradley, Deborah D. Williams, Primo and Genevieve Alghisi and their family, Mother Prioress Marie-Claire Willocx, O.S.B., Diane L. Richardson and her family, Amy Pleiman-Knapke, Wayne Fauchier, Paul and Nancy Chen, Joey and Nora Hizon, Tim and Shirley Song, John and Mary Su, Fr. Louis Suchet Amiotte, M.E.P., and Fr. Francois Dufay, M.E.P.

O my God, You are so great and so good that You would never have been content to offer me the opportunity and the energy to carry on and to win the battle against the atheistic Communist persecution on Your behalf. You continuously bestowed on me this persistent will to put into writing the story of my long and hard struggle and thus to make known Your power to the rest of the world. You even assisted me in the discharge of my responsibility with a better narration of Your loving-kindness and with a more refined edition of my autobiography. Being moved to tears of gratitude for Your mercy, I beseech You, O Lord, to make this book become something edifying and saving for each and every reader. Bless also in a very special way all those, mentioned or unmentioned, who have contributed by some means or other to the realization of this publication. Ultimately, grant, I beg You, Your blessings to all my brothers and sisters who will read this book! Amen!

With respect and gratitude,
Br. Peter Zhou, O.S.B.
St. Andrew's Abbey
Valyermo, California, U.S.A.
May 31, 1999
Feast of the Visitation of the Virgin Mary to Elizabeth

_____

Note: The latest public and official destruction of a new church, giving evidence of another terrifying persecution suffered by the loyal Catholics in Fujian Province, was reported in the June 1998 issue of the *San Francisco Chinese Catholic Newsletter.* This event took place at the Houlu Village in Xilan Township, Louyuan County, near the East Sea, on May 9, 1998. This church, about 600 square meters, was just rebuilt on its original site with the money earned by the hard toil of the several thousand poor and honest Catholics, probably 400,000 yuan ($48,000 US). On that morning, unexpectedly, more than 130 Communist officials and armed police of the county and the township, came by jeeps and trucks, and surged into the impoverished mountain valley to stop the "illegal activities of the underground Church" and to ban the "unlawfully-built church". At first, they forced out of the church all of the praying faithful, wounding them by dragging and beating them, and then, in two hours or so, they destroyed it completely with bulldozers.

FOREWORD BY FATHER ABBOT
TO THE FRENCH VERSION

It is with great satisfaction that I present to French readers this book of faith and courage depicting a major part of the life of our Brother Peter. He is a living sign of the perennial call to follow Christ to the point of great personal sacrifice for the sake of the Kingdom of God. That Brother Peter survived the privations and sufferings of so many years imprisonment and torture is the mystery of God's grace. One can only surmise that his experiences were meant to become a testimony to the faith of the suffering Church in China and an encouragement to many to believe more firmly in the truths of the faith.

Brother Peter's life is in continuity with the lives of so many martyrs and witnesses in the past who suffered for their Christian faith and for the unity of the Catholic Church, the universal community of faith. The Hymn composed by Frederick William Faber (1814-1863) bespeaks the vocation of Brother Peter.

> Faith of our fathers! Living still
> In spite of dungeon, fire, and sword:
> O how our hearts beat high with joy,
> When-e'er we hear that glorious word:
> *Faith of our fathers, holy faith!*
> *We will be true to thee till death.*
> Our fathers, chained in prisons dark,
> Were still in heart and conscience free:
> And truly blest would be our fate,
> If we, like them, should die for thee.
> *Faith of our fathers, holy faith!*
> *We will be true to thee till death.*
> Faith of our fathers! Faith and prayer
> Shall win all nations unto thee;
> And through the truth that comes from God,
> Mankind shall then indeed be free.
> *Faith of our fathers, holy faith!*
> *We will be true to thee till death.*
> Faith of our fathers! We will love
> Both friend and foe in all our strife:
> And preach thee, too, as love knows how,
> By kindly deeds and virtuous life.
> *Faith of our fathers, holy faith!*
> *We will be true to thee till death.*

Brother Peter's story inspires and strengthens us to live more faithfully what we have received as a gift. Each life is precious to God and can transmit to others in this transitory world those eternal truths which promise the rewards of everlasting life. "Well done, good and faithful servant.... enter into the joy of your Lord!" (Matthew 25:21). May the Lord bless those who read this book with many graces.

Abbot Francis Benedict, O.S.B.
Valyermo, California, U.S.A.
February 11, 1999
Our Lady of Lourdes

PREFACE BY BROTHER PETER
TO THE FRENCH VERSION

After the publication of my book, *Dawn Breaks in the East,* in the United States in July 1992, a French version had been envisioned. The enthusiasm and hope for this project lasted for three years. At the end of this period, however, time proves this hope, if nothing else, to be illusory, and I resigned myself to abandon all my expectations, seeing that the project had finally fallen through. As a beautiful mirage, all disappeared in the distant seas, and I found myself alone with only my sighs and regrets for seeing a door closed again. Truly, man proposes, God disposes!

God, the loving and Almighty Lord, had His own plan for me and for my book. On the 29th of November 1995, when I had just begun a novena in honor of the Virgin Mary for the forthcoming Solemnity of her Immaculate Conception, I received unexpected and surprising news from Fr. Werner Papeians de Morchoven, O.S.B. The following day I read a letter to him from one of his friends in Paris, Mrs. Frederique Barloy, expressing her interest in my book, which Fr. Werner had sent her, and her desire to translate it into French. I could not help answering her immediately and directly, personally inviting her to translate my book from English into French. Early in the following January, she sent me a positive reply and promised that she would set to work right away. Thus, my so-long-cherished wish to share the experiences of my struggle for the Lord in the Faith, with my French-speaking brothers and sisters in Christ would become a reality at last and allow me to bring my little contribution and some encouragement to their spiritual lives. This liaison between my book and her was made possible because of Fr. Werner's link to me. In a sense, this added a note both mysterious and wonderful. There exists an old Chinese saying, well describing this kind of miraculous union: "People a thousand miles apart may be linked in marriage through a single red silk thread!"

Since February 1994, when I began to rewrite the Chinese original of the book, I revised carefully the English text, trying to discover and correct any mistakes. From the spring of 1994 to the summer of 1995, with the gracious help of Mrs. Pat Feller, Miss Jean DeBettignies, Fr. Philip Edwards, O.S.B., and Sr.

Karen Wilhelmy, C.S.J., I undertook this work. From the fall of 1995 to the end of 1996, thanks to the generous assistance of Br. Thomas Babusis, O.S.B., and from January 1997 to the planned publication of the English updated edition in August 1999 and of this French version in December 1999, with the precious guidance of Fr. Simon O'Donnell, O.S.B., all the necessary corrections, changes and additions have been completed in time and included in this French version. In fact, I owed this success to Mrs. Barloy's French translation and to her directions and cooperation given me since early 1996, almost for three years. Fr. Francois de Grunne, O.S.B., Fr. Gaetan Loriers, O.S.B., who died on August 27, 1996, at the age of 81, and Fr. Prior Benedict Chao, O.C.S.O., also deserve special mention for their contributions to this translation.

I do not know France and her culture well enough, but in a certain sense, they are not totally strange to me. One could even say that I have had a privileged relation with this country from the cradle. A few days after my birth I was baptized by a French missionary from the Foreign Missions of Paris, called Father Du in Chinese, the pastor of Neijiang County in Sichuan Province. During the following six years, on Sundays and major feasts, my parents used to take me with them to attend the masses he celebrated in the local church. This connection to France continued when, at the age of 12, I was admitted to the Benedictine Monastery at Sishan in Nanchong County, composed of monks of different nationalities, but they had in common the knowledge of the French language. They made use of it and spoke among themselves creating a common bond in their daily lives.

In Chengdu, during the summer vacation of 1948, Fr. Prior Raphael Vinciarelli, O.S.B., (1897-1972) made me take a course of pronunciation of the French language from Mrs. Germaine Braye Yuan, a Belgian lady. Then, our Fr. Prior, Fr. Eleutherius Winance, Fr. Gaetan, Fr. Francois and Fr. Alberic Deloring (1911-1981) helped me to pursue this study. From 1952 until my imprisonment in November 1955, I had the occasion to use French when I corresponded with French-speaking friends, five priests and one sister, in Shanghai, Canton, Hong Kong or in Belgium. Unfortunately, during these seven years, I never had the opportunity to read any works of French literature; instead, my sole literary companion was a French missal I read everyday. Fr. Philippe Charles, M.E.P., the French rector of the Chengdu Minor Seminary, taught me Latin for one year. Fr. Emile Butruille, a French monk in the monastery and Fr. Eleutherius used to hear my confessions in Chinese; the latter has continued to do so in the United States up to this day.

Sichuan, my native land, is a province of China under a strong French influence. Though being known for a long time as the "Far-West China", this province is still one of the most populated and the richest in China. One of the most beautiful, too. In 1897, when Therese of Lisieux was entrusted with the mission to pray for a young priest of the Paris Foreign Mission Society, Fr. Roulland, in his work of evangelizing China, Sichuan was an extremely isolated part of the world. Nevertheless, Chongqing, the province's diocese of choice, became a secondary capital of the country, a sort of center of the Chinese world since November 20, 1937. At that time Generalissimo Chiang Kai-shek (1887-1975) began to progressively establish his rear base to reinforce his position in the face of the Japanese invasion. From a backward province, where Deng Xiaoping was born in 1904, Sichuan became overnight a place where great numbers of Chinese and foreign intelligentsia converged.

Saint Therese of Lisieux (1873-1897) is a great saint in modern times. Her fervent prayers and small sacrifices for the salvation of mankind made her a Patroness of the Missions in 1927, just two years after her canonization. Churches were raised in her honor almost everywhere in China. She was the pride of France and the glory of the French people. In the winter of 1938, every night for a quarter of an hour before bedtime, following the directives of our superiors, our Chinese teacher, Mr. Yuan Helin, read and explained certain passages from Therese of Lisieux's well-known autobiography, *The Story of a Soul,* translated into Chinese by Mr. Joseph Ma Xiangbo (1840-1939) in 1928. He went through the book from beginning to end for our group of ten or so oblate students. Her feast, important to the Chinese Christians and to China, a country in extreme need of continuous evangelization, was celebrated at that time on the third, now on the first, of October, the day which coincides with the Communist feast of the "National Liberation" of China, a date which marks the start of the Sovietization of the country. If my memory serves me, this feast was always the occasion for the local Bishop, Paul Wang Wencheng (1880-1961), to come to the Priory to celebrate together with us.

In the late forties I had read two Chinese books on Saint Therese, published by the *Catholic Truth Society* in Hong Kong.

One was a general biography of her life, entitled *Saint Therese.* The other, *The Science of Love,* by Dr. John Wu Jingxiong (C.H. Wu), J.D., (1899-1986), a famous jurist, was translated in 1943 into classical Chinese style by Mr. Chen Xiangbo (Chan Heung Pak) from the English original. Dr. Wu's booklet was published in Hong Kong in 1940, originally as an article in the April number of *Tien Hsia,* an English monthly, the most influential and best-selling in China at that time. Reading Saint Therese's book, Dr. John Wu was converted from Protestantism to the Catholic Faith during the bombardment of Shanghai in 1937. He remained all the same an authentic man of Chinese culture who sought, through his writings, to show to Westerners a Chinese approach to Christianity. If he was devoted in particular to the value to Zen (Chan) Buddhism, he could also see a new path for Christianity through the original way of the Confucian Lu Zhengxiang (Lou Tseng-tsiang, 1871-1949). In 1927, this Confucian, a former minister of the Chinese Government at the outset of the century, became a Benedictine monk at the Abbey of Saint-Andre in Bruges, Belgium.

In September 1940, three months after the death of Fr. Vincent Lebbe in Chongqing, Generalissimo Chiang Kai-shek and his wife, Chiang-Sung Mei-ling asked Dr. John Wu to make a really accurate and readable literary translation of the Psalms and the New Testament. In 1946, his version of the Psalms came out in Shanghai and was a best seller. Three years later, in 1949, his version of the New Testament appeared in Hong Kong. These new translations in rhythmical or in classical Chinese style, marked a decisive stage in the history of the Church in China whose clergy had become more indigenous since 1926 following the nomination of the first six Chinese bishops. As a ratifier of this totally new Chinese version of the New Testament, Fr. Abbot Peter Celestine Lu Zhengxiang, O.S.B., wrote: "His use of the classical phrases and idioms furnishes the key to a living synthesis of the East and the West, a synthesis like a seamless cloth, like the pieces of coal melted into one fire in the furnace of Divine Love." The whole traditional Chinese culture was henceforth officially grafted onto Catholicism. Something had been born again. If the Communists had not used all their efforts to destroy and annihilate the fruits and work and even the presence of the Church in China, the Church there would have certainly experienced a considerable growth and at the same time would have brought her radiance to the Universal Church.

Dr. John Wu was appointed Envoy of China to the Holy See from September 1946 to June 1949 where he had the opportunity to become well acquainted with Jacques Maritain (1882-1973), French Ambassador to the Holy See from 1945 to 1948 and a great Thomistic philosopher. He was also a good friend of our Fr. Prior Raphael Vinciarelli and was received on March 21, 1940, as an oblate of our monastery. He offered his Chinese calligraphy for the cover title of Fr. Prior's book, *Philosophy and Religion*, published in Hong Kong in January 1948 and translated from French into Chinese in Chengdu in December 1946 by Mr. Li Youxing, a convert and President of the Sichuan Provincial Academy of Fine Arts.

For many centuries, as an elder daughter of the Church, France has given many gifts to her mother, the Church, and many exemplary saints, remarkable in deeds, to mankind. Saint Therese is one of the latest such figures, and she has always been very popular in China as everywhere else in the world. She is truly much admired. She has exerted an extraordinary influence on Church history. Her little approach of spiritual childhood, described in her writings, was her way of predilection and caused her to be proclaimed by Pope John Paul II in St. Peter's Square, October 19, 1997, on the 70th World Mission Sunday, "Doctor of the Church." Thus, she became the 33rd person and the third woman to be honored with such a title. All of us should strive to walk in her footsteps, doing our daily tasks with a burning love for the Lord, for others and for the salvation of all!

If France has made a profound impact on China in the religious field, she was also very influential in the political and social realm. Towards the end of the First World War and in the beginning of the twenties, a number of Chinese students went to France as part of a work-study program. They were greatly influenced by the French leftist leanings found in newspapers, such as *L'Humanite,* which promulgated the theories of Marx and Lenin. They were especially seduced by the propaganda and monetary gain of the Russian Communists who were sent from Moscow to Paris by the Third International, also called the Communist International. This leading organization of all the Communist Parties in the world was established by Lenin in Moscow in March 1919 and was reluctantly disbanded by Stalin in June 1943. Thus, these Chinese students moved towards Communism, participated in the activities of the newly-created agencies of the Third International, and founded their own Communist organizations. Thus it was in France that these students were formed as Communists, and it was Deng Xiaoping who served for three years as the Communist coordinator between themselves in the district of Bayeux, and who in July 1924 succeeded Zhou Enlai as the leader of their Communist group in France. During this French period, Deng Xiaoping, Zhou Enlai and Chen Yi, to mention only them, were among the most active militants. Later, they would ascend to the highest posts of responsibility in the heart of the Chinese Communist Party, and prove to be among the most zealous disciples of Mao Zedong. Finally, they were the source of the greatest tragedy, unprecedented in China and perhaps in the entire world!

The Internationale, well known by the Chinese Communists as the "revolutionary song of the proletarians of the entire world", was the masterpiece of two Frenchmen: Mr. Pierre Degeyter (1848-1932), who composed the music, and Mr. Eugene (1816-1888), who wrote the text. It was precisely in Lille, France, on July 23, 1888, that this song was sung for the first time. Later, it spread abroad to become the national anthem of the Soviet Union from 1917 to 1944 and the universal song of the Communist world. It was in the rhythm of this revolutionary battle song that, from the very beginning, the Chinese Communists crushed democracy, trampled freedom, exploited the people and deceived world opinion, while winning over a number of international sympathizers and foreign friends.

They would not recognize Jesus as their true Redeemer. They attempted vainly to portray themselves as heroes, or rather, to raise Lenin, Stalin or Mao Zedong to be the saviors of China and of the whole world. This would become the inevitable sign of their own future destruction!

Despite the strong influence of these godless and antichristian Frenchmen, who had promulgated these disastrous values throughout the entire world, engendering a real plague, France offered China and many other countries a spirit of charity thanks to her countless priests and nuns. These clergy and religious were full of love, zeal and self-devotion, and came to guide the people in the way of salvation. In the course of frequent persecutions which arose in different regions at different times, some of her missionaries went so far as to sacrifice their lives for their sacred mission of evangelization.

On June 4, 1989, at Tiananmen Square in Peking, the Chinese Communist army killed hundreds of students and workers who were nonviolently demonstrating for democracy and freedom. Just two days before the 7th anniversary of this massacre, on June 2, 1996, Pope John Paul II canonized in Rome, Blessed Father John-Gabriel Perboyre, C.M., (1802-1842), a French missionary, whose Chinese name was Dong Wenxue. He had suffered courageously a cruel martyrdom at Wuchang, Hubei Province, on September 11, 1840. He was the first martyr to have been canonically declared a saint by a Pope in the seven-hundred-year history of the Church in China. It was a great event and an exceptional honor for all of us, French and Chinese alike. I hope from the bottom of my heart, that through the mercy of God, this will very soon bring an end to the current Communist religious persecution!

It was through the continuous and laborious efforts of many French missionaries that my forefathers were led to the Catholic Faith which I have inherited. Furthermore, God gave me the gift to seek admittance to the Sishan Priory established in Nanchong by French-speaking Belgian Benedictine monks. In continuous contact with them, in Chengdu, I acquired a smattering of knowledge of French culture and language. It was at their urging that I threw myself into the holy struggle for the Faith. Ultimately, it was, once more, owing to their help that I was able to pass through the Bamboo Curtain. How can I show all of my gratitude today to them and to all the other French people and missionaries who have lavished on me so many kindnesses and overwhelmed me with so much generosity? Mrs. Barloy has graciously translated my book into French. Her excellent work has made it possible to fulfill my desire to tell them and the whole French-speaking world the story of my struggle in the face of the Chinese Communists and of my witness for Christ in those 33 hard but happy years. I hope that they will welcome my narrative as a concrete fruit of my most sincere thanksgiving! And I continue to pray to Our Lady of Lourdes to fill them with all her maternal protection.

I hope one day I will be able to make a pilgrimage to Lourdes, the sanctuary of the Virgin Mary. Today, more than one century later, the messages and love given by the Immaculate Virgin (conceived without sin from the first moment of her conception) during her apparitions are always valid, important, true and attractive. Through the prayers and penances of sinners among whom we are, we can help others and help ourselves to be converted and to find salvation; and the Holy Water of Lourdes keeps on flowing to cure all sorts of diseases and to perform miracles to make the pilgrims' hearts pure and convictions firm. This is a sacred place of prayer and conversion which shines over the entire world. What a kindness, what a faith-affirming force, O France, have you not lavished on Catholicism and all of us? I wish to come to you one day to mingle with the crowd and to show to Our Lady all my veneration and gratitude!

With interest and fervor, with care and speed, Mrs. Barloy has brought her work to its beautiful end. Her sustained efforts and noble ideal will remain for me an unforgettable testimony and I would like to express my profound and heartfelt appreciation to her as well as to her whole family.

Lastly, I want to extend my sincere thanks to Fr. Abbot Francis Benedict, O.S.B., for his precious encouragement and his gracious Foreword to the French edition; also to Mr. Jim Moeller, the publisher of the English version, for his Note and his cooperation for this new edition; and to all my friends named or not (but not forgotten), for their direct or indirect help.

May the loving Lord bless each one of my friends and all my dear new readers!

With His unfailing love,
Brother Peter Zhou Bangjiu, O.S.B.
Saint Andrew's Abbey
Valyermo, California, U.S.A.
December 8, 1998
Solemnity of the Immaculate Conception Of the Virgin Mary

PART I

THE COURSE OF THE STRUGGLE

INTRODUCTION

Just like Job, the upright man of the Old Testament, whose painful experience was beyond all human comprehension and imagination, the Catholic Church on mainland China knew the horror of the Red Menace when the whole of the Mainland was overrun by the Communists in early 1950. From the very beginning the Chinese Communists fostered a radical hatred and abhorrence toward religions and in particular the Catholic religion. The Catholic Church and her Faith were seen as real obstacles to spreading the Communist Party's own atheistic Marxist-Leninist philosophy, and to carrying out its cruel and despotic rule over the people, because of her sound doctrine and disciplined organization, both of which were difficult to break. The Communists had a need to destroy these obstacles in order to impose their "dictatorship of the proletariat" upon all the country and thus keep the people under the yoke of slavery of both mind and body. In their eyes the Catholic Church, witness of truth and instrument of salvation, became "a thorn in their flesh" and they would not be content until she was driven out of China.

Let me give a brief overview of the history of the Catholic Church in China from the initial period until the eve of the Sovietization of the country, before tackling the question of the concrete means used by the Chinese Communist Government in the persecution of the Church. One will see from this what a spirit, what a love foreign missionaries had to give their lives for the salvation of the Chinese people from the outset and throughout the ages. One will also understand how unremittingly the Church authorities strove to foster and strengthen a native clergy and turn over to them gradually the leadership of parishes, dioceses and archdioceses and thus to get the Church nativized as soon as possible.

Except for Taoism, born on Chinese soil, apparently, like Buddhism, Islam, and Protestantism, Catholicism was seen by the Chinese people as a religion imported from abroad. History, however, would protest against this common view. In 1489, the second year under the reign of Emperor Hongzhi in the Ming Dynasty, in Kaifeng of Henan Province, a stone tablet was unearthed with the inscription of *Yicileye Stele*. "Yicileye" was an ancient transliteration for "Israel" and another name for Judaism. The inscription on the Stele revealed that Judaism had entered China in the Zhou Dynasty, at a time much earlier, more

4 *Dawn Breaks In The East*

than two thousand years ago. After extensive research, Ms. Su Hsuen-lin, a famous Catholic writer, who died on April 21, 1999 at the age of 104 and who was a retired professor of Chinese literature at the National Cheng Kung University in Taiwan, was firmly convinced that the statements and the collected data of the inscription were true and reliable. She held that Judaism had shaped the ancient Chinese notion of monotheism, and acted as the predecessor and foundation of Confucianism, greatly influencing the thoughts of the Confucian School and traditional Chinese culture. Professor Su published her monograph on this theme in Hong Kong in May 1950, under the title of *Traditional Chinese Culture and the Ancient Catholic Church.* In the booklet, to support her theory, she cited powerful and persuasive evidence based on the large number of irrefutable documents from inscriptions on bones or tortoise shells of the Shang Dynasty (1766-1122 B.C. or 1523-1027 B.C.) and from ancient Chinese books, such as the Confucian Classics, and texts of history and philosophy. She also listed many common customs and similarities in social structure between the two ancient peoples: Chinese and Hebrews. Relying on trustworthy material from ancient Chinese books, she even proved Mozi (Mo Di or Mo Tze) (c. 468-376 B.C.), a celebrated philosopher in the Zhou Dynasty (c. 1122-249 B.C.), to be a great master of Judaism and demonstrated that his doctrine had a significant influence on the doctrine of Confucius (Kongzi) (551-479 B.C.) and Mencius (Mengzi) (372?-289 B.C.), principal representatives of traditional Chinese culture. Accordingly, Catholicism in respect to the foundation of its beliefs (monotheism) and liturgy (worship of God), was not new or strange to the Chinese society and its traditional culture, but instead was easily assimilated, understood and adopted.

In 1625, the fifth year of Emperor Tianqi of the Ming Dynasty, the *Tablet of the Nestorian church* was discovered in the course of excavation in the western suburbs of the city of Xi'an, Shaanxi Province. This tablet had been erected in 781, the second year of Emperor Jianzhong of the Tang Dynasty. The inscriptions showed us that Alopeno (or Abraham or Rabban), a Nestorian missionary, came from Persia and introduced the Nestorian church to Chang'an (now Xi'an in the above-mentioned province), then the capital of the country, in 635, the ninth year of Emperor Zhengguan. This schismatic church lasted in China for two hundred years or so and then sank inexorably into oblivion.

It was in 1294, in the early years of the Yuan Dynasty

(1279-1368) that Catholicism entered China officially through Fr. John of Montecorvino (1247-1328). This Italian Franciscan missionary was sent by Pope Nicolas IV and later appointed Archbishop of the Peking Archdiocese by Pope Clement V. After his death, however, very few new missionaries were sent from Europe; moreover, of the few that were sent, none reached China or entered her territory. Some time later, the Church in China gradually began to disappear.

Evangelization in China did not start again until 1583 under the reign of Emperor Wanli of the Ming Dynasty, when two Italian Jesuits, Fr. Michele Ruggieri (1543-1607) and Fr. Matteo Ricci (1552-1610), came to Zhaoqing, Guangdong Province. From then onward, foreign missionaries were sent not only from the Society of Jesus and Italy, but also from many other religious orders and countries, unceasingly proclaiming the Gospel in China. With the painstaking work and training undertaken by the joint efforts of missionaries, indigenous priests and laymen, the Catholic Faith was introduced from the coastal cities, such as Peking, Shanghai, Hangzhou, Nanjing and Canton to cities and villages of inland provinces, and even to the most remote outlying southwestern districts of the "Far-West China." Chapels and churches were built one after another covering the whole country. The Church grew steadily and continued developing even during periods of local or national persecution. From May 11, 1610, when Fr. Matteo Ricci died in Peking, until 1948 when the Communists were preparing to overrun the entire Chinese Mainland, the number of Catholics had gone up from 2,500 to 3,274,000; there were 5,780 foreign and native priests, 1,107 monks, 7,463 sisters, 3 universities, 156 high schools, 2,009 primary schools, 1,063 hospitals and clinics, and 272 orphanages.

In 1640, the thirteenth year under Emperor Chongzhen, Fr. Ludovico Buglio (1606-1682), an Italian Jesuit, arrived in Sichuan and opened our province to evangelization. Since 1752, French missionaries from the Foreign Missions of Paris (M.E.P.) came to pursue the work already begun; some of them even suffered martyrdom and watered the tree of Faith with their blood. In 1949 the whole province had about 300,000 faithful, seven dioceses, three of which were totally administered by indigenous bishops and priests; while the remaining four were managed by French bishops and priests both from France and the local province. Then in the Chengdu Diocese there were nearly 40,000 Catholics, a new French bishop, the Most Reverend Henri Pinault, M.E.P., a number of French and Chinese Sisters from the Franciscan Missionaries of Mary (F.M.M.), a minor seminary, a major seminary, a boy's junior high school, and a girl's junior high school. In the city of Chengdu there were some orphanages and a medium-sized hospital run by the Franciscan Sisters, a cathedral, and six churches: four belonging to the diocesan pastors, one to the Spanish Redemptorists and the smallest one to the Benedictines of our monastery.

The sacrificial rites for ancestors and respectful rituals for Confucius were proper customs in Chinese society and common practices among the Chinese people. But from this emerged a serious conflict, the "Quarrel of the Rites," among different foreign religious orders. Some thought that this ceremony was a superstitious and religious one, while others saw it as only a simple formality and social custom. This controversy was on the increase and became endless among foreign and native priests and among laymen, even between Church authorities and the Qing Dynasty Government. This question remained unsettled throughout almost three centuries and severely curbed the work of evangelization and the growth of the number of the faithful. The conflict was not resolved officially until December 8, 1939, when the Sacred Congregation for the Propagation of the Faith had issued the decree authorizing the practice of the Chinese rites. Moreover, following the Opium War in 1842, another grave problem cropped up, and made the situation of the Church in China much more unfavorable and her redemptive mission much more endangered, as though "adding frost to snow" for her.

Since the "freedom of missionization" used to be included as an item in the unequal treaties forced upon the Qing Dynasty Government by Western Powers, the Manchurian Emperors, many Chinese intellectuals and even the common people began to change their original favorable impression of Catholicism into one of repugnance and even hostility towards the Church, her missionaries, and the faithful. This hostility finally led to the frenzied persecution of the Church in 1900 by the revolt of the Boxers manipulated by Empress Dowager Ci Xi (Tzu Hsi) (1835-1908) and caused the bloody sacrifice of 4 bishops, 31 priests and more than 30,000 faithful, not to mention the destruction of a large number of churches. After the bloody tragedy a certain number of Chinese people still maintained their prejudices and enmity towards the Catholic Church and labeled her as a "foreign religion."

To improve her image among the Chinese people and to

increase the results of the apostolate, the Church continued to urge missionaries to learn Chinese language well, dress themselves in Chinese clothes, adapt themselves to Chinese culture and customs, train and use more and more native clerics. At the same time, she strove to run more seminaries, various schools, publish periodicals, books and newspapers, and establish orphanages, clinics and hospitals. In 1922, Pope Pius XI dispatched Archbishop Celso Costantini (1876-1958) to China as the first Apostolic Delegate and on December 28, 1926, consecrated personally the first six Chinese bishops in St. Peter's Basilica in Rome. After World War II, on December 24, 1945, Pope Pius XII raised Bishop Thomas Tian Gengxin (Tien Kenghsin) (1890-1967) to the dignity of Cardinal, the first one in the Far East, and on April 11, 1946, established the ecclesiastical hierarchy in China. Two months later, on July 6, he nominated Archbishop Antonio Riberi the first Internuncio to China, while for its part, on September 10, the Chinese National Government appointed Dr. John Wu Jingxiong (C. H. Wu) (1899-1986) Envoy to the Holy See. All these signs seemed to herald a certain prosperity of the Church in China. Her brilliant prospects could have been expected and realized, if the Communist Party had failed in its armed rebellion. After the Sovietization of the whole Mainland, the Holy See did not relax its attention to the Church in China, offering the noble and important cardinalate first to Archbishop Paul Yu Pin (1901-1978) on March 28, 1969, second to Bishop John Baptist Wu Cheng-chung on June 29, 1988, third to Bishop Ignatius Gong Pinmei (Kung Pin-mei) (b. 1901) on May 29, 1991, and fourth to Archbishop Paul Shan, S.J., on January 18, 1998. Cardinal Ignatius Kung was given this honor in recognition of his indomitable and persistent struggle for the Church and his flock in the Diocese of Shanghai at first in the Cathedral for six years, then in the Chinese Communist prison for thirty years, and finally under the surveillance of members of the "Patriotic church" for three years. Furthermore, on June 2, 1996, Pope John Paul II canonically declared Fr. John Gabriel Perboyre (1802-1840), a French missionary, Dong Wenxue by Chinese name, the first Saint from the many Blessed martyrs in China.

During the eight-year War of Resistance against Japan (1937-1945) some foreign and native clerics, religious brothers and sisters and faithful directly participated in this hard war and made some contribution, displaying their immense patriotic zeal. Among them Cardinal Paul Yu Pin and Fr. Vincent Lebbe (1877-

1940) are to be worthy of special mention and great praise for their remarkable actions.

Thanks to his frequent and fruitful visits and numerous speeches overseas, the Most Reverend Paul Yu Pin, then Bishop of Nanjing, won foreigners over to the Chinese cause and gained international understanding, sympathy and support for the Chinese war against the Japanese aggression. In the name of the People's Political Council, and in the name of the people themselves, the National Government and the Church, he regularly went up to the front to express greetings, solicitude, encouragement and appreciation to the officers and men. He tried to provide relief and comfort to the refugees and orphans. He did his best to promote the good relationship between the Government and the Church, and to safeguard the safety of foreign missionaries and freedom of their religious activities. He was often invited to deliver his moving speeches to all sections of the citizens. In one afternoon of December 1944, when he came to Chengdu and stayed at the Cathedral, at the invitation of the Provincial Department of Education, he made a speech at Lida High School to us, a group of seven hundred students or so representing all the high school students of the city. Indeed, he was an outstanding Chinese Bishop and made brilliant contributions to the glory of the Lord, to the Church, the country and the Chinese people. He enjoyed great respect, popularity, prestige and praise from people everywhere both within and without the Church, both at home and abroad!

Fr. Vincent Lebbe, originally a Belgian and a religious from the missionary order of the Lazarists, C.M., was called Lei Mingyuan in Chinese, meaning: "A thunder resounds far to a remote distance." Having taken on Chinese citizenship in July 1927, he was a well-known and devoted missionary and one of the great defenders and active promoters of a native clergy for the Church in China. Ordained to the priesthood in Peking in October 1901, he worked for the evangelization of the Chinese people for the first four decades of this century. Having perfectly mastered the Chinese language, he played a considerable role in China both among the people and in the Church through his homilies, speeches and writings, and through his newspapers, magazines, schools, religious organizations and religious orders. To go up to the front to join the War of Resistance against Japan, on August 20, 1937, Fr. Vincent organized a Medical-Stretcher Corps with the monks from his Congregation of the Little Brothers of St. John-Baptist (founded at Anguo in Hebei Province on

December 16, 1928), and the nuns from his Congregation of the Little Sisters of St. Theresa of the Child-Jesus (established also at Anguo on August 15, 1929). On October 1, 1938, at the appeal of Generalissimo Chiang Kai-shek (1887-1975), he recruited volunteers from Catholics and non-Catholics and established a special service corps to arouse the patriotic sentiments of the peasant population behind the lines and to organize them to resist the Japanese invaders. For nearly three years he worked very hard at the front to rescue the wounded soldiers, to serve and comfort them in field hospitals, while training and helping the members of his corps. Unfortunately, in February 1940, twenty odd of these members and twenty of his Little Brothers were arrested by the Communist Army without cause while passing through or working in the Red Area; the twelve strong Brothers were massacred. On March 9, 1940, Fr. Vincent himself was also trapped into arrest in Lin Xian, Henan Province, by the same Red Army. Because of the strong protest of public opinion, and particularly, of the repeated urgent telegrams from Generalissimo Chiang ordering his release, he finally escaped from the jaws of death and was released with ruined health on April 17. On June 14, when he was repatriated from Luoyang to Chongqing (the wartime capital) by a special plane of the National Government, he was so mentally and physically exhausted, that he was too sick to recover. There, on June 24, 1940, as a great Chinese Apostle and brilliant naturalized patriot, he died of exhaustion an honorable and, so to speak, martyr's death. Two days later, on June 26, he was buried at Geleshan, on the Hill of Joyful Song! He was honored with a public proclamation of commendation and compassion from the National Government on July 18, and especially with a memorable gift, a personal elegiac couplet from Generalissimo Chiang:

> "Universal love is what is called humanity;
> Your spirit of saving the world
> Feels no qualms at looking upon Christ!
>
> You could not be subdued by force;
> It is your work, to your last breath,
> To have exerted and exhausted yourself
> to the utmost for China!"

On the very eve of his death, to the question Bishop Paul Yu

Pin asked: "What is your last will for the whole people and your view on the Chinese Communist Party?", he answered in a very weak but clear voice (From *A Biography of Archbishop Paul Yu Pin, Initiator of the Free Pacific Movement*, [p.16], by Fr. Raymond de Jaegher, published in Vietnam in May 1959.):

> "The Chinese Communists are not Chinese!"
> "The Chinese Communists are not human beings!"
> "The Chinese Communists are living devils!"

The experiences Fr. Vincent Lebbe had lived through allowed him to give a just appraisal of the Chinese Communists. Because of his approaching death, it was a pity that he could not fulfill his plan and his desire to come after his recovery to our monastery in Sishan to present a concrete and detailed account of the real situation in Communist occupied areas and of the true faces of the Chinese Communists. During the Sino-Japanese War, they used the National United Front Against Japan, or rather, the War of Resistance Against Japan itself to cover their true intentions: to destroy their compatriots in the National Army, while they expanded their military force and consolidated and extended their occupation over the country. This fact can be fully confirmed by the remarks made by Mao Zedong himself. On July 10, 1964, during an interview in Peking, he confided this secret to certain members of the Japanese Socialist Party: "...Without your Imperial Army's aggression and occupation of the greater part of China, the Chinese Communist Party would not have been able to successfully seize control of the country!...You should not feel any remorse!...The Japanese Militarists had brought awfully significant profit to China!...Your past course of action can be interpreted as something very beneficial because you have done us such a favor!" (From the book, *Long Live Mao Zedong's Thought!*, by some members of the Japanese Socialist Party, in the edition of 1969, pp. 532-534.) Since the establishment of his regime in October of 1949, through endless political campaigns within the Party and without, as well as all over the country, Mao and his followers have never ceased to carry out their fundamental policy of tormenting their fellow countrymen. To this day, however, they continue to deny this fact! Truly, the Chinese Communist Party has said, says, and continues to say every nice word but has done, does, and will continue to do every foul deed!

During the war and afterwards there were also real actions

of patriotism in our monastery at Sishan and in Chengdu. On November 15, 1938, Fr. Vincent de Paul Martin, now a healthy eighty-seven-year-old, went to Chongqing to join Fr. Vincent Lebbe and left with him for the Zhongtiao Shan front in Shanxi Province. He was commissioned as a Lieutenant-Colonel to succeed Fr. Lebbe as the head of the Medical Company of the Chinese National Third Army, Twelfth Division. They were undertaking the demanding work of healing the wounded and rescuing the dying among the Chinese soldiers. In May of 1941, he was captured by the Japanese and imprisoned first in Peking, and then in Wei Xian of Shandong Province until the arrival of victory in August of 1945. During the farewell-meeting held in the sports field before his leaving the monastery for Chongqing along with Fr. Thaddeus Yang, he addressed us, grade school pupils, teachers, philosophic and theological seminarians of the local Chinese diocese, monks, priests and Fr. Prior Raphael Vinciarelli, with only four Chinese words and in an extremely sincere, enthusiastic, exciting and touching way:

"Wo ai Zhongguo!" (I love China!)

At the invitation of Bishop Paul Yu Pin, Fr. Thaddeus Yang Anran (Yang An-yuen) (1905-1982) went to Chongqing on November 15, 1938, to head the foreign section of the editorial office of the newspaper, *Yishi Bao (I-shih Pao),* founded by Fr. Vincent Lebbe in Tianjin on October 10, 1915. Then he accepted the request of Dr. Hollington Dong Xianguang (K. Tong) (1887-1971), Vice-Minister of Information, to launch *Le Correspondant Chinois*, a weekly French bulletin, and two years later, *The China Correspondent,* an English monthly. These two periodicals had the mission to inform the foreigner and especially the foreign servicemen about the spirit of resistance of the Chinese people and to explain their customs and outlook. He was also asked to teach English in the training courses of foreign languages to candidates for interpreters of the military department. In recognition of his fruitful services, Generalissimo and Madame Chiang offered him a trip to the United States from May 1945 to March 1946. His trip allowed him to collect donations to construct the new building of our monastery in Chengdu in the summer of 1949, and also to strengthen mutual understanding and friendship between the American and the Chinese people and between the Catholic communities of the two countries. He wrote a booklet on his trip in English under the title of

Going to America to Become a "Mister". The Chinese translation of this booklet was published at first in Chengdu in the diocesan monthly in installments beginning in the summer of 1946, then in November 1947 in Hong Kong in its entirety. In June 1939, Fr. Wilfrid Weitz (1912-1991) was invited to teach a course of French conversation, two or three times a week for two years in Chongqing, to the wife of Generalissimo Chiang, Ms. Sung Mei-ling, who celebrated her 102nd birthday in the United States of America on March 28, 1999. Then he began his career of teaching English in college and universities until 1949 when he had to leave for Belgium for reasons of poor health. To sum up his teaching experiences and to benefit Chinese students, he published a book entitled *English Syntax* in 1946 in Chengdu. Fr. Eleutherius Winance has been a tireless professor and a fervent missionary to this day, remaining hale and hearty at his advanced age of ninety. He then taught the French language in the Sichuan Provincial Academy of Fine Arts and philosophy in the West China Union University. During summer and winter vacations and on some other occasions, he used to do apostolic work, visiting parishes and Catholic families. After his imprisonment and expulsion by the Communists from China on February 6, 1952, he recorded his "personal experience of brainwashing" in his book, *The Communist Persuasion,* published in the U.S.A. in 1959. Fr. Werner Papeians de Morchoven, a sound and robust 85 year-old artist, was a professor of fine arts in the above-mentioned academy in Chengdu during the latter half of the forties. In 1944 he began to serve as a chaplain for the Catholic officers and men in the American Air Force, Chinese allies and comrades-in-arms during the Second World War. He used to go to the military airfields in Chengdu, Xinjin, Shuangliu, Guanghan and Guan Xian to celebrate Mass for them. He also produced many paintings in China and sometimes offered exhibitions of his paintings. He has never ceased to create new artistic works even now in his old age. Like Fr. Wilfrid Weitz, Fr. Prior Raphael Vinciarelli (1897-1972) was a naturalized Chinese citizen, so that he might serve the Chinese people for their salvation in an easier and better way. While writing articles for the diocesan monthly and three books for the evangelization among Chinese intellectuals, Fr. Prior Raphael laid the foundation for the Institute of Chinese and Western Cultural Studies. To show his most sincere love and that of his Benedictine monastery for China and her people, he conceived of a beautiful plan to establish a Catholic university in the western outskirts of Chengdu.

It is frankly difficult to speak of treason within the Catholic Church or to accuse the Catholics of lacking patriotism. Seeking a pretext for justifying their persecution of and destruction of the Church, the Chinese Communists began to flaunt the banner of Patriotism and shout anti-imperialist slogans. In fact, during their four-year armed rebellion (1945-1949) before usurping power successfully, even during the years of the Sino-Japanese War, they had already openly started their work of persecution of the Church in their occupied areas. In addition to the fate reserved for Fr. Vincent Lebbe, his Medical Corps and his other organizations, the following two examples were the most horrifying among all the disaster-ridden Catholic parishes or communities. In Xiwanzi, 55 km. northeast of Zhangjiakou, originally the most flourishing and oldest parish with the largest population of Catholics in Chahar Province, all the churches and other ecclesiastical buildings were burnt down and many incomplete dead bodies were left scattered everywhere by the Communist troops in December 1946, when they had been forced to beat a retreat once more. At Yangjiaping (Yang Kia Ping), situated originally in the old Chahar Province, 31 of the 75 Trappists of the Monastery of Our Lady of Consolation were massacred directly or tortured to death by the same Red Army from August 1947 to February 1948.

The true meaning of the Chinese Communist expression of "Loving the Motherland" should never be interpreted as "love for the country," but rather as "love for Communism," "love for the Chinese Communist Party," "love for their despotic regime", and as "love for their dictator Mao Zedong himself and for his faithful successors." Regarding the expression of the "Anti-imperialists," it was used to invite, seduce, galvanize and urge people, in reality or at least in their hearts, to fight against all the countries and peoples, except the Soviet Union and its allies, who did not or would not agree with them, nor support them, but rather tried to oppose them or to struggle with them. Just like these two words, "Motherland" and "Imperialism", democracy, freedom, people, truth, falsehood, good, evil and many other terms in their vocabulary, on their lips and in their actions have always an meaning quite different even contrary to ours, to the ordinary understanding or to the customary usage. They have given all the words of this kind totally new, unusual and opposite definitions, intentions and explanations. In playing double-faced tactics, they were able to make fools of the Chinese people at home and deceive the foreigner, the international society and world opinion abroad. Now, let us see what kind of strategy and tactics the Chinese Communists concretely adopted, although vainly, to destroy the Catholic Church in China.

The Communists carried out, step by step, a deliberate plan of oppression under the pretense of "protecting and purifying the Church." They undertook a series of overt and official schemes, such as launching the movements of Opposition to Imperialism and Love of the Fatherland, the Three Autonomies Reform, and the abolition of the Legion of Mary. At the same time, they resorted to covert and contemptible means to destroy the Church from within, by inciting apostasy through personal gain, infiltrating Church institutions with spies and subversives, and sowing discord among foreign and Chinese priests, and among Chinese clergy and laity. Few of the enemies of the Church in her history could match the Chinese Communists in their deceit, ruthlessness, and ferocity.

One might ask why the Chinese Communist Party chose these movements to start its violent offensive on the Catholic Church. At that time in the Catholic Church in China there were two important forces playing a prominent role in the propagation and defense of the Faith. The first was a large contingent of about six thousand foreign clerics, monks and nuns; and the second was the Legion of Mary, a lay association comprised of fervent Catholics who assisted the clergy in their efforts of evangelization. Its members participated in weekly meetings of prayer and spiritual reading under the guidance of priests. They also aided the clergy with programs of home visitation and Bible study. The organization spread widely among the priests and lay people in many cities in China since its establishment in the autumn of 1948. One year later, when the political color of the country began to change, its rapid expansion proved to be quite remarkable. Its founder, the Irish priest, Fr. William Aedan McGrath, M.S.C., had to spend almost three years in jail before being expelled by the Communist Government from China in May 1954.

The existence of the Legion of Mary and the presence of foreign missionaries must have been an ongoing headache for the Communist Party, but were also an ideal excuse to justify the destruction of the Church. They must have thought that if these two forces were completely shattered, they would attain their goal of seeing the Church in China lose her vitality and gradually collapse by herself. As a result, they put a reactionary secret society label on the Legion of Mary, and labeled the Legionaries as "anti-revolutionaries" before cracking down on them.

In the meantime, the Communist Party intentionally identified the Internuncio, Archbishop Antonio Riberi and foreign missionaries and nuns as imperialists before expelling them from the country. After this was accomplished, it then forced the indigenous clergy and laity to sever all relations with the Pope in Rome and carry out the "Three Autonomies Reform." With this strategy, the Chinese Communists asserted that the Catholic Church in China should be freed from the yoke of the Vatican and foreign missionaries in order to be governed, supported and propagated by Chinese Catholics only, in other words, carrying out the three points of the Reform: "Self-Government, Self-Support, and Self-Propagation." In reality, however, they sought to control and enslave the Church.

I, Brother Peter Zhou, was looked upon as one of these "indigenous clergy." On October 15, 1949, I had been admitted into the novitiate by Fr. Raphael Vinciarelli, the third prior of the Catholic Benedictine Monastery of Chengdu. This priory had been built at Sishan on the outskirts of the city of Nanchong (Shunqing Fu), Sichuan Province, in 1929 by monks from the Benedictine Abbey of Saint-Andre in Bruges, Belgium.

I had first been drawn to this religious order in 1938 at the age of 12 when I continued my primary studies at the priory-run school. Finally, in the fall of 1950, Fr. Vinciarelli let me make the profession of my triennial monastic vows. The fall of 1950 . . . the eve of persecution.

When someone refers to my struggle as "heroic," I feel confused and uncomfortable because the heroic character of the battle is without doubt due to the merciful love of God and the circumstances arranged by Him. Were there not the heat and tension of the struggle, even a fighter, however brave and skillful, would not have ample scope to show his skill and courage, or to achieve his goal. Any success I may have had should be simultaneously attributed to all my spiritual brothers and sisters who stood by me with their prayers or any other kinds of help.

The long, drawn-out struggle was fierce, bitter, and complex. Its record is marked by both successes and failures. With a sort of battle hymn resounding in my ears as I write, I will now try to look back and outline what I personally experienced during those long and significant years.

嚮往救主聖誕夜

漁家傲
一九六七年十二月二十四日
於荊光監獄

萬籟無聲將夜半，
雪花飛舞於霄漢，
救主耶穌來降誕。
天使讚，
貞孃義父齊歡抃。

千古公元頭頁展，
罪身從此賢良變，
人類歡呼天地羨。
牧童伴，
往朝欽敬心如箭。

YEARNING FOR THE SAVIOR ON CHRISTMAS NIGHT

To the Tune of Yu Jia Ao
(Fisherman's Pride)
Nanchong Prison, December 24, 1967

At midnight all is quiet,
Snowflakes dancing in the sky;
The Savior Jesus is born.
The angels are praising,
The Virgin Mother and foster father both rejoice.

The eternal Christian era unfolds its first page:
Sinners begin to change
Into righteous and virtuous men;
Mankind acclaims,
Heaven and earth admire.
Accompanying the shepherds,
My heart is bent
On worshiping Him,
On paying Him my homage.

CHAPTER I

PRELUDE TO THE STRUGGLE

December 1950

On December 13, 1950, the Xinhua News Agency of Peking published a document called a Manifesto of Guangyuan. Fr. Matthias Wang Liangzuo, its author, reproduced the official Declaration approved by the Government and spread by Protestants not long before. This Manifesto announced the determination to break away from all ties with imperialism and establish a new independent church, totally responsible for its own reform, resources, administration, and apostolate. The declaration intended to strongly oppose all the interference of the Vatican in the internal affairs of China and affirmed that imperialism would no longer be allowed to stain the holiness of the Church.

Then, twenty-four years old and a professed member of the Benedictine Monastery in Chengdu, I was uncertain whether this Manifesto was truly initiated by the thirty-year-old priest of the Diocese of Chengdu in Sichuan Province and really favored by his five hundred Catholics, or whether it was simply the work of the Chinese Communist Party. The fact remained that the dissemination of the Manifesto began to create confusion, untold trouble and even calamity for the Church in China. This Fr. Wang very soon became a tamed instrument of the Communist Party. It was rumored that he had married. Since the very beginning he had been made the leading figure of the Sichuan Catholic Patriotic Association in Chengdu, and from the sixties onward, one of the vice-chairmen of the National Catholic Patriotic Association in Peking.

———————

On March 31, 1951, the Communist press in Nanjing published a Reform Declaration signed by the vicar general of the Nanjing Diocese and 783 Catholics, favoring the reform of the Church and opposing the interference of the Vatican in Chinese internal affairs. On that same day, as an expression of his strong protest, His Excellency Archbishop Antonio Riberi, Apostolic Internuncio to China, addressed a letter to all the Catholic bishops in China. In this letter he pointed out that the anti-Church Reform Declaration, issued by the Nanjing clergy and laity, allegedly with his approval, was not acceptable. He put them on guard against this Declaration which vainly attempted to carry out plots and schemes and to sow confusion and trouble among the Catholics of the country. He advised them not to let themselves be deceived by it.

The "Three Autonomies Reform" and the "Opposition to Imperialism and Love of the Fatherland" movements swept over the country, in the words of the Chinese philosopher Mengzi (372-289 B.C.), like "fierce floods and savage beasts." Under the guise of these movements, the Communist propaganda stirred up trouble and caused much harm to the chosen people of the New Covenant. Catholic schools were taken over, hospitals and orphanages forcibly occupied, and other properties of the Church confiscated. Many faithful Chinese and foreign clergy, nuns and laity were accused, publicly denounced, jailed, or expelled. Some, like Fr. Vincent She, were even executed.

Fr. Vincent She, Subprior of the Trappist Monastery of Our Lady of Joy at Nibatuo in the county of Xindu, Sichuan Province, was incarcerated in spring 1951 after being accused of irresponsibility in paying the grain tax for the monastery farmlands, a sum of money too huge to pay. He was also blamed for refusing to hand over firearms allegedly hidden in the monastery. During study sessions of prisoners in the Chengdu Prison, he remained worthy of a child of God by upholding the truth without fail that man was created by God, and he had the courage to recite the Creed in public. He was severely struggled against, beaten and handcuffed. On August 7, 1951, he broke down under the weight of many tortures and died as a hero sacrificing his life in witness of the true faith.

Since the summer of 1950 the non-Chinese Brothers of our Community were put under close surveillance and long-term house arrest, while Archbishop Antonio Riberi was finally expelled from the country in September 1951, as were many other foreign missionaries.

Each of these incidents, each of these catastrophes, like the sword that once pierced the Immaculate Heart of the Blessed Virgin Mary at the foot of the Cross, penetrated my heart.

Affliction and indignation increased my desire to make reparation for the Lord. I came to the good Jesus, dispirited because some of His disciples were abandoning Him, repeating with my patron St. Peter, the Apostle: "Lord, to whom shall we go? You have the words of eternal life. We have come to believe; we are convinced that You are God's Holy One" (Jn. 6:68-69). I eagerly longed for the chance to fight for my Lord and wipe out His Church's disgrace. I looked forward in earnest and with all my might to the speedy arrival of the day of the great and holy battle for the Catholic faith.

Despite Communist surveillance and restriction on our movements outside the Priory, we did know about current events through our visitors and the daily mail. Seeing confusion and division growing among the clergy and laity of Chengdu, Fr. Prior Raphael Vinciarelli regularly explained to the community the real current situation of the local Church and the monastery, asking us to prepare at any time for all eventualities. We tried to keep the usual schedule of our daily life in celebrating Masses, reciting collectively Vespers and Compline, teaching, studying and doing all the other works, in spite of living in a near panic under the tense atmosphere. Indeed, the threat of danger hung upon us, and gave us the feeling of a defeated army in full retreat, as the Chinese proverb says, surprised and terrified even "at the sound of the wind and the cry of the crane."

During that October, the Communists had launched an all-out attack on the local Church and our monastery. The agents from the Yangshi Street Police Station used to turn up at any time to inspect the monastery building and the rooms of the monks without warning. One morning when Fr. Prior Raphael was typing in his office, a policeman unexpectedly opened the door and broke in, demanding in loud voice, "What are you writing!"

Fr. Prior, remaining calm, immediately took the paper from the typewriter and showed it to him, saying, "Please read! This is what I was writing. You must know French. Surely you are able to grasp my typing!"

The policeman arrogantly cast a sidelong glance at the paper and put it on the desk. Then he moved forward and stepped into Fr. Prior's bedroom, looking here and there, before leaving quietly.

Later that same month, Fr. Prior Raphael called me to his office and charged me with the task of translating, in secret, two documents from French into Chinese. The first was a prayer written by Pope Pius XII and dedicated to Pope Blessed Pius X. The second document was a three-page catechism written by Fr. Prior Raphael himself at the request of Bishop Henri Pinault with the intention of helping Catholics in time of persecution. This was precisely the document Fr. Prior Raphael had been typing and the policeman had had in his hands.

This little catechism presented to Catholics the basic doctrines of the Church, especially the supremacy of the Pope in Rome over the whole Church. It insisted that constant prayers and the observance of the Commandments should be the necessary and effective way to keep their Faith. However, it also explained that it would be a struggle, a challenge to lead a pure and holy Catholic life and to bear witness to Christ. It gave instructions on how to be reconciled with God, how to act concretely in the situations of marriage or death should the Holy Sacraments be unavailable for them. Fr. Prior enjoined me again and again to keep the work of translation secret. I, for my part, assured him and said to him clearly that I would not fear any danger for having done this.

These two documents alerted me even more concretely to the fact that the Church was indeed approaching a most critical time. They awoke in me a feeling of serious emergency and personal responsibility for the struggle which lay ahead. In my mind I knew that I could not hold my tongue, nor stand by with folded arms, still less become a servant of the Communists. I felt that even Fr. Prior seemed to sense that he and his fellow priests would not be there to aid me. My daily prayers and Scripture readings were reassuring, yet warned me also. Words of warning and encouragement seemed to jump from the sacred text:

"Whoever acknowledges Me before men, I will acknowledge
   before My Father in Heaven. Whoever disowns Me before
   men, I will disown before My Father in Heaven."
   (Mt. 10:32-33).

"Whoever would save his life will lose it, but
   whoever loses his life for My sake will find it." (Mt. 16:25).

"If you find that the world hates you, know it has
   hated Me before you. . ." (Jn. 15:18).

"I am the good shepherd. I know My sheep and My sheep know Me. . ." (Jn. 10:14).

"Blest are those persecuted for holiness' sake; the reign of God is theirs." (Mt. 5:10).

These profound teachings of Jesus Christ went straight to my heart, and His sacred call resounded in my ears. Each word rang in me like the order of a Supreme Commander, or like the instruction of a King, giving strength and courage for the struggle, or still like a bugle call at the hour of the charge.

再訪成都

卜算子
九五三年六月
於四川省成都市

朝食故鄉糕，
暮飲岷江水。
九月剛離又賦歸，
眶滿辛酸淚。

頌主者歡欣，
戰鬼今憔悴。
信仰堅持飲苦杯，
有志青春美！

THE SECOND VISIT TO CHENGDU

To the Tune of Pu Suan Zi
(Song of Fortune Telling)
Chengdu, Sichuan-June 1953

In the morning I took cakes in my hometown,
In the evening I drank water from the Min River.
Nine months later,
There I am again,
With my eyes full of tears.

In times past, I was always happy
To sing Psalms of praise to the Lord;
Now I am wan and sallow
From fighting with the devils of these times.
Adhering to the depths of the Faith,
Drinking from the bitter chalice:
Beautiful is the youth with such high ideals!

CHAPTER II

THE BATTLE BEGINS

October 1951

In late October 1951, fierce persecution of the Church broke out publicly in our city. Throughout the streets of the provincial capital, the Chengdu Military Control Commission posted the official announcement of the suppression of the Legion of Mary accused of being a "reactionary organization." The local Commissions had replaced the Communist armies, as their representatives, to control the cities during the first few years after the capture of the whole Mainland. These Commissions became the local political power of the Chinese Communist Government. The announcement ordered the Legionaries to go immediately to the public security departments to register their resignation, admit the Legion of Mary to be reactionary and break away publicly from this organization. This put into motion the intense development of the Opposition to Imperialism and Love of the Fatherland and the Three Autonomies Reform movements in the entire city.

The Communist Party had originally tried to control and destroy the Church only through its civil officials from the United Front Work Department and the Religious Affairs Bureau. Now with their intentions no longer concealed, it came out from backstage and appeared up front, beginning to enforce its decree of suppressing the Legion of Mary through its military police from the Public Security Bureau. The Communist Government openly assumed leadership in persecuting the Church following the same ruthless procedures of the Government of the Qing Dynasty which ordered the killing in Chengdu in 1815 of Blessed John-Gabriel Dufresse, Bishop, and his faithful priests, both indigenous and foreign, as well as the laity. Thus, the waves of the present and latest persecution swept once more over the historic city of Chengdu which had already bathed in the blood of those martyrs one hundred and thirty-six years before.

At the age of 25, rooted in my Catholic Faith and committed to the Benedictine order, could I remain passive or indifferent, standing on the sidelines? In the monastery Fr. Prior Raphael, Fr. Gaetan and the other monks prayed for us and contemplated our roles for the future. Uniformed, stonefaced Communist policemen and their followers kept watch on us outside the monastery gates. Marching sometimes filled the streets along with loud shouts of citizens protesting our presence. At times the angry groups boldly entered the monastery gates and appeared on the grounds surrounding our quarters and shouting slogans against us.

Early one morning, a notice was delivered ordering our attendance that same evening at meetings in the Yangshi Street Police Station of the Public Security Bureau in Chengdu. All Catholics under its jurisdiction were being called to an "Informal Discussion among Catholics." The purpose was to unmask, denounce, accuse, criticize and struggle against the Legion of Mary. We were also ordered to attend "study sessions" at the Peace Bridge Street Cathedral to discuss the "Reform."

Now, as the struggle for the defense of the Church began, I was filled with an increasing righteous indignation. As a soldier of Christ, I was eager and ready, in the Chinese idiom, "to flourish the whip to urge on the horse," to rush into the battlefield, and armed with the weapons of faith and truth, to do close and deadly combat with the powers of darkness.

Fr. Paul Wu Yong and I walked unescorted to that first of the four consecutive evening meetings. The quiet night badly belied the intense emotions we felt surging inside, yet I remained silent as I walked a short distance behind Fr. Paul. The Yangshi Street Police Station was dimly lit and the room where the meeting would be had barely enough light to see the grim expressions of the faces of those in attendance. The presiding officer aimed his speech at the Church, news articles were read and accusations thrown at the Legion of Mary. After that, we were directed into small groups for discussion. During one of these group sessions, I clearly reiterated my firm opposition to criticism of the Legion of Mary and my flat refusal to attend the study session at the Peace Bridge Street Cathedral.

On the last evening, just before the conclusion of the meeting, Officer Qiang, head of the local police station and in charge of all the proceedings, ordered me to remain behind alone. He invited me to his office to ask whether I would retract and change my "obstinate position" and "rigid attitude" toward the Reform and the Legion of Mary. When I replied in the negative, in a threatening tone and with a stern look, he asked, "Would you dare to put what you have said on paper? If you have the courage, write it down!"

Without hesitation, I requested pen and paper, and wrote the following concise and serious statement:

> "I affirm that the Legion of Mary is a legal and holy organization within the Church. It is an open social institution. I will never join the movement of the 'Three Autonomies Reform' which is aimed at dividing and destroying the Church, nor attend its study sessions."

Then I deliberately added the noble title of "Roman Catholic Believer" before my name. At his request, I also put my fingerprint after my name to demonstrate I would never deny or regret what I had done.

With that he dismissed me without explanation. I turned and walked holding my head high from his office, knowing that my time had come. On the way back, my mind raced with thoughts about the priory and my family, and with increased awareness of my commitment to God and the Church. So deeply absorbed in my own thoughts, I barely knew how I reached the gate of the monastery. Dark and deserted, my only home still offered safe haven to my troubled mind. I gave a brief report to Fr. Prior Raphael, who was awaiting my return, praying the Rosary outside the chapel wall. Once I arrived in my room, I offered my prayers to my gracious Savior and lay down for rest.

For a whole week beginning on November 2 of the same year, the agents of the local police station organized mass assemblies in the entrance hall of our Benedictine Priory at 172 Yangshi Street. Hundreds crowded into the area for a continuation of the four-day "Informal Discussion among Catholics" held at the Police Station. Fr. Paul Wu Yong, Mr. Jia Zhizhong, our manual worker, myself, and two other persons of the Priory were called faithful "imperialist running dogs." From the beginning officials forced us to attend these meetings every evening, at times ordering us to a center table where we faced a thousand accusing fingers and were targets of all kinds of abuses. For hours each evening, officials, extremists and fellow Catholics who had gone over to the Communists took turns standing and shouting invectives at us, attacking our monastery and denouncing the Church.

During the first two evenings, anti-Catholic documents were read and explained as usual by the police and the officials of the neighborhood commission. The attacks were directed against the Legion of Mary, the Pope, the Apostolic Internuncio, bishops, priests, nuns, and the Catholic orphanages. All were ridiculed, maligned and insulted. The assembled crowd was incited to cry out without fear and expose without mercy the various "crimes" supposed to have been committed by the Church as a whole against the country.

While my ears were stung by all these calumnies, my heart was filled with anger. Overflowing with these intense emotions, I could not restrain myself from writing a lengthy declaration to defend the Church (See Appendix I). Since we had been told we could air our own personal opinions to the public, at the third evening meeting, I stood up from my seat, took the floor and read my text to the crowd.

After briefly introducing myself, I stated the three points which manifested clearly my position and attitude. First, I categorically refused to join the so-called Reform, a movement which neither before nor after its establishment had received the approval of the Pope of Rome, the one and only head of the Catholic Church. Moreover, this movement was flatly and totally disengaged from the authority of the Holy See, having a radically different orientation and goal. Secondly, I dutifully recognized and respected the legal, pure, and sacred character of the Legion of Mary, an organization of Catholic laity, which had been approved by the highest authority of the Church. Finally, I openly professed my most sincere affection for Jesus Christ; to Him I pledged my total loyalty and love. I affirmed my desire and willingness to sacrifice everything, including my life, for Him.

As soon as I finished speaking, the whole audience was stirred up and the crowd began shouting. Extremists among the throng vied with one another in shooting many questions in rapid succession, demanding immediate answers.

"You believe in a foreign religion! You are a Chinese! Why

should you defend this foreign religion?"

With the help of the Holy Spirit I had the strength to answer them one by one, withstanding their onslaught, "I do not believe in any foreign religion, but in the Catholic religion, which belongs to the entire world and the whole of humankind. She teaches people the truth, promotes their goodness and holiness and leads them to everlasting life. As a simple Chinese, especially as a loyal Catholic, I should undertake the serious duty and responsibility to speak in defense of the Church."

"The Communist Party and the People's Government have never been against your religious belief, but against the imperialists' aggressive acts done through the Church and endangering the Chinese people. How can you be ignorant of it?"

"The Church has never been a cat's paw for imperialism, nor participated in any activities harmful to the Chinese people. How could this be unknown to you?" I countered.

"Why should you tell a bare-faced lie? How can you deny the countless crimes jeopardizing the Chinese people, exposed in all the press and committed by the imperialists in the garb of religion?"

"The sources of the newspapers are not infallible. It still needs to be verified whether the related reports are true are not. Foreign missionaries have been engaged only in lawful religious activities. They have served the Chinese people enthusiastically in the salvation of their souls. They have never worked on behalf of imperialism!"

During the following evenings, they continued to question me. They tried in vain to wear me down by keeping me constantly on the run; they hoped to make me unable to withstand them and so finally to defeat me. In my responses, I sought to refute their calumnies and bring to light the unfairness and untruth of their statements about the Church.

"If you speak truly, how can you explain to us the actions and attitude of the imperialist in Nanjing, expelled from the country just two months ago and called by you pompously as 'Apostolic Internuncio'? He has done everything to hinder brazenly Chinese Catholics from joining the patriotic movement of the Catholic Three Autonomies Reform."

"Archbishop Riberi, as the delegate to China of the Pope in Rome, the sole supreme leader of the whole Church, had the responsibility to uphold the Faith and unity of the Church. He was obliged to put an end to the campaign of rebellion, orchestrated to split and destroy the Church. He was fully justified in doing so. It is a downright mistake and an improper attribution to the wrong person, just like "putting Zhang's hat on Li's head," that he has been labeled as an imperialist!"

But they switched to another subject, "It is undeniable that there have been imperialist activities in the Catholic Church. Why must you flatly deny it? Right at present, there is another evident example. The Legion of Mary, a counter-revolutionary secret organization in the Church, has now been banned by the People's Government. You can by no means deny it, can you?"

"Though I did not take part in the Legion of Mary, I know very well that it was approved by the Pope and that it is a legal and holy organization. It encourages its members to practice special devotion to the Blessed Virgin Mary, to observe the Commandments of the Lord, to remain faithful to the teachings of the Church, to take part in evangelization and to serve the world."

Just at this point the extremists brought up the emotional and burning issue concerning the Fenghuang Hill orphanage deaths.

"On Fenghuang (Phoenix) Hill in the northern suburban district there is a mass grave confirmed to be a burial place of ten thousand corpses. There countless murdered babies were buried. It was just your French Sisters in charge of the orphanage at Madao Street who have done this outrage. Do you still try to persist in denying the guilt of these imperialist slaughterers, capable of killing without blinking an eye?"

Over the shouts and moans of the overheated, indiscriminate and uncritical crowd, I answered, "In spite of being ignorant of the exact situation in the local Catholic orphanage, what I can absolutely affirm is that these French Sisters have had nothing to do with the so-called 'slaughterers' of those Chinese orphans. Having left their own country and traveled all the way across the oceans, they came to China not to plunder nor murder, but to practice Christ's teachings about universal love and redemption of the world. With these high and holy ideals they have done their utmost to establish charities, bring up abandoned orphans and save the souls of the dying. They have come with a self-sacrificing spirit to enter the service of the Chinese people, ready to remain faithful without respite until the end of their lives. About the so-called 'Phoenix Hill mass grave affair,' I believe, history and time must give a reasonable explanation and a fair judgment, and one day the whole truth must be revealed and come to be known to all. If only people would take off their colored spectacles, which can confuse black and white, and have a correct observation and understanding of the objective world around them!"

During the last two meetings we, the "obstinate ones," were obliged to stand in the center as the crowd surrounded us, threatening, criticizing, scolding, and insulting. In this way, they hoped to achieve an honorable and triumphant ending to the weeklong general public criticism assembly.

At the outset, I had a presentiment that imprisonment, even martyrdom, was imminent. But, as events unfolded, I understood that the will of God deigned otherwise. Even if this might come to me one day in the near or distant future, for that moment, it was only a question, only a good, but unfulfilled wish.

I did not keep a copy of my public declaration. It was a fortnight later, however, at the request of Fr. Prior Raphael Vinciarelli, who on November 9 had been imprisoned, that I rewrote it. He, together with several French missionaries and Sisters of the Chengdu Diocese, had been taken to a temporary detention house in the Battalion of the Criminal-Police in Hongqiang (Red Wall) Street. They had refused to accept the official description of the Legion of Mary as an outlawed reactionary organization. This was the first step toward their expulsion from the country on February 6, 1952.

After the first two weeks of acute and intense conflict with the Communist Party and its militants, God in His wisdom and mercy provided me with a respite of over two months to prepare for a new struggle. During this period, all the foreign members of the community either left the country "voluntarily" or were expelled. My monastic family was dispersed. Only two Chinese members, Fr. Paul Wu and myself, were left to take care of the deserted building. We were totally aware that we would have to move out sooner or later. We boarded with Mr. Vincent Yuan Nengding. Upon failing to obtain a passport to leave for Belgium with his Belgian wife, he resigned himself to remain behind and live alone in the old houses of the monastery.

We had no daily duties. After attending Fr. Paul Wu's early morning Mass with the others still lodging in the monastery, we spent our time in our respective cells reciting the Divine Office and reading holy books. During the day we went out frequently to visit some of the loyal laymen and sisters.

In the afternoons as the sun was setting in the west, the monastery looked more abandoned and desolate than ever. Facing the miserable scene, I could not repress sighs of sadness. It was truly like the scene described in an ancient poem:

> "The house becomes hollow when its host is gone,
> Even though white clouds should remain over it
> For one thousand years!"

From the very beginning, the Municipal Committee of the Communist Party in Chengdu decided to occupy our monastery. At first, it commanded the Catholic Three Autonomies Patriotic Association to act on its behalf to confiscate the traditional Chinese-style structure. Since it was Church property, it belonged officially to the Patriotic church. In this roundabout way, members of the Patriotic church took over the premises but only in name, because in fact, none of them were allowed to enter to live among us. Fr. Gaetan Loriers, our acting-prior and last foreign brother, had been forced to hand over to them all the keys of the building just before his expulsion from the country on March 2, 1952. Then they began to transport our utensils, furniture and books of the library to the nearby cathedral on Peace Bridge Street. In cooperation with the Municipal Committee, the local police station of Yangshi Street ordered us and the other eighteen people living on our property to evacuate the Priory by the end of April. We had a very short time to comply and find other housing.

The month of April 1952 was radiant and enchanting. The spring was warm. Flowers were blooming everywhere in the city of brocade. The Exhibit of Flowers at the Qingyang Temple was coming to the height of its grand festival. Then, when everything was alive and most beautiful, the Municipal Committee of the Communist Party made their decision to take possession of our magnificent monastery building. I had no choice but to tearfully bid farewell to the monastery where I had lived joyously for nearly fourteen years, including six years at Sishan Monastery. At the end of the month, I moved back to Suining to live with my father, Paul Zhou Zinan, and to assist him in setting up a stall for his eyeglass business, hoping that one day I could escape to the haven of the West.

The situation in the local parish was as serious as that of the parishes in Chengdu. I was continually harassed and pressured to change my thinking. Wu Bogao, an old schoolmate from the Nanchong Provincial High School and close friend of mine, was then drifting with the tide and came to question me. Failing to coerce me into accepting the Reform, he became aggressive and hostile. From then on whenever we met in the street he glared angrily at me and showed me his hostility. Another time I was given a review of the Reform movement published in Changsha, Hunan Province, by a religious sister who was actively participating in the study meetings of the Reform. Finally, on the Feast of Our Lady, Help of Christians (May 24, 1952), the local Reform Association of Chengdu scheduled a mass meeting to celebrate its official establishment. The extreme elements of the Association continued to sabotage the Church and harass those priests and laity who remained faithful to the Holy Father.

All these incidents struck a deep chord in me, bringing tears to my eyes, sorrow to my heart, and bitterness to my soul. I felt the increasing need to voice my dismay. Choosing the only means in my possession--my pen--and hoping to reach others, I addressed those who like myself, struggled to maintain their faith in the chaos surrounding their daily lives. Delivered to all Catholics in China, my letter emerged as if required by the times.

I tried to analyze the Three Autonomies Reform Movement from all possible perspectives and to clearly point out how this movement, under the pretense of "self-government, self-support and self-propagation," and "opposition to imperialism and love of the fatherland," sought to deceive simple people and to attack and slander the Pope, the Vatican, and the Apostolic Internuncio. At the same time, I showed how the Reform had craftily and unscrupulously denounced, falsely accused, and wrongly condemned the priests, nuns, and laity who were loyal to Rome; and I indicated how it scandalously attempted both to appoint and remove members of the clergy.

I wrote that through these means, the movement was breaking and destroying the unity, sanctity, Catholicity and apostolicity of the Church. It brought the Church under the absolute control of the Chinese Communist Party and turned the Church into a mindless and obedient political tool of the State. Such shameful actions of those who embraced the Three Autonomies Movement were evidently against the commandments of God and the laws of the Church.

Recalling in pain and agony the devastating persecutions of the Church in the past, I suddenly realized that I had become an anxiety-filled witness of the Church in danger of imminent collapse. Finally, looking to the possible destruction of the Church in an uncertain future, I uttered a loud cry of warning to all Catholics in China. I appealed to each and all to distinguish truth from falsehood, right from wrong, and to use all their power to break with and fight against any acts and words of their own and of others which might lead to betrayal. I urged that they should not hesitate to pay a high price to stem the raging tide, and if necessary, to shed their blood to write a heroic and moving page in the magnificent history of the Church.

My four-page open letter was completed in August 1952, when I was in Suining. In September I went to Chengdu and distributed more than twenty copies among my acquaintances: priests, seminarians, sisters, and lay people who remained faithful to the Church. Copies were also sent to Sr. Marie-Claire, a French Sister from the Franciscan Missionaries of Mary. I corresponded with her from the autumn of 1952 until the spring of 1954 when she was expelled from Shanghai. A French priest in Canton, Fr. Pierre Narbais-Jaureguy, translated my letter into French after having received it that fall. He was imprisoned by the Communist Party on August 26, 1953, nearly one year later, and then expelled from China on April 21, 1954. Three years later this document, my declaration and appeal in defense of the Catholic religion, was used as "evidence" of a "counter-revolutionary crime," and as an "attempt to overthrow the People's Government." It was the principal charge held against me, playing a decisive role in my arrest and in my sentence.

Not long after, in that same fall of 1952, I still felt I had not given adequate and clear expression to my concern about the Church, my thoughts about China, and my detestation of the world and its ways. All kinds of thoughts and feelings swept over me. I expanded them in a work entitled *From Paradise to Purgatory* in which I insisted on denouncing the real intent and activities of the Reform. I also condemned the general and specific policies and the tricky and deceitful tactics of the Chinese Communist Party. I pointed out that all these policies and tactics had no other purpose than to oppose God, destroy the Church, suppress thought, enslave hearts, and bring calamity to the country and its people.

As the manuscript was progressing, I sent drafts to fellow

strugglers in Chengdu for their criticism and correction. By August 1953, the first draft was completed. Since my request to pursue studies at the seminary in Shanghai had been refused by the Suining Bureau of Public Security, I had no choice but to return to Chengdu. After a three-month stay in the provincial capital, I registered as a permanent resident at 184 Changshun Middle Street, the home of Mr. Vincent Yuan Nengding, my old and close friend from the last days at the monastery. There I finished the correction and recopying of my manuscript.

In January 1954, when I realized it was impossible for me to go to Shanghai, I asked Zhu Chaoqian to deliver my manuscript and "Letter" addressed to my fellow Catholics in China to Fr. Aloysius Jin Luxian, S.J., Rector of the Seminary in Shanghai, for examination and publication. This rector was at the time a brave and firm warrior of the faith. But, unfortunately, after his arrest in September 1955, he began to change his position, accepting a compromise and in the end, becoming a member of the Patriotic Association. Since his appointment in the eighties by the Chinese Communists to the dignity of the "bishop of Shanghai", he has even become an active and effective propagandist and apologist of the Chinese Communist "religious freedom". How was I to know that Zhu Chaoqian, who appeared to be a faithful Catholic, was, in fact, a Communist spy sent to infiltrate the Church?

This forty-year-old Chinese had lived in Hongqiang (Red Wall) Lane in the vicinity of our monastery. He was introduced by a certain reliable Catholic in 1951 to Fr. Prior Raphael and Bishop Henri Pinault, M.E.P. Shortly afterwards he received baptism and was given the Christian name of Peter. All of this was, in actual fact, only a masquerade designed to win the confidences of Bishop Pinault and our Fr. Prior. His feigned faith and pretended opposition to the Communist Party gained him a position of counselor, and his opinions were valued by both churchmen. Bishop Pinault appointed him to collect house rent for the diocese, spoke with him about all that related to the Church and asked him for advice in many situations. Fr. Prior looked upon him as a fervent Catholic and sought his opinions whenever he had dealings with the Communists. They even recommended him to their own successors before their deportation, instructing them to put trust in him and enlist his help in case of necessity. All their successors, Fr. Lawrence Li Wenjing, Fr. Robert Xue, Fr. Gaetan Loriers, and Fr. Paul Wu Yong, followed the recommendations to the letter. Other loyal priests, seminarians, sisters and laymen in Chengdu also regarded Zhu as one of their own and kept in close contact with him. We frequented his house to attend the Masses celebrated by the underground priests. I myself gave him all my confidence, very often calling on him for counsel about almost all matters, large and small.

For their part, the Communists allowed members of the Patriotic Association to treat him as their enemy and occasionally to cause him some trouble so that he might more easily conceal his real identity and thereby efficaciously keep watch on and destroy the underground Church in secret. One day near the end of 1953, I went to see him at his house. He told me that he had been an officer in the Kuomintang's army and that he had hidden his military uniforms and all his credentials under the floor of his bedroom. He even added that his loyalty to the Church could withstand the test of time!

Even Fr. Lawrence Li, the underground acting Bishop of the Chengdu Diocese, was totally deceived just as everyone else. Fr. Li, appointed in secret by Bishop Pinault just before his expulsion, had received a letter written in Latin from Fr. Francois Dufay, a French missionary living in Hong Kong after his deportation from Chengdu on March 31, 1952. This French missionary requested Fr. Li to dispatch someone to Shanghai as soon as possible to pick up a large sum of money from the hands of another French missionary, Fr. Louis Suchet Amiotte, expelled from China on May 5, 1955, who has been serving as a church's pastor in Singapore since 1956 to this day. The amount, about five thousand American dollars, was badly needed for the diocese.

After much consideration, Fr. Li appointed me and Zhu Chaoqian to fulfill this extremely important and confidential mission. Taking also into account that my departure might in all likelihood be hindered by the local police station, he finally decided to let Zhu set out on the journey in advance and stop in Chongqing to await my rejoining him. All my efforts to travel to Shanghai, however, failed and Zhu continued his travel alone.

In retrospect, this was obviously all pre-arranged, plotted and controlled by the Communists. Zhu carried with him, along with my two manuscripts, letters of recommendation by Fr. Li, another priest, and myself! Thus he was able to obtain the large sum of money, and also to come into contact with all our friends in Chongqing, Wuhan, Shanghai, and Canton and in this way, to have access to all the information on the Church in those great cities. The money was put into his care and control from the very start and when, in fact, it reached the diocese, Fr. Li used only a very small sum before his arrest in November 1955. The rest probably fell into Communist hands.

A month after I had entrusted my manuscripts to this supposed friend, the fellow Zhu was home from his trip to Shanghai and re-appeared in Chengdu. He gave me a message that he had delivered my manuscripts to Fr. Aloysius Jin. He also claimed that Fr. Jin told him that, because of the possibility of his own imminent arrest, the manuscripts should be put into the care of some other person. What actually took place, I do not know. The two manuscripts, however, written for the defense of the Church, simply disappeared, never to be seen again, as the Chinese proverb says, "A clay-ox enters the sea and never returns."

Not until the summer of 1955 was Zhu's mask thrown off and his true character revealed by Fan Tingsen, his accomplice and my former fellow novice. We were all extremely surprised and greatly shocked. We couldn't imagine this to be credible until we thought back carefully and repeatedly, stage by stage, on all our dealings with him from the beginning, even the most minute. Eventually, we were obliged to yield to the facts that Zhu Chaoqian and his two fellows, Li Zhenyu and Fan Tingsen, truly were secret Communist agents working among us. These three regularly reported to the Battalion of the Criminal-Police and gave the Communist intelligence officers the latest situation of the underground Church. When they frequented that Communist branch, they did their best to avoid meeting with one another. If they happened upon each other by chance, they would keep silent and dared not even say hello. They were absolutely forbidden to consult with each other and were ordered to limit the field to their own espionage. They were to be responsible only to their common and immediate superior and to deliver to him their independent reports. From him they received instructions as well as their monthly subsidies.

Fan experienced such sentiments of guilt that he could continue his deception no longer. At long last, he revealed this "state secret" to our underground Church, and, as a result, was thrown into prison by the Communists in mid-November 1955, a week after my own imprisonment. In August 1958, he was sentenced to a fixed-term imprisonment and then sent to one of the many labor-reform camps of the Communists.

During the entire year that I lived in Chengdu, I tried my best not to arouse any suspicion. In addition to my close connections with the underground Church, I lived the simple life of an honest citizen, praying, reading, studying and writing. In March 1954, I launched a small business transaction with Mr. Vincent Yuan Nengding, Sr. Anna Lei Jingyuan and Sr. Assumption Jiang Qifang, two sisters of the Franciscan Missionaries of Mary. We had a grocery, selling various household supplies such as peanuts, eggs, seasonings, soap, matches and toilet paper.

I used to go, without a stop, to state companies, wholesale stores, or suburban marketplaces to stock shops with goods. I regularly had to make my way to the office of the trade association of grocers to attend meetings and listen to lectures. I also had to keep up my relations with the people in the same trade. All these obligations were so heavy physically and mentally that I was weighed down, not difficult to imagine, by excessive fatigue and the rigorous strain. After half a year we lost money, and I took the blame and resigned. I then resumed the study of philosophy, which revived my soul, lightened my spirit and gave me much contentment.

My financial condition continued to deteriorate. I had neither any bank deposit, nor any other source of income. I had only a couple of dollars as ready cash. My monthly board, a sum of seven dollars, was generously paid each month by Fr. Lawrence Li. I lived a hard life; however, I did not become discouraged, nor did my will weaken. The following spring I began to write to Fr. Paulinus Li, O.C.S.O., Prior of the Trappist Monastery in Hong Kong and to Fr. Gaetan Loriers of the Abbey of St. Andre, Bruges, Belgium. Both of them promptly responded. They gave me the required advice and met with my needs. The former remitted me a certain sum of money several times, while the latter sent me a new missal in French and in Latin, two little copies of the breviary and some other sacred books. This correspondence not only improved my living conditions, but also raised the level of my confidence. During this distressing time, I was able to make frequent contact with fellow strugglers in Chengdu. As we encouraged one another, my spirit rose and my hope soared.

Less than two months before being taken into custody, I received the bad news of the arrest and imprisonment of the bishop, priests and lay people in the Diocese of Shanghai who remained loyal to Rome. The iron hand of Communist oppression began tightening its hold on my freedom, just a week prior to my own arrest, when a few of the extreme elements of the Patriotic Association in Chengdu called on me unexpectedly and tried to persuade me to retract my stand, and to incite me to betray the true faith. All this presaged that the time of my imprisonment was imminent.

The cup I had been willing to drink at the start of my struggle four years before, but unable to reach out for, was now at hand and would never be denied. I was totally ready to raise it and empty it with joy for the Lord. In order to have thoroughly cleansed my soul and worthily celebrated the feast day of my Patron Saint, I had made a three-day spiritual retreat at the nearby Trappist Monastery four months before. There, I had made a general confession in preparation for whatever was to come, and in the desire to well dispose myself, with courage and peace, to welcome God's will.

夢聖誕

七律
一九六七年十二月二十四日
於南充監獄

救主生時雨雪霏，
歡迎玉笛朔風吹。
牧童見謁貞萱樂
天使聞歌養父怡。
仰視奇星賢士愕，
沉思聖誕信徒傳。
夜闌因語南柯逐，
身在鐵窗醒始知！

A CHRISTMAS DREAM

In the Poetic Style of Qilu
Nanchong Prison, December 24, 1967

Amidst squall of rain and snow,
The Divine Savior is born;
In greeting Him,
The cold wind plays a jade-flute.
Seeing the shepherds bow down,
The Virgin Mother rejoices;
Hearing the angels sing,
The foster father exults.
The wise men are astonished
Looking up to the mysterious Star;
Believers are happy
Pondering deeply over the Holy Birth.
In the dead of night
The inmates' whispers shatter my dreams,
I wake to find my body in jail!

CHAPTER III

IMPRISONMENT IN THE JAIL OF CHENGDU

November 1955

That favorable and blessed day the Lord had prepared for me from all eternity finally arrived on November 7, 1955. At three o'clock in the morning, I was suddenly awakened first by the sound of a car horn, then by a violent knock on the door. Sr. Anna Lei Jingyuan, who slept downstairs in a small room near the kitchen, got up immediately at the harsh sound of the knock, turned on the lights and stepped forward to open the door. No sooner had I arisen from bed and dressed than two persons, revolvers in hand, rapidly rushed up the staircase four at a time. Looking at them intently, I recognized one as Mr. Zhang, the policeman in charge of our neighborhood. Pointing their revolvers at me, they shouted, "Raise your hands!"

Then the other official, unknown to me, appeared and loudly read out my arrest warrant, specifying that I was arrested for the crime of "opposing the revolution." Without delay, they put me in handcuffs, searched my desk and bed and took away my photographs and notebooks. I remained speechless and dumbstruck for those few minutes, then was ordered gruffly to go downstairs. They walked me out of the house to a small jeep parked near the door at the side of the street. The official I did not recognize pushed me into the back, and the driver instantly started to drive northward. I was on my way to the No. 2 Detention House of the large prison on Ningxia Street. That same day and on the days following, a number of the clergy, seminarians, and laymen were also arrested and imprisoned.

The news of our imprisonment and our crimes was published in the November 25th edition of the *Sichuan Daily*. The authorities instructed Cheng Min, the chief prisoner of my group, to force me to read the newspaper. Across the front page the headline read as follows: "Anti-Revolution Group Headed by Li Wenjing. . . " The report occupied more than a page. On the second page, there were articles by some new defectors accusing us of "crimes" and denouncing our religious position. I am unable to recall the details of all these reports and articles and I only remember that I was considered the backbone of the "counter-revolutionary group" and treated as the faithful "running dog of the imperialists." My letter addressed to the Catholic clergy and laity of China and my manuscript, *From Paradise to Purgatory,* were presented as unquestionable evidence of my intention to "destroy" the "Three Autonomies Patriotic Movement" and of my "unbridled attempts to slander and attack" the Communist Party and the People's Government.

———————

As I stepped into the Ningxia Prison, I entered into a world totally strange and unlike any other I had before comprehended. Very old and divided into several different parts, some for male prisoners and others for females, the prison seemed to cover a vast area. The place where I was imprisoned at first, had five rectangular single-story barracks arranged in a fan-shaped form with post sentry at the entrance. Each of these barracks was called a "Daozi." Each Daozi had a long corridor running through the center, with exposed electric lamps suspended from the ceiling. The door of the Daozi was left open in the day but locked all night. The rapid change of my environment made a profound and tremendous impact on my whole being. I had never lived in luxury, but I had never been short of what a simple life would require. Here, I was thrust into the midst of a company of ten other prisoners with whom I was compelled to live. In our Daozi there were also thirteen other companies.

Each Daozi had seven cells on either side of the long narrow corridor that ran down the center of the rectangular building. Each cell, dimly lit through the window by the corridor's lamps, was about fourteen square meters, and each contained ten or more prisoners. We had no beds. We slept on the wooden floor. One chamber pot was left in the cell for our needs and only once each day were we allowed to go out, collectively, to use the common lavatory. Two meals, breakfast and supper, were provided daily. For each meal there were vegetables and unpolished rice mixed with wheat bran. In the beginning, I could barely force myself to eat the bad tasting rice, but because I should keep on living and struggling for the Lord, I, as a hungry man, could not be choosy about my food, and gradually my system adjusted to living on this brownish and dry mash.

During the day we had to sit silently on our seats, doing self-examinations or writing our confessions. We could be called out for interrogation at any hour, day or night. In the evening various appointed items from the newspaper were read loudly in the corridor, and then we were to discuss them in our small group. At 9 p.m. the official on duty came to take roll call and after that he bolted the door of the cell: it was bedtime. Each morning at 7, the door was opened again and we got up to start another day of our monotonous life.

The iron gates and the enclosing walls of the prison seemed to strip me of my courage and fighting spirit, creating the false illusion that the struggle had come to an end. The abrupt and radical change in my life, my lack of knowledge of the law and my ignorance of the judicial process gave me great distress. The threatening atmosphere into which I was thrust created tension and fear within me. What is more, I had known for several months that the Communists knew everything about me, our monastery, and the local Church through their three spies, Zhu Chaoqian, Li Zhenyu, and Fan Tingsen, who had been sent or bribed to infiltrate the Church. In my confusion, I consented to write without protest a "confession" at the order of the interrogator on the third day of my detention. I even gave a free hand to the chief prisoner of my group, Cheng Min, to go over and revise the material to his liking.

When I recall what I did, even now, I feel so deeply ashamed and regretful that I can find no place to hide myself. I can do nothing but sorrowfully ask for the infinite mercy of God, Our Savior, to forgive me once more. Once revised, this "confession" to the crimes with which I had been charged was handed over to the prison officials. My spiritual distress and mental confusion lasted for another month and a half. After this sad period, I began to awaken, to recognize what was happening, and to correct myself. I stopped and reconsidered before the situation got out of hand and before it was too late to turn back.

To maintain and revive my inner faith, I began to rely upon the firm foundation of my prayer life established during my years in the monastery. Each day I recited the basic prayers I had chosen in the early fifties along with Compline and the daily regular parts of Holy Mass that I memorized. At different times, I turned my soul to Our Saviour to adore Him and to receive Him spiritually in the Sacrament of the Holy Eucharist. Whenever possible, I recited the fifteen mysteries of the Rosary in place of the Divine Office. I seized any opportunity or place to pray. For example, I prayed during large meetings and during small group study times; I prayed while walking, resting, or going to sleep. Several times due to my carelessness, I moved my lips when I was meditating, and, unfortunately, it was noticed by some of the other prisoners. Because of this, I was cornered and became the object of their ridicule, insult and attack.

The prayers I spoke to the Lord in that small cubicle, fourteen square meters, where I had been confined, was truly similar to that of the prophet Jonah who was swallowed by a large fish and remained in its belly three days and three nights. From the belly of the fish he cried to the Lord, singing the glorious song of His praise, and offering himself to God as a sacrifice (Jon. 2:1-2).

On the eve of the first Christmas I spent in prison, around 7:30 p.m., I was called to the office of an interrogator. He ordered me to accuse a priest incarcerated in the same prison. He distinctly stated that this would be considered a meritorious service to atone for my own crimes. I flatly refused his request because the precepts of the Church would not allow me to do so. In answering his sharp interrogations, I said very clearly that if the priest had really committed some crime, the People's Government would need to bring him to justice, and that after having ascertained the facts, the Church authorities would also deal with him according to Canon Law. I resisted his repeated threats and absolutely refused to "expose, condemn and criticize" the so-called crimes and errors against the commandments that were attributed to this priest. Finally, the interrogator ended his hour-long questions with a concise phrase: "Those who are incorrigibly stubborn will certainly come to no good end!"

From that time I made a decision to avoid all improper terms and susceptible wording that could be turned against the Church in the various statements that the prison officials forced me to write.

One such "statement" written at the request of the Communists in March 1956, concerned the Benedictine Order. Over thirty pages were written in full accord with the view and position of the Church. When Cheng Min, the chief prisoner of my group, read these pages, he whispered to me, "What you have written is well done, philosophical and interesting!"

Even though this was true, I could see that I should not al all narrate to the Communists the formation, goal, structure, rule and lifestyle of the Benedictine Order and the development of our monastery in Chengdu. Such behavior, I believed, could be perceived as an expression of bowing my head and admitting my "guilt." The mere fact that the chief prisoner approved of my text, made my action questionable and consequently blameworthy.

During this period, like the other prisoners, I attended daily the political study sessions. On these occasions I often made speeches and sometimes even spoke in praise of the Communist Party.

For my small group, I occasionally read the newspaper and recited official documents. I also agreed to take part in the examination of current events. Nevertheless, whenever I heard slanders and insults from other prisoners against the Catholic Church, whether inside these study sessions or outside, I stood up at once to defend righteousness, refute these attacks, and uphold the truth.

I remember clearly an incident of this kind which occurred during the summer of 1956. I entered into a heated debate in the course of a study meeting with a member of our study group by the name of Li, who knew both English and Russian. After the meeting he drafted a "written accusation" to get recognition and praise from both the prison officials and the other prisoners. One official of the detention house called me in to ask me for some explanations about what was going on and he showed me prisoner Li's "written accusation" so that I might learn my lesson.

In His mercy, God extended His helping hand to me. He reversed the course of events after all. Before I fell into the trap, He helped me retrace my steps and enabled me to recover my bearings and see the daylight once more. In the beginning of the summer of 1956, I decided to write only a part of the "materials" which the interrogators had asked me to write. At the end of the same year, I was determined not to write anything more at all. In October, when I was asked to go over my earlier statements, I did exactly the opposite by requesting to be allowed to correct the errors I had made in this deposition. Although I did not win my case, my determination to strike out on a new path was strengthened, and the hope of rallying all my forces was overflowing in my heart.

In December 1956, I seized the occasion of the yearly "general review" to write a two to three page "Summary of My Thoughts in the Year 1956." There I forcefully defended all the words and actions I had undertaken in the past to defend the Church. I emphasized that I was imprisoned only because of my religious beliefs. I renewed my petition to thoroughly revise my statements written from the outset of my imprisonment. I further solemnly declared that if my request was not granted, these "writings" were all to be regarded as null and void. I practiced self-criticism and retracted all my assertions and actions, erroneus and susceptible to confusion, I had made while participating in study meetings, while "speaking" at these meetings, and while accepting "political examinations." In the same way, I explained the sheer religious basis for my observance of the prison regulations and participation in manual labor. I intended to make the "Summary" the turning point in my life as a prisoner and the milestone in my battle on God's behalf.

Later, on my own, I wrote and presented another document to the authorities of the No. 2 Detention House to rectify my past mistakes. By the beginning of 1957, I refused to write anything at the command of the interrogators. I also completely refused to participate in daily study meetings and in "regular reviews" or to yield to the "reform of thought." I devoted the obligatory time reserved for political study to acquire some knowledge of Russian and to read books and magazines. Since my improper "deposition" at the very start had haunted me and prevented me from having a peaceful conscience, I twice, during the summer of 1957, took up the matter strongly with the prison officials for permission to correct the errors made in my deposition of 1955. During an interview, however, Mr. Wang, Chief of the Interrogation Section , rejected my request with the excuse that the files of my case had been transferred to some other department.

In 1957, the month of the Holy Rosary, my second October in prison, a clear and crisp October, came around. In honor of Our Lady of the Rosary and in repentance and reparation for the serious mistakes I had made during the first period of my imprisonment, I decided to take further steps to reinforce my resistant will for the struggle to come. First, I would declare openly, whenever an occasion would present itself, that I was jailed for the Church. Secondly, I would strongly refute all the slanders against the Church made before me by other prisoners. Thirdly, I would oppose other prisoners calling me "criminal" or referring to me as a "fellow criminal." Finally, I would refuse to participate in the nightly "roll call" by the official before bedtime. To carry out this prison ritual, the official on duty used to come in at bedtime with a roster in hand and call out each prisoner by his full name. Every prisoner was expected to walk to the door and answer. As soon as the ten prisoners assigned to the room had responded in proper order, the official closed the door, our signal to rest.

Because of my refusal to participate in the "roll call," I was accused of obstructing the "normal observance" of the prison rules. After the head of the detention house and some of his subordinate officials had failed to persuade me to change my attitude, they organized a small public meeting on October 14. It was supposed to be a denunciation and criticism meeting attended by about ten model prisoners who were striving to reform themselves.

Once one became the butt of public criticism and denunciation, a whole series of punishments would come upon him in the course of forced "confession" and "examination." Usual punishments might include: being struggled against in small or big public meetings; standing up; lowering one's head; bowing down to one's waist for hours; enduring slander, insults, abuse, beatings; suffering reductions of daily provisions and monthly allowance; being put under close surveillance; being tied with rope; being handcuffed, shackled, or confined; having demerits recorded; having an increase in sentence; or at worst, being very simply shot. Among these brutal measures some could continue one or more hours; some several days or even weeks; in certain cases some could go on months or years. Generally speaking, the punishments did not cease until the victim bowed down and bent his knees, "admitting his crimes." Then he had to give in and make a "complete confession"; otherwise, he would be tormented unto death for his ideals.

The Communist prison authorities were terrifying, arrogant and persistent. They racked their brains and resorted to all their tricks trying to undermine the prisoners' thoughts and spirits, and to ruin their physical and mental health. Indeed, O Lord, it was truly impossible without Your special grace and assistance to resist them over a long period of time and to defeat them in the end. Without You, all resistance would have reminded me of "a small ant trying in vain to topple a giant tree." Consequently, it was not surprising nor indeed matter for criticism, but rather a fairly common sight when one observed people drifting with the tide or falling short of success for want of a final burst of energy. Model prisoners were those who had yielded to the tide, and now these ten model prisoners from our company readily joined with the officials to attempt to sweep me into their reform.

My tenacity in refusing to follow the "normal observance" of prison rules forced the officials to tightly handcuff my hands behind my back. It was about four o'clock that October afternoon.

Silently praying to Our Lady of the Rosary, the Queen of Martyrs, I peacefully endured the wounds and pain of my swelling arms and hands, and came out victorious over the cruelty of the Communist officials. I remained five full hours with both arms painfully cuffed in bronze rings behind by back. I did not cry, yell, groan, or sigh. Still less did I "acknowledge my mistake" as the officials and other prisoners demanded, or "ask for mercy." Just before bedtime, the official, Gao, had me brought to his office. Of his own accord without any conditions, he loosened my handcuffs slightly, but still leaving me in the awkward and painful position, my arms behind my back.

For twenty-nine days my arms remained cuffed in these bronze rings. Eating, sleeping, standing or sitting, all these movements of ordinary life became painful for me. One kind prisoner helped place food in my mouth. I could not sleep unless I had my legs stretched straight out in front of me and my back against the cell wall. Every day I had to bear the ridicule and jeering of the other prisoners. Yet, neither physical torture nor psychological pressure could in any way shake my fighting will.

The chief prisoner of the company, Yi Zuyou, pointed me out several times in the prison passageway and taunted me, " You haven't changed your clothes for quite a while. Lice must be multiplying on your body. If you continue to be obstinate, what a terrible thing it will be! Why not run to the official at once and acknowledge your fault so that you may get free from this 'teaching aid'? It is you who started the trouble, you must end it yourself, as the proverb runs, 'Let him who tied the bell on the neck of the tiger take it off himself'!"

In my mind I reasoned, "The dark night will not last forever.

To persevere means ultimate victory."

On the night of November 12, after nearly one month, my handcuffs were finally removed. Before the release, I promised only to answer the evening "roll call." Nevertheless, I refused to confess, reform, or participate in the daily study sessions. I did not make any concessions to the demands of Official Gao.

I realize now that the month-long handcuffing was directly due to my unwise action of non-cooperation in the "roll call." I know also, however, that I acted with the good and holy intention of honoring the Blessed Mother and of doing penance for my sins. On this account, I do not regard my protest as without significance, without value, or as totally wasted. Much more, it provided me an occasion to give my will a crucial test, and rendered the merciful love of the Blessed Mother more generous, available and present to me. This experience further strengthened me for the long and arduous struggle that was still to come.

The handcuffing punishment was unable to quench the raging fire of the love for the Lord that burned in my breast. It only kindled my enthusiasm for defending the Church. After another month and a half my third Christmas in prison arrived. I handed to the detention authories house a "memorandum" of about twenty pages.

In this document, I systematically and point by point refuted all the "accusations" levelled against me. At the same time, I pointed out the righteousness and lawfulness of my past actions and words in defense of the Church. I asked the officials once more to correct all the mistakes I had made at the beginning of my imprisonment and cancel all the previous "confessions" I had uttered. In this memorandum, I clearly manifested that my tenacious attitude and just position from then on would be final and irrevocable. In front of my signature I wrote "the persecuted one" both on the outside paper strip seal and the inside document itself. This in itself was another direct challenge to the Chinese Communist Party.

Unfortunately, the manuscript of this "Memorandum" as well as that of the "Summary of My Thoughts," written a year before, were confiscated during the prison search at the end of April 1958. The Communist officials, however, could never destroy my sincerity in confessing my sins to the Lord and doing penance, nor take away my great desire to defy them to the end in fighting for the Faith. On the contrary, my sincerity and desire were kept evident and bright ever before the eyes of all.

My two and one half years of militant life in the No. 2 Detention House of the Ningxia Street big prison came to a victorious ending in April 1958. I was then transferred to the No. 1 Detention House in Wensheng Street in the same city. This change marked the beginning of the second and more terrifying stage of my struggle against the Communist Party. In this new prison, the prisoners were required to attend daily public accusation meetings that continued without interruption. Following these accusation meetings, there was a series of cruel punishments such as reducing prisoner rations, forcing victims to stand still for extended periods of time, or handcuffing arms behind the back; even fetters and binding ropes were employed with great frequency. The prisoners were frightened and demoralized. In this setting, everything seemed intimidating. As the Chinese proverb says: "The grass and the trees were all troops!"

As far as I was concerned, my position and attitude were resolute and unchangeable. Daily, the officials and the prisoners of my unit put strong pressure on me to confess my crimes, to accept reformation, to write required materials, to give speeches at study meetings, and to make my self-examination and self-criticism. I persistently resisted their pressure.

One day in the height of summer, an inmate, Gao Xiantan, wantonly vilified my stubbornness in a study meeting of our small group. "Why should you, Zhou Bangjiu, go against the trend of the times? Why shouldn't you change over to new ways? Open your snobbish eyes and have a look at the excellent situation of today! The 'Great Leap Forward` campaign initiated by our great leader Chairman Mao has already set the entire country ablaze like wildfire. The whole nation conscientiously carries out the general line for socialist construction with high spirit and energy. Who can oppose this? Who will dare to refuse to follow the Communist Party?"

"We need not look to those far away! Let us see certain people here present! Chu Yitian was a journalist and a writer; Zhang Renlun, a certified public accountant; this maimed prisoner, also a well-known and learned figure. Even I myself, to tell you the truth, was an engineer, a high-ranking intellectual. We all have already bowed our necks to the Party. And you, who do you think you are? Nothing! Only an ignorant and incompetent greenhorn, young and inexperienced! It is too hard to imagine that you dare to challenge the Communist Party to the end! Truly, you are downright presumptuous and hopelessly stupid!"

When Gao concluded his tirade, the whole group with a roar against me chimed in together. Some sternly condemned me, while others tried to persuade me gently. No one ventured to show the least sympathy for me. I did not return fire, but kept silent to avoid incurring more censure and "pouring oil onto the fire."

After four months of pressure and threats, I was called to court and publicly tried. In the presence of three judges, an official from the procuratorial bureau called "state public prosecutor", and two "people's assessors," I was found entirely alone, without support of attorney either private or public, to refute their false accusations. After the official trial, I knew well that because of my resolute refusal to yield to the Communists, I would be sentenced to a long-term or even to the death penalty. I also realized very clearly what I should do was to persistently adhere to my stand, namely, to remain loyal to the Church. I must leave all the rest in the hands of the good God Himself.

In the middle of September, I was asked to appear in court once more to hear the pronouncement of sentence. No sooner had the pronouncement been read than I took a little slip of paper from my pocket. Just as I opened my mouth to begin to recite the message prepared on the paper in advance, one judge suddenly hurried down from the judicial platform toward me. Wresting the slip from my hand, he proclaimed, "You needn't read it. Just submit it to us!" With this the sentencing procedure was abruptly ended, and I was sent back to my cell.

My declaration's main points written out on that seized slip of paper were this: "It was because of my defending the Catholic faith that I was imprisoned. I strongly protest any kind of judgment,which flies in the face of all facts, made by this court. I will never accept any false charge held against me. I decide, however, not to lodge a basically ineffectual appeal to the higher court that can implement nothing else than the same wrong policy of the same Communist Party. To follow the holy example of Our Savior Jesus, I am ready to serve any sentence, even to sacrifice my life for the truth!"

It did not surprise me at all that the Communist judges condemned me to twenty years of imprisonment—the longest limited-term sentence. They wanted to severely punish me on one hand and incite me to reform myself on the other. By limiting my imprisonment to a definite term, according to the words of the judgment, they intended to leave me some room for turning over, hoping to see me repent and to be won over to their side. They wanted me to have a chance to change my views and surrender, consequently, in my view, to sell my soul to them. Their tactics were manifestly clever and their plan truly insidious!

Ten days after my sentencing, I was sent to the reform-through-labor camp called the Red Flag Ironworks at the New West Gate in Chengdu. I was assigned to clean up the sand of castings and to do sundry labor in a foundry. One year later I was moved to a newly-built Power Machine Factory, belonging to the same camp and located in the countryside outside the North Gate.

These one and a half years in the labor camp were far from peaceful. Because I stood firm in my resolution, every day became a day of struggle for me. I became an object of attack. I was questioned and threatened by the officials. I was always watched by my fellow prisoners and ceaselessly harassed by them. I was often criticized at the study meetings, and was once penalized with a big demerit. Besides this criticism and struggle in small or big meetings and besides the tortures of handcuffs and shackles, the Communist prison or labor-reform camp authorities usually penalized disobedient and anti-reform prisoners with official disciplinary sanctions, such as warnings and these demerits. According to the prison stipulations, three recorded warnings should be regarded as a small recorded demerit; three small recorded demerits as a big recorded demerit; and three big demerits were enough to justify an additional penalty.

My little monthly allowance was reduced. The Chinese Communist Party claimed that no wages should be paid out to labor-reform prisoners. Only some monthly allowance might be taken into consideration to encourage the prisoners to work hard and fervently. The allowance varied in amount and depended on their contributions, great or small, and on their manifestations, good or bad. Usually the allowance was two dollars a month for each person. Since I opposed the Reform and had been penalized with a big demerit, my monthly allowance was reduced to forty cents.

All this pressure, however, produced no effect. Despite the increase in punishment and threats, the Communist officials were not able to make me write the anticipated "Confession" or "Self-examination," or state publicly in meetings my repentance of "crimes" and my acceptance of the "reform." What most incensed them was my refusal to put my fingerprint on the criminal's registration card without adding a declaration that I neither admitted, nor denied anything by attaching my fingerprint. This process was another of the many rules inflicted upon prisoners to demoralize and subdue them—another of the many rules that the vast majority of prisoners could not defy.

In fact, from the time I entered prison up to the time I passed through the Bamboo Curtain—throughout those long years, I did not observe with my own eyes any one of the priests or faithful with whom I was imprisoned, continue to be loyal to the Lord. Why? Great and protracted pressure was applied by the Communist Party! I more particularly witnessed the heartbreaking end which befell three such people who abandoned the narrow and right path either from the very start or halfway through their struggles, to follow the current of the times. One died tragically in a mountain quarry of the Peng'an Labor-Reform Camp after a sudden collapse of rocks late one night. The two others were permitted to leave prison due to their "acceptance of reform," but the first not so long ago died while the second was kept under surveillance and had no real freedom.

This harsh reality with its impressive lesson made my heart ache, but it also made me take one step forward in my determination to fight for the Lord until the end. From this point of view, I vowed to the Lord saying, "Lord, on the Cross Your agony reached its extreme limit quite early. How could I by any word or act of ingratitude and betrayal drive still further the nails into Your hands and feet? I could never barter away the truth just 'to save my life to live dishonorably in this troubled world,' in the words of Zhuge Liang (183-234 A.D.). I have determined to fight until death for You, to be ready at all times to throw myself into the battle for You even at the cost of my life."

One incident in particular made a painful impact on me during all those difficult years. It happened on January 10, 1960. That day I had been requisitioned to work overtime in the foundry. About four o'clock in the morning, while I was cleaning up the sand of some just-poured and much-needed castings, Wang Hanchen, a well-wishing prisoner, my acquaintance and the assistant inspector of the shop castings, coming to the shop to check the castings, informed me secretly of the grave message that my Benedictine brother, Fr. Paul Wu Yong, had been asphyxiated by gas and had fallen to the ground just ten minutes previously while carrying a diesel engine. All rescue measures had failed; he was dead!

The sad news struck me like a sudden bolt bringing back memories of Fr. Paul. I thought again of our more than thirteen-year life in the Priory and of our four-year struggle together for the same faith in Chengdu and in our respective hometowns since the end of October 1951. We had been arrested at the same time and put into the same jail. Fifteen months before, we had been sentenced to the same twenty-year term and sent to the same labor-reform camp. Now, we found ourselves in the same Red Flag Ironworks. We met each other frequently in prison, but could never talk; much less exchange views. Yet now, at the age of forty-five in the prime of his life, he suddenly was gone forever without saying good-bye. How could my heart not be broken? My deepest sorrow was that he had persisted in his former concessions.

According to what I had seen and heard of him, especially from his short article posted on the prison wall in the No. 2 Detention House in Ningxia Street of Chengdu in the summer of 1957, I learned with regret that he had apparently submitted to the pressure of the detention house authorities. He had made a confession, admitted his mistake, participated in the study meetings, and expressed the intention to accept ideological remolding. In this way, he had withdrawn from his original position and had hurt his integrity. His error, however, was far from apostasy. It was a compromise. It was the one I myself had committed in the early period of my incarceration.

All these distressing events made more clear my purpose and gave me a deeper perception of the arduousness and significance of the current struggle. I must be more vigilant. I was determined to view Fr. Paul's experience as a warning and exert myself continuously in the struggle. I was prepared to withstand the Communist pressure at any price and to eventually accomplish the noble cause of defending the Faith, even if it should mean the shedding of the last drop of my blood.

Indeed, a compromise could never resolve cardinal questions of right and wrong, nor ensure safety in life for the conceder himself. This would only endanger his own integrity and mar the glory of God. For this reason, I affirmed the way to go and made up my mind to pursue the way of fighting and not the way of conceding. It was only through walking this way unswervingly, through fighting at all costs with an unconquered spirit the formidable power of the Communist religious persecution from start to finish that I could achieve my high goals: consoling the loving Sacred Heart of Jesus, recompensing Him, making reparation for my own sins and those of others, working for the glory of the Church and for the removal of the disgrace heaped on her and giving my little contribution to the salvation of humanity.

In the spring of 1960, I received from the Procurator's Office of the city of Chengdu an indictment which was supposed to increase my penalty in the near future. On account of this new indictment, I was sent back to the former factory near the New West Gate to do "self-examination" and "self-criticism" and to await court trial. Yet, for a reason unknown to me, the original plan was changed, and the proceeding rescinded. Instead, I was sent to the maximum security prison for serious offenders. Very likely, the Communist officials thought that in this new setting and with new pressures I might sooner or later walk their so-called way of "abandoning evil and doing good" and of "turning over a new leaf". Much to their disappointment, however, they soon learned that their hope was an illusion, and that as a Chinese saying puts it, all their efforts in forcing my surrender were as futile as "drawing water with a bamboo basket."

Does not a Chinese proverb also say, how can "a frog at the bottom of a well" grasp and fathom the mysteriously profound decree and intricately subtle plan of our Father in Heaven who sees all? Or again, as another Chinese saying goes, how can "a mantis stop a chariot with its arms"? Who can thwart the wonderful design of the Almighty God?

發暫願二十六週年感懷

滿庭芳

一九八六年十月十五日聖女德蘭慶節
於達安勞改營單獨囚禁中

神往西天，心傾容市，萬千感慨胸間。
緬懷當日、發願景眉前。
觀禮諸賓濟濟，
今安在？晤否塵寰？
長遭佔 樂園樓守
何日得旋還？

多年、殫力戰、神杯暢飲、鬥志仍堅。
復吟詠詩詞，氣概昂然。
惟望凱歌早唱
於天國，大願終宣。
孤囚裏，哀求天父，
三願守維虔。

THOUGHTS ON THE 26th ANNIVERSARY OF TEMPORARY PROFESSION OF MONASTIC VOWS

To the Tune of Man Ting Fang
(Fully Fragrant Court)
In Solitary Confinement—Peng'an Labor-Reform Camp
Feast of St. Teresa of Avila, October 15, 1976

My spirit arches through the western sky;
My heart leans toward the city of Chengdu;
Within, a multitude of feelings swells.

Looking backward to that day,
To that scene,
I see myself:
The novice bowed,
Binding myself to be a monk in holy vows;
I see the many guests who saw me then—
Where are they now?
Can ever on this earth I see them again?
I think over "the Building of Paradise,"
My monastic home,
Now occupied so long—
When may I see there my glorious return?

So many years now
To struggle vigorously with the Wolf,
Still constant is my will to fight,
Though from the divine chalice, full to overflowing,
I have already drunk my fill.
Yet fuller still the mettle gained
From wrestling with words to craft these poems.
Believing, hoping, longing
Soon to sing the songs of triumph,
So that in the Kingdom of Heaven
I may profess forever
And at last my Solemn Vows.

In my solitary cell,
I implore the Heavenly Father with all my heart
To keep me faithful to my three vows.

CHAPTER IV

STRUGGLE IN THE
NO. 1 PROVINCIAL PRISON OF NANCHONG

June 1960

Handcuffed and escorted by an official and two guards, I left the labor-reform camp in the northern outskirts of Chengdu along with three other prisoners on the afternoon of June 12, 1960, and started out on my journey to an untold destination. Missing the last train to Chongqing, we were sent to a detention house close to the railway station overnight. The next morning we took the first train of the day and arrived at Jianyang County at mid-day. We passed the night in the waiting room of the county bus station. At bedtime we were ordered to lie down on the floor of the waiting room and bound with ropes to the long, hard wooden chairbeds all around us. Then the door was locked. The three escorts took turns standing guard outdoors, guns in hand.

With the sun rising in the eastern sky, a painful and sleepless night ended. The guards unbound our ropes replacing them with handcuffs, and thus, we four prisoners got onto the bus to continue our way to Nanchong. Although we were strictly forbidden to talk with the other travelers, the passengers could, at a mere glance, understand our situation and avoid approaching us in any way. None of us ventured to be unruly in word or deed, knowing the result would be a taste of cuffs and kicks from the guards.

Having suffered much from the painful jolting of the bus, the smothery lampblack and the suffocating mugginess, I began to feel dizzy and vomited. I not only had lost my appetite for lunch, but also had to endure the uncomfortable position, cramped in my seat. In deepening dusk our bus entered the county seat of Pengxi. Like most of the other passengers, we stayed overnight in the bus while the two guards, with their guns, again took turns keeping watch on us nearby, without relaxing their vigilance. At dawn, as the morning breeze began blowing, the bus moved on to complete its last run of thirty miles. Under the blazing sun we finally reached Nanchong and had our lunch at the station area. We walked, carrying our own baggage, through the urban district towards the riverbank. Soon after crossing the Jialing River by boat, we arrived at the end of our journey, now known to us, the No. 1 Prison of Sichuan Province. It was on June 15, 1960.

Situated at Hedong Village outside the city of Nanchong, this prison was one of the four biggest and most important in the province. Its secret code number was 2085, but officially it was known as "New Life Leather Shoe Factory." Inside were a tannery, a leather shoe factory, machine factory, and a farm. The leather shoe factory produced various high-quality leather shoes for export, mainly to Russia. They were designed by specialized technicians and should be made and assured on schedule and according to a fixed quality and quantity. If something went wrong with the production, the responsible prisoners would be accused of sabotaging the state production and exportation plan and punished severely without mercy. Divided into eight or nine companies, this prison housed over two thousand inmates. Most of them were condemned to either a suspended sentence of capital punishment or life imprisonment. The remaining few were under limited-term sentences. Most of these were regarded as "obstinate" fellows, hard to reform.

Coming into this new battlefield, I determined to acquit myself in all respects in the same way as before, and not stray or waver in the midst of all the apparent changes. In view of my attitude towards "study" during the first few days, and especially because of the fact that I had written on the registration form two remarks, "arrested for no reason" and "imprisoned for the Church," the officials in charge observed me closely and were forewarned. They assigned me to unskilled labor in the leather shoe factory, closing the door to my chance of learning any new knowledge, any trade or skill. I was then only thirty-three years of age and already had some education, and was capable of growth and development. This was denied me, at least for that time.

────────────

Fifty-five days later, on the 10th of August, fell the Feast of St. Lawrence, Deacon and Martyr. About four o'clock that very hot afternoon, I was working in the factory workshop wearing only short pants and an apron tied about my waist. I was summoned from the workshop to the small rock desk near the west side door of the large prison administration building. There I was questioned by the chief of the section in charge of discipline and education, Mr. Liu. In answering his questions, I reaffirmed the lawful and honest nature of the Legion of Mary. I also refused his order to write anything about Sr. Lucia Shu Dejun, who had fought very bravely for the Lord in Chengdu during the 1950s. Although highly criticized and long harassed by the Communists, she was never imprisoned and had continued working in a hospital until leaving the Mainland for Hong Kong in September 1987.

When the section chief recognized that his sharp words and threatening manner had produced no result, he ordered me to return to my company. However, as I moved away from his desk and neared the main entrance to the administration building, he ordered me to stop and wait. He entered the large office structure and, in a moment, came back with handcuffs hidden in his trousers' pocket. Calling two men from his section to back him and boost his morale, he asked me three more times in rapid succession: "Do you admit that you have committed a crime?"

Three times I replied resolutely and strongly, "I have not committed any crime! I have only defended the faith of the Catholic Church!"

Having listened to my last, clear answer, he immediately motioned to his two assistants. They roughly grabbed my wrists and stretched them behind my back while Mr. Liu locked the metal handcuffs in place about six inches above my wrists. The backs of my hands and wrists were forced together as he cruelly tightened the cuffs and stretched my right hand to its extreme limit.

I could especially feel the bronze cuff compressing my right forearm painfully as Liu sneered, "This punishment should have been given earlier upon your arrival when you wrote the words 'arrested for no reason' on your registration form! I did not order punishment then considering you were a new transfer. I thought to wait patiently for your change of heart. But ha! Little did I imagine you would persist in your blindness and obstinacy and refuse to come to your senses! These cuffs will help you reflect and eventually confess! Now, back to your company!"

To watch over me strictly, he immediately sent for two prisoners who were more than willing to reform themselves and to be entirely submissive to his order. That was the harbinger of the life under torture that I was to live for the next five years. In such ways, an ever-faithful heart is formed!

Relying on the grace and strength of the Holy Spirit, I did not sigh or groan; I did not cry or shed tears; I did not pour out endless grievances against injustice; still less did I ask pardon or appeal for mercy. I remained calm and successfully weathered the storm of the first harsh afternoon and the first restless night of this most painful and arduous period of my life in prison.

With my arms bound so tightly behind my back, especially the right forearm with the bronze ring of the cuff cutting off circulation, my body worked to combat not only the growing intensity of the pain but also the extreme heat of the August afternoon. I ate no food and only tried to rest on the single large bed of my group.

In this prison about two hundred prisoners were housed in a long rectangular building similar to the Daozi of the Ningxia Street Prison in Chengdu but a little larger. Instead of individual cells for each group of more than ten prisoners, the rectangular building was used as a common sleeping room for all the groups. On each side of the narrow corridor were eight square wooden platforms raised approximately twenty-seven inches from the ground. Each of these platforms served as a group's common bed. There was no separation of one group's bed from another's. We slept side by side, stacked like so many cans of sardines lining each side of the corridor.

When bedtime came that hot August evening, because of the pain and position of my arms, I was obliged to sit on a small bench with my right upper arm leaning on the bed side and my back stiffly propped against one of the support columns in the center aisle of the building. After about an hour the prison guard on night patrol duty brusquely called out, "Get up! Take your place in the bed!" The chief prisoner of my group sat straight up from his place and forced me to get up into the bed and lie down. Finally, after an excruciating hour or two, I fell into a half-sleep of fatigue and pain. At the sound of the morning bell when I totally awoke, my right hand had gradually become numb causing the pain to be less acute and making endurance a little easier.

About 8:30 the next morning, I was summoned to the prison office building once more. Another official interrogated me. I refused to answer his questions. I simply pointed out that my position had been clearly made the day before, and I had nothing new to add.

Faced with my strong and unexpected stand, immediately the prison authorities decided to form a small special group. Composed of about ten prisoners, the group began denouncing, criticizing and struggling against me day and night. I often repeated my flat refusal to make a critical examination of "my errors" and confess "my crimes."

Railing and insult became my daily fare. My life, full of difficulties, pains and sufferings, became a living nightmare. Because my spirits remained high and my attitude persistent, I was always required to stand during the daily meeting. My legs became sore and my body weakened. Days seemed to drag on like years. When night fell, with the torture instruments on my body and with the pain of my wounds, I could not sleep. Sometimes I could not even close my eyes throughout the night. My body was worn out and very weak. My health deteriorated from day to day. Fortunately, God lavished His grace on me in great abundance, and I was filled with divine consolation. God's joy was my constant companion. Consequently, my spiritual strength never failed me, and my courage never faltered. Burning my bridges, I made up my mind to struggle on all the more, even if I should be regarded merely as a cornered beast that could still fight in desperation. My mettle was firm, my confidence full; so eventually, I was able to overcome all the cruelties imposed by the Communists and shown in handcuffs and other punishments.

Five endless days passed to the afternoon of the Solemnity of Our Lady's Assumption, August 15. During a "criticism-struggle meeting", the head of the group of ten prisoners assigned to break my spirit, Mr. Chen Chaodian, tightened the cuffs' bronze ring on my already swollen right arm to the fifth and last notch. On a nearby bed sat a lame prisoner who pointed his finger at me and said in the presence of all, "Now, see whether Jesus Christ, in whom you believe, will come to save you. If you can endure such pain until this hour tomorrow and remain tenacious in your purpose, I will respect you and regard you as a heroic person, and I will even believe in Jesus Christ like you!"

The day and the night passed quietly with my right arm bound even more tightly behind my back. As a soldier of Christ, I remained more calm than ever continuing my silent prayers. The next day as I stood before my accusers, "faithful in my purpose" all the same and successful in enduring the pain, the lame prisoner lay silent on the bed, deliberately or unwittingly, forgetting his promise. I was unable to wear my glasses and thus could not clearly see the expression on his face, nor could I fathom the real feelings hidden in his innermost being. In any case, the bitter reality of being in prison under the grim control and constant menace of the godless Marxist-Leninist Government, would not allow me to pass whatever, if any, judgement on his behavior. Even if Christ performed such a miracle as to release my cuffs and heal my withered hand in a marvelous manner, what goodhearted prisoner would dare stand up and speak from a sense of justice on my behalf and openly profess his faith in Jesus Christ? Furthermore, should this occasion arise, the Communist officials would not, as a Chinese proverb says, "lay down their butcher's knife and suddenly become Buddhas!"

On the contrary, they would rather have put another cuff on me and adopted more severe methods to intensify their pressure and attain their objective. This episode, however, created waves in my mind which plunged me a little more deeply into the loving embrace of our Heavenly Father and gave me another confirmation: only His support and approval were sincere, reliable and powerful; any sympathy or hatred, any praise or slander from this world were all transient and of little importance, just as fleeting smoke or a passing cloud. Now that our Heavenly Father stood by my side, what battle,even the fiercest, could not be won? What cross, even the heaviest, could not be carried?

The heat at that season in Nanchong was intolerable and turned tigerishly harsh, especially for me. My right forearm and hand, which had been tightened to the maximum, began to rot and breed maggots a few days later. As a soldier of the Kingdom of Heaven, however, I remained tranquil with head up and chest out, facing others with a steadfast gaze. The Communist officials were obliged to do something in this grave situation; so, in order to make a show of humanitarianism, they changed my handcuffs to armcuffs.

My festering right arm was an oozing open sore that ran smelly pus. The two rings of the new armcuffs began to dig one large and one small hole in each arm. The difficulty of eating and sleeping, combined with this, physically wore me down. My overall fatigue increased day by day.

The same group of ten prisoners continued to desperately pursue and attack my "obstinate attitude" as the Communist prison officials attempted to deliver another heavy blow. Railings, insults and clamor constantly rang in my ears, day and night, inside the "struggle meetings" and outside. All this bedlam, though, became for me a graceful symphony of praise to God, a magnificent and triumphant marching song, leading me on the way to Paradise. It would be hard to find better music than this in the world; music that, in the Chinese idiom, "resounded so melodiously as to stop the passing clouds."

After two attempts to break the will of a prisoner—my will—by torture, the formidable Communist officials apparently had their first experience of failure. On the one hand, they had to indicate to me that they would not take their defeat lying down; on the other, they had to cover the appearance of having gone too far in their cruelty towards me before the other prisoners. So, after four weeks of punishment, they showed a little generosity by removing the cuffs from my arms and replacing them with shackles on my feet. They even ordered me to go to the clinic everyday to get medication to reduce the swelling and to stop the oozing sores on my arms.

A month of torture and continual harassment by the group of ten prisoners severely damaged my already very weakened body. Not only my arms but my entire body was racked with fatigue and disease. The distressing conditions of prison life wore down even the most healthy, able-bodied prisoner. How much more misery would there be for one whose body was beset by infection and deprived of even minimal sanitary necessities!

I distinctly remember one anecdote. One morning in the first part of September, I felt a roundworm climbing up my throat. I was forced to react, pulling it from my mouth and throwing it to the ground! A few times when I went to change bandages, the doctor, noticing my sick body seeming too weak to hold up, gave me injections of cardiotonic shots to strengthen my heart before changing the bandages. All these various signs seemed ominous both to others and to me. I was nearing my end like "the sun setting behind the western mountains." There was no guarantee in the morning that I would last until evening!

Another clear indication of just how near death I was during this critical time, remains very fresh in my memory to this day. I went one afternoon to the prison shop to buy some small articles. I was surprised to find out that my account had been cancelled by the person in charge under the pretext that "my soul had already returned to the Western Paradise." I was, in his mind, no longer living, but already dead! Fortunately, the Lord in His goodness did not see it that way. This must have surprised everyone. He appointed for me the path of the Prophet Daniel— conquering the lions, overcoming death, preserving life, so that I might live to this day. Without any doubt, His design will unfold in time.

After a month and a half of medical care, the smelly pus infecting the sores of my right arm finally stopped. The four wounds, one on each forearm and one on each upper arm from the hand and arm cuffs, were slowly scarring over, but my right hand, on the contrary, had become permanently crippled. Seeing their hopes of breaking me down through torture and "struggle meetings" vanishing, the prison authorities disbanded the small special group and stopped bothering me with the meetings which had lasted everyday from morning to evening for nearly thirty days.

The fetters, though, remained on my feet to keep me company like a shadow. The officials probably fancied that I would eventually be brought to betray my faith, or as their teacher Mao Zedong said, "I would carry a granite-like skull with me to meet my God." In this way, their fierce, month-long attack launched against me ended in failure and was reluctantly abandoned. With the meetings halted, my adverse and painful condition began to improve somewhat. This early victory strengthened my faith a little more for the final victory.

For two more months I continued to stay with the production company of two hundred prisoners which made leather shoes. In late December 1960, with fetters still on my feet, I was transferred to a unit composed of old, weak, sick and maimed prisoners who needed rest and care. I stayed in their company for more than two years, and there the atmosphere remained relatively quiet. My independent attitude did not cause much trouble or harassment. As a result, there were few serious conflicts. Besides, I enjoyed some freedom to move around. The only irritation and annoyance to others was the noise of my fetters, and I still had to endure the other prisoners' frequent scolding for my resistance to prison authorities.

The living conditions were, of course, no better than or different from those of the regular prisoners. The convalescent company was made up of sixteen small groups in one building. Ten to twelve men were crowded into one group, sharing one common plank bed. The food here was worse both in quality and quantity than in all the other production companies. It was always thin rice gruel mingled with vegetables. Only once a month could I have a little bowl of cooked rice with a couple of small slices of pork, a dish of fried vegetable and a bowl of soup. We washed our faces with a little hot water in the morning. Showers or baths were not a regular part of prison life. Only a washbasin of hot water was provided for a bath usually once a month. I was always infested by lice from my neighbors sharing the same big bed and I was incapable of protecting myself.

———————

One afternoon in late May 1963, the official in charge of our company, Mr. Zhu, suddenly appeared in our building without notice. He was accompanied by another official unknown to me. I was called to them, and they proceeded to ask me to follow the example of a fellow prisoner, Fr. Lawrence Li Wenjing. They demanded I change my obstinate stand and take Fr. Li's path of throwing in my lot with the Communist Party and the Chinese people. By that, they intended to persuade me and, at the same time, to lure me with a bright future. Seeing my refusal to satisfy their expectations and my unshakable attitude of non-submission, they immediately put me in solitary confinement. I was ordered to reflect carefully and do serious self-examination in this new situation.

This unexpected and sudden development must have had a reason. A Chinese common saying goes:"There are no waves without wind." After two and a half years of trial by shackles on my feet, the officials had not been able to make me confess my crimes, nor write material of self-examination at every appraising time. They had long regarded me as "an irritant in the throat" to be spit out. So they chose solitary confinement as the stronger and harsher measure, thinking it would force me to lay down my arms and surrender at the end.

I was led hastily to an area near the prison wall some distance from my company and apart from all other prisoners' buildings. No sounds, only the clanking of the metal shackles on my shuffling feet, could be heard. The two prisoner guards hurried my difficult walking by pushing me along and showed me no kindness. Neither would they meet my resolute gaze nor utter any words of either support or criticism. The cell itself was dark with only a light through a little window near the ceiling at the top of the back wall. In the door was a small opening through which food could be passed. Only the guard's voice and no other sound could be heard.

No sooner had I entered solitary confinement than I thought that the hour of sacrifice must be finally at hand. I wished very much to make my last oath before laying down my life for the Lord, and to write a profession of faith to be a testimony of my fidelity and, at the same time, to manifest to the Communists my sincere ideals. Unfortunately, Official Zhu, making one last check, caught me writing. He immediately opened the locked door of my cell and ordered the prisoner on guard to rush in and snatch my pen and paper and the little bench upon which I was writing. Not until the end of the year, more than six months later, was my desire to write the oath fulfilled.

When the annual overall appraisal took place, prison officials distributed writing materials for the prisoners to use for that purpose. I had finally been given paper to attain my goal. On the Solemnity of Epiphany, January 6, 1964, I presented Official Zhu the "Nine-Point Declaration" as my eternal oath and ultimate profession of faith. It was ten pages, about 10,000 Chinese characters. Although I do not remember all its details, I have kept its outline.

1. "I stand justified in my past actions and words put forward in defense of the Church."
2. "I reiterate the lawful nature of the Legion of Mary. I condemn the so-called 'Three Autonomies Reform' and 'Opposition to Imperialism and Love of the Fatherland' movements as treacherous, divisive, and destructive to the Church."
3. "I reaffirm that the speech I made at the public mass meeting held at Yangshi Street, Chengdu, was utterly correct and necessary."
4. "I declare that the letter I addressed to the clergy and laity of the Church in China was proper and true."
5. "My manuscript, *From Paradise to Purgatory*, is in conformity with the Church's doctrines and objective reality."
6. "I argue that my Memorandum written in prison was based on facts."
7. "I declare anew that the 'testimony, confession and speeches at the study sessions' I had wrongly made during the first period of my imprisonment were made out of

ignorance and under duress and, therefore, are inaccurate and invalid."

8. "I state that I completely accept and uphold forever the Scholastic Philosophy of Realism of St. Thomas Aquinas. I reject atheistical views stemming from the 'Philosophy of Idealism' and, even more, from the 'Philosophy of Materialism.' "

9. "I refute the statements of Mao Zedong, to wit: 'All the stubborn can remain obstinate for a certain time, but never forever,' and 'The obstinate can only carry a granite-like skull to meet God.'"

"Finally, I solemnly assert to Mao's followers that I am willing at any time to offer my life for God and for truth, and I ardently hope that some day I will meet them again in Paradise as soon as they have abandoned the darkness of their atheism and have accepted the light of Christ."

————————

With each day totally at my disposal in the peaceful and secluded surroundings, I profited by an excellent opportunity for prayer and meditation. Thus, this cubicle, a prison in prison, became, as it were, my monastic cell where I could enjoy both peace and happiness. I gave no thought to life or death, to good or bad fortune. I entrusted my destiny to the hands of my Heavenly Father. After finishing the Nine-Point Declaration, I still kept in my heart the desire to express the many feelings surging inside. Consequently, I devoted my time outside of prayer to conceive and create cheerfully a long manuscript in poetic form I entitled *The Song of Life*. My intent was to write verses to praise God, extol our Holy Mother Mary, honor the angels and saints, and to pay homage to the Holy Souls and the living. Although I use the word "write," there was actually no pen or paper. *The Song of Life*, in its totality of 9 parts, 93 paragraphs, 1,416 stanzas and 5,664 lines, was engraved in my mind, but never transcribed on paper even after my release from prison many years later. To facilitate the memorization, I gave every other verse a rhythmic form. There was also a preface and introduction.

I revised the "Song" over and over for six years. I would recite lines according to a precise schedule. Everyday after my prayers and meditation, I would first recite the lines composed the previous day and then the memorized verses up to that point. After that I continued to create new rhythmic lines in the same or new rhymes. With a small stone I etched into the wall characters with the same rhymes so that I could choose suitable words as I needed them. I used all my time outside daily prayer in pondering and singing this *Song of Life* which lay in the depth of my heart. In just this way, the "Song" took shape and continued to evolve and grow until it matured and blossomed into the flower of my life one year later in January 1965. My regret is that I have not been able to recapture the "Song" in its entirety. Fortunately, the main ideas of each paragraph in each part have left traces in my memory, and I hope some day to be able to reveal its full and true face to the world. At present, though, there are only traces. . .

Prison Cubicle — Monastic Cell

The Lord, Holy and good,
Created the world and saved mankind;
His favors are deep and lasting,
His loving-kindness boundless.

How should I repay the Lord?
Allowing myself to be thrown in jail,
Covered with shame,
I remain loyal in the sorry plight,
Returning Him my love with heartfelt sentiments.

In the footsteps of Jesus
I shall follow resolutely, closely;
With the help of Our Lady,
I find the courage to take up my cross.

In my solitary cubicle
No sky no sun:
I turn pale
And lose all my strength.

In summer I am on familiar terms with the heat,
In winter I make a friend of the cold.
Rats are my constant companions
While mosquitoes buzz all around.

The stink from the chamber pot in the corner
Fills the whole space;
The bunk is so low
The dampness penetrates to my bones.

With fetters on my feet,
My movements are hampered and hard.
It is difficult to change my clothes,
My body stinks.

Salted vegetables,
Very sour and so harmful to teeth,
Are my frequent dish at meals:
Causing many painful toothaches.

Two prisoners
Guard me round the clock;
They shout at and scold me,
They add ridicule and slander.

Such pains and troubles
Are only physical and external;
They can in no way reach and disturb
My soul or my inner life.

Though able to take my life,
They cannot forfeit my integrity;
They only make my love for the Lord
More fervent than ever before.

My spirit flies to my monastic cell,
My body remains prisoner in my isolated cubicle;
Saying prayers, composing poems,
I feel happy and content.

When this "Song" will be entirely resuscitated and written down, I cannot at this moment predict, and I am not indeed one hundred percent sure it ever will be possible. What is absolutely certain, however, is that my own experiences have taught me the profound meaning of the phrase of Laozi (604-531 B.C.), a philosopher from the Zhou Dynasty, "Good fortune lieth within bad; bad fortune lurketh within good."

———————————

New situations continued to develop and changes happened all around. Almost five years of torture and nearly two years of isolation were not able to crush my high ideals and my fervent heart. Even the pernicious movie, *Cut the Devil's Claw,* directed against the Catholic Church, which I was obliged to view on the evening of March 6, 1965, failed to shake my indomitable faith and my conviction in certain victory. This movie was produced in the early fifties when the Chinese Communist Party had already begun persecuting the Church. It was a fictional story contrived by the Communists about a foreign missionary in Shanghai starting with his involvement in anti-communist activities and ending with his arrest. This man was seen as the epitome of an enemy of the Chinese Communists and the Chinese people. Among his many crimes, he was reproached particularly for having concealed arms and for having gathered information on behalf of the American imperialistic government.

In the movie's plot this character prevented Catholics from participating in political campaigns or from joining the Communist Party. He was even portrayed as dissuading them from engaging in the war to resist U.S. "aggression" and aid Korea, and from taking part in the Movement of the Three Autonomies Reform. To make things worse, he was accused of rumor-mongering and finally was arrested at his parish and punished under the law!

Just one week after this episode, an official of the prison administration named Ji came to my cell unexpectedly about mid-morning to inform me that my stay in solitary confinement had come to an end. He declared to me," We recognize that thought reform takes a long time. In order to give you a very full opportunity to accept reform and to manifest our patient waiting for your change of heart, we have decided to take off the fetters from your feet and let you out of your solitary cell. Now we offer you a better environment in which to reform yourself. However, after you leave solitary confinement, you are required to observe strictly the prison regulations. Do not act the fool!"

I steadfastly replied, "My position and view have been well known and shown from the beginning. It is not necessary to repeat this. Regarding the prison regulations, my attitude remains unchanged, that is to say, I am ready to observe them as long as they are not against the faith of the Catholic Church."

In this way, I victoriously left my solitary confinement without making the slightest concession. I returned happily to the original company of prisoners who needed rest and were convalescing. These five long years of furious battle came at last to an end. As a Chinese proverb says, with "banners lowered and drums muffled," the prison authorities were ceasing their attacks and beating a retreat.

After my release, an official of our company, He by name, gave me some toilet paper, soap, a toothbrush and toothpaste and showed me special concern. Of my own accord, I did not participate in any hard labor. My physical condition was about the same, no better but no worse than it had been five years before. My right arm and hand withered and remained numb and stiff especially during the cold winters.

On the eve of the International Labor Day, May 1 of that year, when Political Instructor Tan and Official Wen asked me to join the mending unit to repair old clothes, I tactfully objected that my withered right hand rendered such work impossible. In the summer of 1966, when assigned by Official Zhang to straighten small curved nails with a little hammer with the straightening-nail unit, I declined his order with the same excuse.

Not engaged in forced labor, I relished living a quiet and carefree life. Discussions at study sessions, confessions, self-examinations in reorganizing prison regulations meetings, self-criticism in regular appraisals, all such activities did not concern me. At ordinary study sessions and in small or big criticism-struggle meetings, there were times when shouting and screaming became deafening or times when the atmosphere was so tense and terrifying that one's hair literally stood on end. I tried to remain calm and sat in silence. I prayed inwardly or revised and recited quietly in my mind *The Song of Life*.

In my company there was a prisoner of a certain education and culture, by the name of Zhao Hanye. Though he was blind, he had an extremely good memory and a righteous heart. We became good friends. One day in June 1966, he loaned me a copy of *The Poems of Chairman Mao*. Using the rest time of four naps after lunch, I secretly, since I regarded reading Mao's writing in public as shameful, read the book and recited it repeatedly. I finally memorized all thirty-seven poems and engraved them in my mind. I also carefully read and memorized the classical poems sometimes found in newspapers and magazines. From these poems I discovered what I thought were the poetic rules and gradually mastered them.

I now enjoyed free time and had models for imitation, I conceived my plan to create my own repertory of poetry. This project buoyed up my spirits and became the source of my interest and inspiration. Thus, the poems with absolute sincerity began to take shape and to emerge one by one. As though they were arrows from a bow, poems shot out of my mind. After experiencing ten years of struggle, there were many things I wanted to unburden to the Lord, many feelings I needed to express. There were also many struggles and achievements of others and of my own that could be recorded, many mistakes and blunders, too, that could be recounted.

Poetry seemed the most suitable tool to express all these feelings and ideas. Classical Chinese poetry in particular seemed to me a passionate and beautiful literary style to express one's emotions and ideas. This literary style had been used for centuries to express sorrows and joys; to voice partings and reunions; to pour out sentiments and plaints; to paint the scenery of wind, flowers, snow, and moon; to picture the tender feelings between a man and a woman. Why should this literary form be used only for these things? Why should we not also use it to praise God and let it serve the cause of man's salvation? Insofar as even nature, by its goodness, praises day and night the Creator, why should not poetry with its meters also give praise to God and thus participate in this grand mission?

When I was confined in the Communist prison, I could only compose verbally and store the compositions in my brain. There was no way to put my compositions on paper. In such a situation, poetry, which could be easily committed to memory because of its style and form, was naturally my best choice. I regret that I was only an amateur. In no case could I manipulate poetry as "driving a light carriage on a familiar road" or as "using a familiar instrument at will." Neither was it easy for me to make poems sound and rhyme sonorously and forcefully to give a lively and vivid reflection to the sentiments that lay deep in my heart and soul.

With the passage of years, the number of poems gradually increased from 100 to 200, to 500 and to 1,000. Five years afterwards, the number grew to 2,000. The burden of reciting all of them at a scheduled time became for me heavier and heavier. Later, when I was engaged in hard labor, there was less time for reciting, and the burden was too heavy to be carried. I was very painfully obliged to give up something I loved to do. At least for that time, I had to lay down the burden and part reluctantly with what I treasured, leaving the future of my poetry to God and letting Him decide its destiny of surviving or perishing.

Up to the eve of my departure from China, more than 600 new poems were added to the 2,000 composed in prison. Thanks be to God that 858 of my poems have already been written down. There are still 1,800 more that need to be recalled when time permits. I hope that one day I shall be able to write all of them down so that they may do some good both to me and to others, and that all my energy and effort spent in those years will obtain some fruit.

———————

One morning in the month of July 1966, Ni Huashan, a prisoner in my unit, maligned some clerics of our Church in the presence of four fellow prisoners and myself. When I heard this, I was so angered, as the popular proverb says, that "my hair stood up and tipped off my hat," and I promptly refuted him. My roused emotions lasted till evening. Then, departing from my normal behavior and breaking my usual silence, I berated Ni again during our small group study meeting. At the same time, I restated the just position that I upheld consistently and recalled my persistent attitude in the past when I was cuffed and shackled. The chief prisoner in my unit, Guo Xiaohui, was very surprised at my unexpected outburst. As in the Chinese proverb, he believed "he had found a priceless treasure," therefore he was both very joyful and anxious to appropriate it, and he hurried away to record my remarks in detail. Thanks to this report, he received a "merit" from the prison's leading officials.

About two weeks later, when Official Lin checked and read the minutes of our small group study meeting, he found what I had said in the meeting questionable and even objectionable. Immediately, he ordered our small group of about ten prisoners to move to a place removed from the other groups. It was simply a question of protecting the other prisoners from being "adversely" influenced by what I might say. He sought to use the group meeting to criticize my speeches and clean up the "spreading poison."

During the next four days of a public criticism meeting, held in the manner of a gentle breeze and a mild rain, I calmly repeated my positions and answered the questions of other prisoners. Refuting their false accusations levelled against the Church, I recited to them a Qilu, an eight-line poem with seven characters to a line, that I had composed:

"Almighty Son of God, good Jesus,
You descended to earth as a slave to save mankind.
Worshipping the Lord, honoring Your parents,
You set a holy model for us;
Bestowing Your benevolence, preaching Your doctrine,
You transformed our narrow and blind hearts.

Oh, Master, You died on the Cross
To ratify the New Covenant;
I, Your disciple, accept the Good News,
Walking the Way with confidence.
Thankful for Your loving-kindness,
Defending Your honor,
Only to be imprisoned, insulted—
Now I am ready to lay down my life for You!"

The criticism meeting of the small group did not give the official and his colleagues satisfaction. My little poem recited in public stung to the quick and irritated them so much that, as a Chinese proverb says, like "a cornered dog trying to jump up a wall," they resorted to extreme and desperate measures. They decided to increase my penalty. Proceedings were initiated against me, and they requested the court to send someone to interrogate me. Two days before increasing my penalty, they organized a mass meeting of the whole company to criticize and struggle against me. But their crafty strategy could not bend me. On the contrary, it rather tended to spread my spirit among the prisoners of the company. They could all witness my steadfast confidence and faith in spite of the menace imposed by the Communists.

At the end of September 1966, a general rally of the entire prison population was called. It was aimed at punishing certain prisoners and coincided with the overall development of the so-called "Great Proletarian Cultural Revolution," a large-scale campaign, more frightening still and setting the whole country ablaze.

At this rally a few prisoners including myself were sentenced. I received an additional penalty of five years. In the sentencing statement I was accused of sticking to a reactionary stance, making indefensible speeches at the study meetings and writing reactionary poetry to slander venomously the Party and Government. All this was not surprising. The Chinese Communist Party, though highly appreciating those of its adherents who used poetry to sing its own merits and to praise its own virtues, a fortiori feared and hated people who used poetry to defend justice and fight oppression. Once it faced such people and such poetry, it was apt to resort to any measures of suppression. This was done in my case.

Not long after this new sentence, Political Instructor Tan and Official Lin ordered me to accept the new verdict. I refused. Furthermore, to redouble my protest, I even returned to them the first two indictments and the first written judgment which I had kept for eight years. To retain those documents any longer, I thought, would be an error and a sign of compromise.

This increase in penalty was the most difficult stage of my struggle during that period. It lasted three months and brought about ten days of special supervision. But by the middle of October, the storm began to abate, and I resumed my former relatively carefree and pleasant rhythm of life.

It was possible that the officials of our company, while examining my exceptional behavior during those five years of torture and solitary, changed their view of me and began to regard me in a more favorable light deciding to leave me alone and pay little attention to my case. From time to time, Official Lin, who was responsible for discipline and education, called me in for questioning, but our talks generally wound up unsatisfactorily. Each of us spoke his mind and stuck to his own version, not really seeking to debate, neither willing to give ground in the least. Most of the time, the interview ended in a stalemate.

I recall an incident, which occurred one morning, probably in the fall of 1968, in the course of a public "struggle meeting" against prisoner Chen Decai. Official Wen, who presided, wanting to force prisoner Chen into making a true self-examination and confession, said, "My view is that it is most expedient for you to confess earnestly at first on your own initiative. Because if you remain obstinate, you will be subjected to punitive sanctions, like the handcuffs, and I should be surprised that you will be able to endure them. You surely will cry out in pain and call upon heaven and earth. You will still eventually have to confess all the same. I should be also surprised that you will be able, like that Roman Catholic we have in this company, to remain obstinate to the end. Indeed, I have never met a second one like Zhou Bangjiu. No matter how tightly one handcuffed him, he could always bear it without uttering a sound, without shedding a tear, without any groaning or yelling. Still less could one see him admit his mistakes and ask for pardon. What stubborness! And you, how can you do that?. . ."

To the best of my memory, Official Wen had never seen me with his own eyes undergo those tortures. He could only have received this information through other officials and prisoners who directly witnessed my trial. Now he unexpectedly spoke on my behalf and in my presence. I heard his words with my own ears. I saw with my own eyes the admiration and respect which the other prisoners showed me from all sides. I had the impression that finally, through me, our loving Mother Church which had suffered so much humiliation was obtaining some glory. Realizing this phenomenon "I put my hand on my forehead," as a Chinese proverb says, and felt a surge of jubilation. This incident aroused my ardor and strengthened my resolve to fight on and push forward in the flush of the victory to obtain even greater triumph.

If only those prisoners and officials, so astonished and led astray, might realize that it was really Almighty God who manifested in my weakness His extraordinary spiritual power and accomplished this silent miracle! If only they could through this event come to know Him, believe in Him, and receive His salvation! Should this be the case, I would ask for nothing better than to suffer again this trial of the first summer of the 1960s. I would do so to offer to the good God another opportunity to display His power so that He might once more be glorified in all things.

––––––––––––

Insofar as no human path has ever been straight and level, how could the road of the holy and difficult combat, which one rarely encounters, be easier and smoother? The bumps and windings do but make the poetic path richer, just as the rise and fall of waves, with their musical melody, give a vivid description to the sea, and as the ebb and flow, with their rhyme, give more power and majesty to the movements of the ocean.

In March 1970, the annual general review in prison had lasted over two months and was coming to an end. The newly-arrived Political Instructor Li and Official Wu, in charge of education and discipline, objected to my unusual and persistent refusal to write the year-end self-examination. They flew into a rage at me. They ordered the prisoners of my unit to organize a series of criticism meetings, day and night, so as to force me into writing this self-examination.

After a week, when Political Instructor Li saw the tenacity of my resistance, he convened a large public meeting of several groups in the open field to increase the pressure. At this occasion, he addressed me publicly, "You are absoulutely not allowed to resist the general review nor refuse to write anything about your self-examination. We are not asking you to fulfill all that we require from other prisoners. Whether you write much or little, well or poor, we do not mind at all. Only one thing is required: to agree to write. That is all."

As soon as he finished speaking, all the prisoners spontaneously and simultaneously shouted at me. They yelled at me to express myself, to put into action what I was requested and to obey immediately. I had arrived at a crossroads, and I had to make a quick choice. Since the opposition had given up a good part of their demands, I trimmed my sails and adjusted my position, and in a particularly tense atmosphere I gave the following reply: "I can indeed write this summary. But I will do so only with regard to prison regulations and manual labor. Furthermore, I shall write from the Catholic viewpoint as it has been my usual way of doing things."

After I had given my reply, neither the political instructor nor the prisoners raised any objection to me. The public meeting broke up and I returned to my unit. I put on paper without delay what I had promised to write--a three-quarter page statement entitled "The Summary Self-examination of 1969." I handed it over to the authorities of the company. With this, the week-long sharp and fierce battle, as a sudden violent storm, came to an end.

As I thought over the whole incident carefully, I realized how far I was from coming out victorious. The outcome of the conflict was a compromise that would jeopardize my principles. This was the first time since December 1956 that, under the pressure of the officials, newly assigned to our company, I gave in and wrote unwillingly a self-examination for an overall appraisal. During the first general review of that December I had written on my own initiative the first Summary of My Thoughts, which was aimed to correct the serious mistakes I had made during the first period of my imprisonment. Moreover, the Summary Self-examination of 1969 set a bad precedent to the Year-end Self-examination which I wrote twice during my next labor-reform camp days at Peng'an.

The most vexing thing was that the "fortress of obstinacy" I had been called all those years actually had been penetrated and broken by these officials. In fact, this was exactly what happened. Political Instructor Li and Official Wu were greatly overjoyed with their victory and pleased with themselves so much as to make a big fanfare. Both of them mentioned this fact at the meeting of the whole company, and a great number of the prisoners manifested their approval in various degrees.

Even today I still feel regret for this and am reminded of the beautiful verses of Tang Yin (1470-1523), an artist and writer of the Ming Dynasty:

> "A single slip may cause lasting sorrow,
> It will be too late for one to repent
> Though he lives for a hundred years!"

─────────────

It was just in the beginning of the decade of the 1970s that I met with this painful setback of my Self-examination of 1969. The first spring days seemed quite somber and dispiriting, and I did not spend them in my usual joyful way. Yet, despite the mingling of my mood and the very uncertain spring weather, I was neither disheartened nor dejected. Rather, I rallied my forces and waited for the first opportunity to fight again.

Since the last incident, the officials of the company had not given me any other trouble. They left me to live my untroubled life as before. During the several collective daily readings of *Chairman Mao's Quotations,* which like a tidal wave swept over all the companies of the prison, I continued to place myself outside the group activity and kept the same old behavior.

During this period of time, the number of new poems I composed increased rapidly. The annual rate was, on the average, at least one per day. Each poem required frequent recitation, correction and commitment to memory. Usually the time it took me to memorize each poem was three to four times the amount of composition time, so the rate of one poem each day was rather good.

Soon the second spring of the 1970s came around. The battle drum of the general review, a highly sensational and violent campaign once every year, was heard again. Xu Hun, a poet of the Tang Dynasty (618-907), says: "The wind sweeping through the tower heralds a rising storm in the mountains." His verse expresses very well the tension reigning before the imminent announcement of a fierce battle. This battle, without any doubt, would come from the dogged will of the prison authorities. The soldier of Christ was preparing himself to brave this storm and die in the tempest, if necessary.

To avoid committing the same mistake of the past year and travelling the same disastrous road, I determined to change my plan. I would take the initiative by writing down in advance what I wanted to say and as I thought best so that I could use it as a reason for refusing to write anything else. I wanted to gain the advantage by striking first and thus pass through the squall in one bound.

For this purpose, I wrote a poem in eight lines and fifty Chinese characters. I entitled it: "Summary of My Thoughts in 1970." Four years previously my penalty had been extended on account of a poem which I composed. This brief and rather unusual summary self-examination followed as a model, the style of the "Ci" of Xi Jiang Yue, meaning "Moon over the Western River," but in its number of lines and characters only. I had deliberately left aside its rhyme and meter, which were not included in the Chinese original until 1985 when I was able to commit it to writing in the United States.

Summary of My Thoughts in 1970

"The Church is good and benevolent, saving mankind;
I have lived under her wings ever since my childhood.
Jesus, Creator of the universe, redeems the world;
I have vowed to worship Him forever!

When the year has passed away like a river flowing,
I am glad that my ideals remain unscathed.
I can see before my eyes the glory that is to blossom;
I push forward towards the future with full confidence!"

Official Wu read this entirely new Summary Self-examination. A few days later, he called me into his office to question me and to force me to rewrite my summary. I categorically refused.

That February 24, Ash Wednesday, the very evening before starting the general appraisal of the self-examinations just written by each of the prisoners, Official Wu called a meeting of the whole company to dispose of the work of investigation and judgment of all the units in the company. Just before the close of the meeting, he suddenly accused me before all present of having composed the poem as an attempt to sabotage the general review movement. At the same time, he reproached me for not reading *Chairman Mao's Quotations*, for refusing to admit my guilt, and for opposing reform. Then he declared that I should be both cuffed and shackled and sent to solitary confinement for reflection and self-examination. Thus, with handcuffs on my wrists and the clank of the fetters in my ears, I took again the road to a cell and to solitude.

The solitary life which I had lived six years ago was resumed. Yet, this time my cell was no longer situated near the prison wall but was within the compound of the company building. And, besides the shackles on my feet, I was also handcuffed. Although at first glance, all this looked like "snow plus frost" or one disaster after another, in reality, it was one lucky event after another. I felt both apprehensive and joyful. For a while, I was unable to discern which of these two feelings was uppermost. My heart rose and fell, passing from one extreme to the other, unable to decide.

At first, all this seemed to presage that I would die a martyr soon as I had expected from the very start of my struggle. How was I to foresee that at the general meeting of the whole prison population, which was organized a month later for the purpose of rewarding the well-behaved and punishing the disobedient during the year-end general review, I would be given only "two big demerits" as punishment? There was no way I could fathom how mysteriously Divine Wisdom molded my life, even to the minute details. There was also no need for me to sound out the way God works. Yet, I knew deep in my heart that my destiny was not controlled by itself nor by the Communist Party. It was totally in the hands of the Good and Almighty Jesus Christ. This was why I had no reason to feel anxious or uncomfortable, or panicky, and still less to react as if sitting on pins and needles.

With these optimistic thoughts, I seemed to be back in my monastic cell at Chengdu, which I yearned for day and night. I imagined I was transported far away from the turmoil of the world to the Land of Peach Blossoms, to a realm of unique beauty. In the beginning of my solitary confinement, I set myself a new daily timetable made up of prayer, meditation, recitation of my former poems, composition of new ones and review of my *Song of Life*. Every day I faithfully followed this schedule and lived a quasi-monastic life in peace, joy, and recollection. Half a year later, at the time of my release, I was able to offer three hundred more poems to Jesus Christ to express my innermost feelings.

From time to time, officials came to make an inspection of me. Prisoner supervisors sometimes stared at me with ferocious expressions and shouted orders and reprimands. Accompanying me like the shadow following a person, the chains on my wrists and feet obstructed my every move. My life was filled with difficulties and pains. My face grew pale and even more haggard. My body was filthy. Winter and summer took turns in their attack on me with cold or heat. The mosquitoes and dampness of the prison cell were a constant irritation. All these troubles, however, were aimed only at the repeated training and unceasing shaping of a faithful heart totally offered to the Lord. They, too, served the mission of paving the road for other brothers and sisters to receive the Gospel one day. They were the bricks and mortar for Jesus Christ's great work of salvation. But, as a matter of fact, for the Communist officials who were bent on breaking me, could there be anything else left to expect?

Time and seasons never stand still. They fly at full speed just as fast as "the passing of a white colt glimpsed through a crack in the wall," according to the saying of Zhuangzi (369-286 B.C), a philosopher in the time of the Zhou Dynasty. Seven months had passed before I knew it. The Feast of Our Lady of the Rosary, October 7, took me by great surprise and filled me with immense joy. About nine o'clock in the morning, I was unexpectedly summoned to the office of the company. I was unconditionally released from my cuffs and shackles and from my solitary cell. The flimsy reasons the new Political Instructor Zeng gave to justify this new decision, in all seriousness, but unconvincingly, before releasing me, were the following. First, during my confinement, I did not get off the track but kept the prison rules quite well. Second, prison officials did not want me to eat free rice and do nothing the whole day. Third, they intended for me to be reformed through hard labor.

These reasons Political Instructor Zeng had advanced before my release were actually high-sounding excuses to justify the officials themselves and to deceive themselves as well as others. Afterwards I found out the real reason: they were ordered in fact by their superiors to transfer all the prisoners serving a limited

宿蓬安縣城

覃鴻秋
一九八一年七月二十五日
於蓬安

蓬中十夏驕陽似，
孤房五月甜如醴。
加利威脅難移态，
鄉繩毆辱惟傷體。
夜景賞街心，
遐想飛天際：
歷程戰鬪何時記？

AN OVERNIGHT STAY
AT THE COUNTY SEAT OF PENG'AN

To the Tune of Sai Hong Qiu
(Wild Geese over the Northern Frontier in Autumn)
Peng'an, July 25, 1981

Ten summers in the prison of Peng'an
Were hot as the burning sun,
But five months in a solitary cell
Were sweet as honeyed wine.
Added penalty,
Threats and pressure
Did not wear down my will;
Binding ropes,
Beatings and insults
Harmed only my body.

I enjoy the night scene at the crossroads,
My reverie flees to the ends of the earth:
When will the course of my struggle be recorded?

CHAPTER V

HARD BATTLE IN THE PENG'AN
LABOR –REFORM CAMP

October 1971

Only five days after I had left my solitary cell, October 11, 1971, I said good-bye to the Nanchong Prison No. 1 in the province where I had spent eleven years of warfare. Over 130 male and female prisoners were transported with me by seven long-distance buses, specially rented from the local "Motor Transport Company." We were escorted both front and back by two motorcycles, three military vehicles and one jeep and surrounded by about ten officials and some dozen armed guards carrying loaded rifles, ready for all emergencies. The large company looked like a long procession of an enormous and powerful revolutionary army as we drove the more than thirty miles to the Jinping Labor-Reform Camp in Peng'an County. There I was going to write with the sweat of my brow, the ink of my tears and of my blood a new page in the epic of my struggle.

This labor-reform camp was said to have been originally constructed with the purpose of moving the prison of Nanchong there. Therefore, the Communist officials responsible for its construction, knowing that this site was of strategic significance, took certain security measures to conceal the buildings among the trees. For a reason unkown to me, they gave up the original plan and made a fresh start. Thus, there emerged a new labor-reform camp with the code name: "P.O. Box 91."

Arriving in a strange environment and meeting many new faces did not change my attitude towards life. I was quickly spotted in the midst of the crowd, as a Chinese proverb says, like "a crane standing among chickens." This would necessarily attract public attention, invite trouble, and even stir up discontent among other prisoners, especially among those who were actively striving for a bright future.

The third day after our arrival, during the time of registration when I had to give the reason of my imprisonment, I wrote as usual "imprisoned and sentenced for having defended the Catholic faith."

Two prisoners in my unit who were also transferred at the same time from the prison in Nanchong knew the details of my case. They were doing all they could to display their zeal to "be reformed totally well." When they saw what I had written down, they suddenly got very angry with me and violently reproached me in unison. Their scolding sounded like thunder. They grabbed me, immediately dragged me to the responsible official of the company and accused me face to face. They were so familiar with my past that, "as if enumerating their family valuables," they could review and list a series of my "actions contrary to reform" from the past, such as my "refusal to confess my crimes, to read *The Quotations of Chairman Mao,* to study the press and other official documents, to take part in the study meetings, to write confessions, and to make self-examination at every appraising time." Furthermore, they pointed out that I had been punished very often by handcuffing, foot-shackling, demerits, an extended sentence, supervision, public struggle and criticism, and even solitary confinements. They wound up requesting that the government take severe sanctions against me.

After listening to their report and accusation, Official Ren called me to the office. He questioned me and then ordered me to write at once a self-criticism concerning the registration incident. When I resisted his order again and again, he did not directly retract it, nor did he obstinately seek to impose it on me any more. To save face, he merely asked me to return to my group and reflect. Unable to solve the matter, he had to leave it unsettled. Thus my first skirmish ended in victory. Fortunately, the news of what had happened spread quietly.

This labor-reform camp was a genuine labor camp, meaning it had no convalescent company. Every prisoner was assigned various jobs, more or less laborious. Physical labor in prison did not in itself constitute a particular danger to my faith. For that reason, from the very beginning, I changed my usual behavior. I withdrew my ten-year-old refusal to do hard labor on account of my physical condition. Then I took the resolution and the initiative to make a concession and take part in the hard labor assigned. When the old Official Pu of our company, who, rough and irritable by nature, had a tendency to hit obstinate prisoners, saw me willingly participate in hard labor to the best of my ability despite my handicap, he expressed extreme satisfaction and praise. He even gave me public recognition and commendation saying that even though I was stubborn psychologically, my attitude toward work was not bad at all.

The prison authorities always sought to compel a prisoner to acknowledge his crime, submit to the law, accept reform, do hard labor with all his might, and faithfully keep the prison rules. With this aim in view, they arranged two hours of study every evening. During this time news and articles reported in the press and "Quotations" of Mao Zedong and his other works were read aloud. In particular, various reports on big or small campaigns given by the wardens or other leading officials and certain special documents had to be studied. The meetings of self-criticism of the daily life took place every Sunday. Strengthening regularly the prison rules, launching the seasonal review and the mid-year appraisal, and especially undertaking the year-end general comment were all important programs of the evening meetings of study.

The methods of study, after listening to newspapers, reports and documents, were to voice our understanding and impressions, to measure ourselves by documents, to make our self-criticism, and to deeply analyze over and over the ideological roots of our crimes. All these study meetings would be carried out usually by listening and speaking, but on some specified occasions, by submitting written accounts, too. At the same time, prisoners were obliged to denounce, accuse, and criticize their fellow prisoners.

———————

One morning in the fall of 1972, during one of these study meetings, the official in charge of our platoon made attempts to force me to accept reform and get me to publicly read Mao Zedong's books. This action of the official was the direct result of a speech of Fr. Nie Jidao, an inmate of my group, who had chosen the road of compromise. In his intervention he said once more that I showed no understanding of the times, that I was out of step with what was evolving, and that I was going against the powerful current of history. He reproached me for refusing to read *The Quotations of Chairman Mao* and for still doing exactly what I pleased.

Official Pu, who was the head of the platoon and chaired the meeting, on hearing what Fr. Nie had said, played the same tune and brought up again my unresolved matter, analyzing it up and down, obversely and reversely. He wanted me to turn over a new leaf, to repent and be saved. He ordered me to read and study *The Quotations of Chairman Mao* with the other prisoners, to accept reform, and "to strive for a bright prospect so as not to be crushed to pieces by the wheel of history."

Hearing Official Pu's statement at the study meeting, the active elements of my group at once sided with him and took the occasion to concur with him so entirely that they would, as the Chinese proverbs say, "make the stormy sea stormier," and "wave flags and shout battle cries" for him. Two of the thirty platoon members dragged me back to the prison dormitory and compelled me to take out *The Quotations of Chairman Mao* for joint recitation. As soon as I took that little book out of my suitcase, I gave it to them and tried to return to the meeting place. Nevertheless, grabbing the book, they attempted to force it into my hands. When they could not, they forced me to sit and placed it on my knees. Instantly I threw it to the ground. They regarded this act as an insult to their great leader and as a humiliation to his brilliant literary work.

Using this incident as an excuse, under the initiative of their chief prisoners, Chen Desheng and Ren Gongbi, they rushed headlong into mass action. Some used their fists and others their feet as they struck and kicked, intent and competitive in showing their power and valor, their hatred and anger to me as well as their submission and allegiance, their love and support to the Communist official. In a deafening noise, the whole meeting-place turned wild and was thrown into great confusion. Fists and palms were flying at me from all directions, hitting me in the face, head, shoulders, and back. Under their blows, I fell to the ground on my back.

Because I had firmly refused to accept their "precious book" and dropped it whenever they put it forcibly into my hands or on my knees, they gave me a violent beating upon each refusal. Even Official Pu joined personally in the foray, kicking me with the tip of his leather shoe. The next morning at the study session, still fuming, the chief prisoner Chen Desheng cruelly gave my already bruised and swollen face three more slaps.

How could the brutality of the Communist officials, the abuse and beatings of their adherents overcome a soldier of Christ? How could Mao Zedong's heretical and pernicious writing, though bewildering the people and harming them, be forcibly imposed on the real holder of truth? My firm determination and fighting fervor in refusing to hold and read that little red book proved ultimately stronger than all the fists and claps. As a matter of fact, that was the opportune occasion for me to rid myself of the "precious book" once and for all. I felt as if a heavy load was now off my shoulders. As the Chinese idiom says, "with light pack and vigorous strides," I could pursue my way and brave a hail of bullets from all sides on the battlefield.

Official Pu, probably realizing after the close of this tragic and painful farce that he had not achieved the desired results, on the same day ordered a few prisoners of my unit to go to the infirmary. He instructed them to get medicines for my contusions and bruises, and to have my pair of broken glasses repaired. The next morning, when he called me in for questioning, his countenance wore the hypocritical look of "one bewailing the misfortunes of his times and pitying the sufferings of mankind," as people say in China. Having regained his composure and put his views aside, he reasoned with me thus, "Regarding the reading and studying of the Chairman Mao's quotations, this question can be looked upon as a matter for further thought and later discussion. We can wait patiently for the day when you will wake up and do it on your own."

And with these words, the unexpected and violent storm passed and all was calm. Moreover, it was the very one, the troublemaker, Mr. Pu, who terminated of his own accord what he had started in the first place. Nevertheless, the Communist Party in complicity with its submissive and docile prisoners added only another very shameful and inglorious page to its guilty history!

———————

At the outset of 1972 and 1973, under repeated pressure, I also acted against my principles and bowed in compromise. I wrote at the beginning of each of those years a short year-end summary, thinking wrongly that it was the best thing to do under the circumstances. Even though these two summaries were totally similar in all respects to the one I had written under duress in March 1970 in the prison at Nanchong, mentioning only the subjects related to manual labor and prison regulations and avoiding touching on the pointed questions of confession, study, thought reform, and political consciousness, I regarded them as thorough defeats. Like what had happened in 1970, they cut me deeply and left in me a wound, a real mark of bitterness, and even profound regrets to haunt me for the rest of my life.

Thanks be to our Mother Mary who in her merciful love gave me the strength, the determination and the bravery necessary to get out of this desperate situation. Helping me recover from my fall, she made me stand firm each year, starting in 1974, by rejecting to write my annual summary. With her assistance, I was able to reverse the unfortunate situation of those previous three years, to recover all my fighting vitality, to pursue my struggle and to rewrite my militant epic of the early 1970s even to the point of being moved to sing and to weep. I was also able to continue my long road with indomitable will, with lighter and happier steps.

It was true that I had to pay a high price each year for not writing my year-end summary, and for fighting the battle to its very end until at last I was released from prison. The high price I paid during those years was the repeated criticism and the repeated struggle I had to endure in my group meetings and in the general public meetings. During these meetings there was a series of reproaches, slanders, jeers, insults and beatings from the other prisoners present who also forced me to stand or even bow down from the waist while they criticized and struggled against me. In addition, I was sent to solitary confinement, received two big demerits, and was sentenced to another increased penalty. Despite this, the officials of the company could no longer break me, whom they had been nicknaming "stubborn fortress." The image of the resistant soldier of Christ was once again established, and this represented in itself an important victory worth celebrating.

In the early hours of September 9, 1976, Mao Zedong died of illness in Peking. Always the head of the Chinese Communist Party from 1935 until his death, Mao imposed his despotic and cruel reign, first on a part and then on all the mainland of China for nearly forty-one years. His dictatorship was a real and grave catastrophe not only for the vast number of Chinese people but also for the Chinese Communist Party which later and reluctantly acknowledged this in December 1978 and in June 1981, during the Third and the Sixth Plenary Sessions of the Eleventh

Central Committee. Could they do otherwise? No, they had no alternative! The tragedy officially began in the latter part of 1957 when the great campaign of the "Struggle against the Bourgeois Rightists" was launched. Then it was intensified and reached its limit in 1966 when another campaign with no historical precedent—the notorious Great Proletarian Cultural Revolution took over.

During the noisy and gloomy ten years of the Great Cultural Revolution, Mao Zedong brought struggle and oppression to its highest pitch. He pointed the finger at his own inner camp, turning against the large numbers of his leading officials both of central and local authorities. A feeling of imminent danger and a state of great panic were created among them, making them uneasy whether sitting or sleeping, causing them to denounce and accuse one another, to form cliques, to pursue selfish interests and to scramble for power and profit. All was in chaos.

The common people were the first victims, as a Chinese proverb says, "plunged into deep water and tormented by scorching fire." Subjected to all kinds of sufferings, the Chinese drank to the full the cup of bitterness and pain, and in large number experienced the tragic lot of summary execution. On the death of Mao Zedong in 1976, political turmoil reached its peak. The country's economy was on the verge of collapse, and agriculture and industry were crumbling.

Though Mao's body, like a withered tree or a rotten stump, had collapsed, his formidable influence did not relent. His partisans panicked as if foreboding the arrival of their end. To preserve the regime and to guard themselves against possible danger, they redoubled their oppression all over the country. Terrifying waves of suppression fell upon the people to crush them. Countless innocent Chinese were struggled against and thrown into jail. Both the decent and the indecent were tortured and killed without distinction. The atmosphere in the prison suddenly became very tense. Every company set up an office for round-the-clock surveillance. The officials were on duty day and night. The control over the prisoners was tightened. Terror was intensified. The reform-through-labor prisoners of the whole camp lived in constant fear.

The seventh evening after the announcement of Mao Zedong's death, during a study session, Official Jiang, in charge of discipline and education in the company, came to our unit to make trouble. He wanted to compel me to read out in public a newspaper proclamation from the *Sichuan Daily* regarding the death of their "great" leader entitled "Letter to All the Party, All the Army, and the Chinese People of All Nationalities." He ordered me to give my personal views to this article. I turned him down point-blank and, seizing the opportunity, I restated on the spur-of-the moment my definitive and unchanging position in upholding my Catholic faith forever. After half an hour of pressure, which ended only in deadlock, he then gave order to send me to solitary confinement. He advised me to "reflect carefully" and "confess conscientiously" during my confinement.

With me, three other prisoners from our company, Yan Luxiang, Wang Lin, and Tang Runchao, who were stubborn in thought and less submissive in attitude, were also put in solitary confinement that evening. It was certain that some prisoners in other companies suffered similar oppression. Since all news was severely controlled, there was no way of verifying this.

My life there in solitary confinement was exactly the same as in my two other confinements in Nanchong Prison. It provided me with the ideal conditions to pray, meditate, recite poems and compose new ones. The dreary scenery of the isolated cubicle had a strange charm; its peaceful and soft environment many times made me dream, and even visualize my return to a monastic cell.

The officials of the company and those prisoner guards who helped them to do evil redoubled their efforts to break me, but without success. Though sentenced to solitary confinement, I was still obliged to attend public struggle meetings. During these meetings of our platoon, the week-long attack of criticism, insult, scolding, beating and forcing me to bow low did not produce the desired result. As in the time of my first struggle, I could only patiently long, day and night, for the glorious moment of my martyrdom. I looked forward so eagerly to seeing that moment arrive that my eyes were strained by dint of expectancy. But it was in vain. My desire was not realized.

The will of Heaven is irresistible. All will be entirely accomplished in the fullness of time. The camp authorities in the end could do nothing but release me from my solitary cubicle and allow me to return to my original unit in the company as confidently as I had left. They decided this the morning of February 10, 1977, after a public meeting of the entire camp which was to conclude the year-end general appraisal. In the public meeting they gave me two big recorded demerits and, at the same time, declared that they had achieved a big victory over me with this punishment. In reality, they were only deceiving themselves, as "one plugs one's ears while stealing a bell." Thus, they ended their oppressive acts which had brought sufferings upon me for almost five months. This showed they were unable to find a way out, and this is well pictured in the poem of Yan Shu (991-1055 A.D.) of the Northern Song Dynasty:

"Flowers will die,
Do what they may!"

After leaving my solitary confinement, I had only a short respite and time to repair my martial attire. Meanwhile, I still had "to lie with my head pillowed on a spear, waiting for day to break"—as the Chinese idiom runs — and to be ready at any time to meet the even crashing battle to come.

At this time the new head of the Chinese Communist Party, Hua Guofeng, stirred up people to redouble their efforts to study earnestly the many-published works of his "great teacher" Mao Zedong. The bluster of this turbulent wave knew no limit and no restriction dashing into the prison with the momentum of an avalanche. Prisoners went out of their way to greet this new campaign and to curry favor with the new Communist head. At the call of the officials, they responded enthusiastically. They competed to buy and learn Mao's books which they held as golden rule and infallible precept. As a result of daily political study, they saw in these books unequalled tactics and powerful weapons for ideological remolding and real foundation of a glorious future.

Facing this new situation in the compound of the prison and resisting the onslaught of this new windstorm of madness that swept over the country, I tried to "remain as grave as a maiden," in the words of Sun Wu, a famous military strategist of the Eastern Zhou Dynasty (770-256 B.C.), and to stand as solid as a rock. I kept quiet and recollected, paying no heed to it. I repeatedly repulsed the temptation and pressure of the other prisoners. I had to calmly bear the unceasing taunts, reproaches, irritations and disturbances inflicted upon me at their whim.

During the middle of April 1977, the fifth volume of *The Selected Works of Mao Zedong* appeared in print and was issued in great quantity. This event made the already volatile situation reach its peak. The officials in charge of each company all rushed to the local Xinhua Bookstore of the state to buy their copies of the book.

On the evening of May 1, Labor Day, an exceptional meeting was organized to distribute the works of Mao to the whole company. Before the distribution, the officials lavished praise on Mao. Their flattering words resounded in my ears: "His writings mirror his person; his reputation fills the whole universe; and his influence acts as the wind making the grass bow before him!"

They asserted that his writings enjoyed the renown of a precious book, something rare and unique in the world and hard to come by, and everyone must have a copy in his hand. It was to be read carefully, studied thoroughly. The officials also announced that each prisoner would be called according to his rank in the unit to receive a copy. Upon receiving it, one had to show his reverence by bowing down!

As far back as the time of subscription for purchase of the book, I had already clearly manifested my non-compliance. But Official Jiang in charge of distribution feigned ignorance of my protest. When my turn arrived, as if nothing had happened, he in all seriousness called my name and urged me again and again to go up to get the book. In face of this intentional challenge, I met him head-on with a firm attitude and a sharp reply. I stood up on my seat, flatly refused to obey, and said in a loud voice: "I do not want to buy it!"

When he questioned me about the reason for my refusal, I replied that it was my duty to faithfully uphold my Catholic faith. Suddenly aware that I was pouring cold water on this happy and enthusiastic occasion, he flew into a rage. He belligerently gave an order to all the prisoners to write and hand over at once after the meeting an accusation of my wildly arrogant attitude and my extreme audacity. He finally added that the necessary meeting of criticism and struggle would follow soon.

Official Jiang was indeed a man of power. When he spoke, people obeyed. His orders, unshakable as a mountain, were carried out to the letter. After the meeting, many prisoners immediately held their pens in their hands to hastily write down the "crime" I had just committed. They demanded that I be severely punished. As for the prisoners of my own unit, they incessantly harassed me in order to pressure me to change my attitude. They did not want to stop their pestering. I was thoroughly upset and extremely exhausted. But the matter was important, the cause just. How could one bow one's head and yield? How could one bend one's knees and surrender? If a high price should be paid, "the game was worth the candle!"

With God's help, the first barrier was victoriously crossed after all. What followed my resolute resistance was more scolding, screaming and punishment. I was forced to stand in the center of the meeting place while the prisoners of my group heaped sharp criticism upon me. For the next fortnight , they continued their work by keeping me as the target of every nightly meeting. Could my fellow inmates by these means reasonably expect to compel me to change my early determination and give up my principles? No, nothing could affect me, not the blows from prisoner Liu Aimin, not even the harsh words and stern countenance of Official Chen Gongbo, not still Official Chang's intervention in the middle of a struggle meeting. Two months later the trial by the conceited officials from the local court did not avail either. Still less could they hope to achieve their goal, even though they were able, as a Chinese proverb says, "to shoot an arrow through a willow leaf a hundred paces away." My "conversion" remained no more than an inaccessible dream for them!

At the beginning of June, two or three weeks after my ordeal, I was reissued my savings account book from the prison. I was surprised to find out that the book payment which had been forcibly deducted from my account was put back. The sum appeared in the new balance. This showed that the officials of our company had backed down and candidly admitted failure. Do not people say that only in a fierce wind is the strength of the grass revealed, and that pure gold proves its worth only in a blazing fire?

You must not think, however, that those officials would rest and stop at this. It would not be long before their unmerciful faces exposed their secret plan of adding five years to my punishment. On September 3, 1977, they fully made their plan public at a general meeting of the entire prison. That afternoon I tasted particularly their cruelty and suffered untold humiliation. They bound me tightly and brutally with ropes for an hour. Official Zhang and a prison guard dragged me with haste to the front of the platform and forced me to keep my head bowed and wait for the announcement of the sentence. Only after the turn of the other eight prisoners who suffered the same fate had passed was I pushed away from the platform and ordered to sit in the last row of my company. After a while, the ropes were loosened and then, as the meeting continued, they were unbound.

Soon after I was sentenced to an added five-year imprisonment, another tempestuous wave swept over me. The document containing the judgment against me was placed before me and I was ordered to put my fingerprint on it. To this new attack I gave head-on blows. I protested with all my might and absolutely refused to obey the order. Official Jiang and Official Chen reproved me with their repeated threats while the other prisoners of my unit made war against me for two days. But all these attacks were shattered and all these efforts were without success. Unfortunately, during the "criticism meeting" on the last evening, the chief prisoner Chen Zuobin, with the tacit consent of Official Chen Gongbo, set up a crafty plan. Suddenly, by previous agreement, he and a few of his fellow prisoners rushed at me in unison, seized me by the hands and forcibly placed my fingerprints onto the document. This made me sick and drove me mad, but I was helpless in the face of their savage acts.

By such base means the Communist officials obtained my fingerprints. But what value had such prints? Would this prove in any way my voluntary approval of their judgment, or demonstrate the justification of their action? No, never! It would only "drag their prestige into the dust," as the Han Shu, the History of the Former Han Dynasty by Ban Gu (32-92), says, and only completely discredit them and expose to the light of day their true nature and inner-self for the world to see and scorn! The Han Shu says also, "An arrow shot from a powerful bow at the end of its flight cannot pierce even thin silk such as that of the Shandong Province!" Then, what to say of an iron will?

———————

Deng Xiaoping, in 1978, reappeared in the political arena. When he captured the reins of power, things began to change. Following the Third Plenary Session of the Eleventh Central Committee of the Chinese Communist Party, he gradually seized the supreme power and introduced a more moderate and long-range policy. He launched a campaign to rectify all the unjust, false, and misjudged cases both within and without the Party and he urged the rehabilitation of the victims. He shifted the focal point of work from the question of exposing and criticizing the Gang of Four to the question of the Construction of the Four Modernizations. It was important and urgent for him to restore the Communist Party's image, rehabilitate its prestige, and show a more pleasing and more open face both at home and abroad. In consequence, some of the dark clouds was disappearing and the cold storm, full of cruelty and violence, was relenting. This wind of change also penetrated into the prison and lessened much of the tension of the atmosphere. From this time on, things began to change for many and even for me, Your faithful servant, O Lord, who continued following Your way. Without veering, without catering to this new situation, I persisted in opposition to the confession of crimes, to participation in study of Mao's works, and to acceptance of reform. Despite this, whether during the ordinary meeting for regular study, or for weekly review of daily living, or for prison rules to be re-established, or in the very tense atmosphere of a certain campaign, the authorities of the company no longer had recourse to rude means against me. They limited themselves to gently criticizing and educating me when they did not just simply close their eyes, taking no further interest in my case. My general life began to know a considerable change and a clear improvement.

In the beginning of 1979, the labor-reform camp began to adopt some relatively open measures. One of these was to allow the prisoners to learn foreign languages. Thanks to this freedom granted by the new policy, I subscribed to two foreign language magazines, the *Beijing Review* and *China Reconstructs* in both their English and French editions. I also bought, at the local Jinping Xinhua Bookstore of the state, a small copy of an English-Chinese dictionary and a few copies of the *English Language Broadcasting Teaching Materials.* During the next two years I was even able to buy, through the mail, dictionaries and books of foreign languages from Peking, Shanghai, Chongqing and other major cities in China. In this way, I could take up again the English and French languages which I had studied more than twenty years before.

In our company three young prisoners earnestly asked me to help them learn English. It was difficult to refuse. I finally agreed with reluctance, trying my best to teach them. It was a wonderful grace for me to help others and this allowed me to increase my enjoyment day by day in rediscovering the foreign languages I had learned before. There was very little time at my disposal to study and to teach, and my progress was very slow, as if with "the step of a snail or an old ox," as the Chinese proverb says. In spite of this, the officials of the company, and even those of the camp, seemed to have changed their behavior towards me. No more did they stare at me with hostility. They viewed me in a new, more favorable light.

Two months afterwards, Section Chief Deng, in charge of discipline and education in the camp, inquired about my English study and teaching during a private talk. Also, certain officials in our company at times showed me the imported watches they were wearing on their wrists so that I might translate for them the English inscriptions, such as "waterproof, antimagnetic, stainless steel, made in, Switzerland." At their suggestion, a couple of the officials from other companies and even from the camp came to consult me as well.

Who would have ever thought that my very limited knowledge of English could one day make the Communist officials throw off their animosity and condescend to beg for a little learning from their subordinate? As a result, I felt my status rising suddenly in the eyes of the other prisoners, and my small voice, as the Chinese proverb says, "becoming out of the blue like the loud clap of thunder, no longer the muffled sound of an earthen pot." The grace of God spreads with mighty power, permeating all the world, and the loving God deserves eternal praise!

The great winds of change began to blow with the warm breeze of spring throughout the Mainland of China. The result could be felt especially in what touched unfair and false legal cases, and cases where mistakes had been made. Even the high walls of the jail could not resist such a powerful wind. For having refused to buy and to study the fifth volume of *The Selected Works of Mao Zedong* and for having opposed the annual summary examination, I had been condemned to an additional punishment. The leadership of the labor-reform camp felt from then on that this condemnation was a mistake made by the extreme Left and intended to correct it resolutely.

In the latter part of March 1979, Section Chief Deng confided to me during a private interview that there would be a retrial of my case of September 1977, in which I had been given an additional punishment. He assured me that all the mistakes must be corrected whenever discovered. On the evening of October 7, 1980, exactly a month before completing my twenty-five year sentence including its first prolongation, Mr. Wang Mingxue, the official in charge of discipline and education in our company, called me unexpectedly into his office for a conversation. Coming straight to the point, he spoke of the penalty inflicted upon me by the local court three years before. He persuaded me to make an appeal to the People's Law Court of Peng'an County requesting a retrial of my case. He declared in passing his willingness to bring me assistance so that the matter could be resolved as soon as possible. He also suggested that I write to my friends and relatives to find a suitable place to stay upon my release.

Seeing that his words really sprang from good will, I agreed right away. The next day I handed him an appeal addressed to the court asking for the rectification of the mistakes made in my case, along with three letters written to seek a place to live after leaving prison. The first one was sent to Fr. Prior Paulinus Li at the Old Folks Home in Kowloon, Hong Kong. The second letter was addressed to Mr. Vincent Yuan Nengding and two religious sisters at 184 Changshun Middle Street in Chengdu. The third was mailed to my fourth brother, John Baptist Zhou Bengu, in Suining. After a while my letters to Chengdu and Hong Kong were returned undelivered because the addressees were no longer there. But I did receive a reply from my brother in Suining who invited me to come to live with his family.

It was surely owing to my ongoing insistence on defending the Catholic faith and views that the county court in Peng'an took time to deliberate my case and hesitated to come to a decision. So, the reply did not arrive when expected, but kept me waiting. During the next six months I wrote a few more appeals pressing them to act quickly, and I even set out once again my consistent position in detail on March 8, 1981 (See Appendix II).

A curious incident occurred in the early summer of 1981 when I was about to be released from prison. At an evening meeting of the company, Official Wang Mingxue made an unexpected announcement: "Some of you know English. The country needs people with such talent. We have no reason to keep such persons in jail. We must do all we can to let them out of prison so that they can do some translating and enjoy travelling by plane today here and tomorrow there and living a free and happy life. Thus they can make their contribution to the national efforts of the Four Modernizations Construction of the country."

During his announcement, Official Wang did not allude to

anybody in particular, nor even hint whom he had in mind. Yet, I myself and the more than one hundred prisoners present who were acquainted with the real circumstances in the company knew for a fact to whom he was referring and could hear his implication and understand his intention.

As he spoke, through my mind flashed a past event contrasting so strongly with what I was hearing that I did not know any more whether to laugh or cry. Six years before, on March 25,1975, ten minutes before starting a public meeting to criticize prisoner Wang Lin, this very official read to us the latest news item from the Sichuan Daily concerning the release from custody of two hundred and ninety-three war criminals under a special amnesty. After finishing the reading, in all seriousness, he declared to the audience: ". . .Now, three days after criticism and struggle against in the public meeting of the company, Zhou Bangjiu remains as obstinate and unrepentant as ever. He is a prisoner who wants to set himself against the people forever, and who pretends to be able to resist the ideological reeducation until the end. As far as a prisoner like this is concerned, even if one day there is any general amnesty, it will never apply to him. He will never benefit from this chance, and never be one of those who will be pardoned. . ."

The official who had uttered these words also changed his attitude and treated me henceforth differently, as if he was two different persons. He was even offering his most devoted assistance in obtaining the rectification of my case. My poor knowledge of English obviously played a determining role and produced an unforeseeable and undreamt-of effect. Lord, this is one of the many wonderful arrangements Your Providence has made for me and one of the numerous living manifestations Your infinite love has shown me.

Finally, the hour dictated by God arrived at last. On the evening of July 22, 1981, no sooner had our company's public meeting concluded than Official Wang called me before him to hear, in the presence of many prisoners, the new decision of the Peng'an Court settling my case once and for all. The new verdict indicated clearly that my case came under an ideological category and accordingly should be handled only by reeducation, not by condemnation. In this connection the decision rescinded my original sentence of the extra five years of imprisonment and implied my immediate release. After having read the new verdict of the court, Official Wang handed me the document together with the statement of release plus a two-month living allowance.

Thus, in His wisdom and in His mercy, God eventually realized my most cherished wish and my least accessible dream. What a complete surprise! Indeed, I was overjoyed and moved to tears of gratitude. I could only turn towards the Lord, bow my head before Him and offer Him every one of the remaining days of my life.

重臨故地，市區徜徉；
可愛修院 注目遠方。

漫步蓮花池畔，
當年就讀中學回想；
佇立大北街邊，
昔日主教座堂凝望。

往事舊景，腦海翻滾；
千情萬緒 心頭湧進。

斯城滄桑，
何深何鉅！
感慨無限
難言難敘！

舉目望藍天，一切何主獻；
心靈趨寧靜，無憂又無怨。

CHAPTER VI

VICTORIOUS EXIT FROM PRISON

JULY 1981

After two days of preparation and packing, early on July 25, 1981, I triumphantly and cheerfully passed through the iron gates of the prison, carrying in my heart all my allegiance to the Lord. I felt neither haughty nor humble with regard to the prison officials. I did not hold any grudge against them, but rather a feeling of forgiveness for them. Just like a miracle, I bade farewell to the battlefield where I had fought for the last ten years. As I looked ahead, the future still appeared quite uncertain. But I felt full of hope and joy for the path which lay ahead of me.

Not long after leaving the labor-reform camp, I arrived at the bank of the Jialing River. On the other side was the county town of Peng'an where I stayed for a night. The next morning I took a bus to Nanchong.

> *On coming to the old place,*
> *I stroll about the urban district;*
> *I view from a distance*
> *Our lovely monastery.*
>
> *Pacing around the Lotus Pond,*
> *I recall the middle school where I studied;*
> *Standing still at the side of Great North Street,*
> *I gaze at the former Cathedral.*
>
> *Images and recollections of the past*
> *Overwhelm my thoughts;*
> *Emotions in great number*
> *Well up in my heart.*
>
> *How this city has changed*
> *During all these years!*

勝利出獄

眼免媚
九八一年七月二十五日
於蓬安

出牢謝主望晨星，
虎口慶餘生
漫長黑夜，
頑強戰鬥，
終見黎明。

主前成敗詩文獻
毀譽任人行
展望前路，
昂然挺進，
壯志霄凌。

How hard it is
To tell my countless feelings!

Lifting up my eyes to the blue sky,
I offer my all to the Lord;
Now in my calmed heart
Worries and complaints disappear.

VICTORIOUS DEPARTURE FROM PRISON

To the Tune of Yan'er Mei
(Charming Eyes)
Peng'an, July 25, 1981

Leaving jail with gratitude to the Lord,
I gaze up at the Morning Star.
How fortunate to have escaped from the tiger's mouth!

Throughout an endless night,
In a tenacious fight,
I see the dawn rising at last.

Successes and failures, poems and articles—
All I have dedicated to the Lord;
Blames or praises, no matter to me!

On my way ahead,
I rush forward, high-courage,
My hopes reach the clouds!

CHAPTER VII

CONFLICT IN MY FAMILY

August 1981

One week after my release from prison and return home, when I went to the Public Security Bureau in Suining to apply for a permanent residence, Ms. Liu Sufen, an official in charge of my file, suggested that I make a careful consideration and wait until I was definitely willing to live together with my fourth brother. This official lived very close to his house, right next-door but one, and so she knew quite well his disposition. At that time, the beginning of August, I did not take this judicious warning into account. I even thought, "Why worry? Why take the trouble to do that?" As a matter of fact, for me there was no other solution, all other ways of access were closed before me. I had to be finally approved to stay in my brother's family and for a while I felt elated. Unfortunately, this elation did not last long, just as a beautiful flower never keeps on blossoming. When I saw the real situation I was in, all my joy evaporated. Then, I wanted to leave Suining as soon as possible and move back to the place whence I had come: the reform-through-labor camp. Yet, it was too late. As a Chinese phrase says, "the raw rice was already cooked." It was no longer possible to change or go in reverse.

I found that in my own family my fourth brother had become an active supporter of the religious Reform. I learned at the same time that a few months earlier he had been designated to participate in a provincial meeting of the Chinese Catholic Patriotic Association in Chengdu. He took delight on several occasions to speak to me about this meeting, vaunting the preferential treatment he and the other delegates had enjoyed from the United Front Work Department of the Provincial Communist Party Committee. He pushed the provocation even to the point to sing to me a song praising the exploits and the virtues of the Communists, without realizing that he was mistaking the audience. I gradually discovered he was totally under the guidance of the local pastor, Fr. Huang Woze.

This pastor had long ago yielded to the pressure of the Communist Party and fallen into their embrace. He was proud of the honorary title of Member of the Standing Committee of the County Political Consultative Conference. He received from the United Front Work Department of the local Communist Party Committee a monthly salary of about $50, which corresponded to the median wage for the worker of Mainland China and could actually pay the living expenses of two persons. He was totally loyal to his Communist superiors. He said yes to whatever they wanted, submitted to their direction in all his activities, and always reported to them what was going on. If necessary, he did not hesitate to openly attack the Vatican and foreign missionaries during his homilies or some other speeches. Obviously, it was impossible for me to put trust in such a priest, to have any contact with him, to attend the Masses he offered, or to receive the Holy Sacraments from his hands.

From the very start, my brother and Fr. Huang were opposed to my unambiguous position and unyielding attitude in the face of the Reform. They immediately adopted the tactic of overt pressure and covert attack against me. Really, it was not at all surprising. Such conduct seemed to be very naturally and normally part of their logic and illustrated perfectly the word of Holy Scripture: "Let us beset the just one, because he is obnoxious to us; he sets himself against our doings, reproaches us for transgressions of the law." (Wis. 2:12).

My brother was an accomplice of Fr. Huang and acted in collusion with him. He hated me deeply. So far from regarding me as a soldier of the Church and a true Catholic, he also forgot to treat me as his own blood brother. Rather, he looked on me as a foe and was hostile without declaring war. Under the instructions of Fr. Huang, he spied on me behind my back.

He prevented me from writing letters. Once he actually stole from me a few letters written by one of my prison friends who had been released. He ventured to do this with the excuse that my behavior was anti-revolutionary. He even threatened repeatedly to report me to the government authorities and to request that they settle the matter lest he and his family be involved in a criminal case, dragged into blame, and meet with a misfortune together with me, like "the fish in the moat suffering for the city gate's catching fire." He insisted many times in clear terms on reminding me that I was not allowed to send letters overseas to make contact with the priests of our priory, whom he called imperialists.

My brother did not want me to stay at his home and tried every means to drive me out. Once when I was under heavy pressure from him, I went to Ms. Liu Sufen, the official who had already dealt with my file, and I asked her to show me a way to find a job. I thought that if I got a job, I would be able to depart from my brother's house. Unexpectedly, instead of answering my request in a positive way, she used this occasion to scold and lecture me, saying, "You complain today that you were not able to find work. Why did you commit crimes in the first place?" What was the use of arguing with her or trying to respond to her? Much less could I blame her for not having any way to find work for me. At that time there were several thousand young people unemployed in this region. Therefore, there was no solution left for me but to ask permission to move out of Suining and to go elsewhere to find work and another residence.

During the second half of 1981 and at the beginning of the following year, when the local Police Station Chengguan twice sent out a policeman to investigate my situation, I told him the whole truth every time. In the spring of 1982, the policeman was transferred. When the new policeman in charge of household registration of our residential district came to question my situation, I told him the same thing. Not long after, this policeman came again with another official, and I explained once more my predicament showing them the letters I received from Fr. Bernard Hwang and Fr. Felix Tang, two Benedictine monks. I stated specifically to them that I had received a sum of money from them. I also informed them that I had found my fifth brother living abroad through Fr. Hwang. I pointed out my difficulty in staying in my fourth brother's home, thus the urgent need to find new lodging. I answered all their questions without concealing the slightest detail.

In February 1982, I even went so far as to visit two of my former units of confinement: the labor-reform camp in Peng'an and the Provincial Prison No. 1 in Nanchong. A month later, I went back to that camp for another visit. But my request to return there to work was refused. Hence, I had no alternative but to live under my brother's roof and continue to swallow his insults and vexations.

Shouting that the Communist Party had never persecuted the Church and that I was not in any way imprisoned on account of religion, he forbade me to buy books. He did not permit me to read or write, nor would he let me learn foreign languages. He declared that since I kept my own way of thinking and refused to change for the better, all my learning was of no use even if I was able one day to master foreign languages. The government would never employ me or give me any work whatsoever. Whenever I retorted, he flew into a rage, even raising his hand against me. He used all kinds of means and pretexts, hard to describe, to coerce me to depart from the right way.

The hostility of my blood brother, John Baptist, gave a glimpse of the scale of the repercussions of terror the Communists exerted over all the people of China. Since he was afraid of the Communist Party and of suffering its persecution, he had to follow its line, join the Patriotic church and thus walk in Fr. Huang's footsteps. In his mind, the Communist Party was opposed not to the Catholic Church herself, but to the intervention of the Vatican. My brother regarded the re-opening of the local chapel and the permission to celebrate and attend Mass on November 1, 1981, as the tangible proof of religious freedom. At the same time, he claimed that my steadfast loyalty to the Lord and my flat refusal to follow his way were evidence of my being anti-communist. According to his reasoning, my course of action would get me nowhere and apart from an inevitable second imprisonment, bring me nothing very positive for a future. In addition, since I was staying in his house, these consequences would surely fall on him and on his whole family. Accordingly, to take preventive measures, he felt it necessary to draw a clear line of demarcation between him and me, and to strive to persuade or even force me to change my mind. If his plan should succeed, he would gain certain prestige, probably improve his status and receive some awards. Even if his efforts should be futile, he would have shown in all this his allegiance to the Communist Party, and thus would be able to avert all suspicion of compromise and avoid all complication.

Little did I know that having left prison and escaped the den of the lion, I was to come home and fall into the tiger's lair, equally dreadful. This verifies the proverb:

"Blessings never come in pairs;
Misfortunes never arrive singly!"

Fr. Huang Woze, who hated me to the bone, was both tricky and sinister. He never ceased to scheme and to sow intrigue, using base tactics to frame me. He instructed my brother to launch an offensive against me from the front, while at the same time, inciting my sister-in-law and my niece and her husband to pressure me from behind each one in his turn. He brought all his skill into play, attempting vainly to drive me to the wall and to compel me to follow their dubious road. Perhaps, if his plot failed, he would try to get me imprisoned. He knew perfectly how to hide his intentions and his tricks were both clever and dreadful!

The mail and money I had received from abroad escaped his attention and obstruction during the initial period. But when he learned of them from the report made to him by my brother, he worked hard to ruin my established overseas contacts. He deliberately spread a slanderous rumor that I was making contact with the imperialists to get their money.

In order "to shoot two hawks with one arrow," as a Chinese saying runs, he tried to perturb and frighten both me and the family with another rumor which it was then impossible for me to verify. The rumor was that at a study meeting for Catholics of Chengdu, the officials from both the United Front Work Department and the Public Security Bureau of the city had raised my past problems, recalling "my attempted sabotage on the Reform and close affiliation with the imperialists." The rumor continued to say that these officials had already asked the same two authorities in Suining to keep me under close surveillance and certainly not allow me to leave the country, because I still persisted in the same reactionary thinking. This measure was taken to avoid a new incident such as that of the Archbishop of Canton, the Most Reverend Dominic Tang Yee-Ming, S.J., which had arisen not long ago. His leaving the country was considered by the indignant Chinese Communist authorities as a serious harm to the nation and the Patriotic church.

After a twenty-two year imprisonment for Christ, the Archbishop of Canton, the Most Reverend Tang had been released from prison on June 9, 1980. The following November, he was allowed to go to Hong Kong for medical treatment. From then on, he did not return to the Mainland. On June 5, 1981, he was appointed by Rome, Archbishop of the Canton Archdiocese. A week later, the Chinese Communists began to attack the Vatican for "interfering in the internal affairs of China" and at once launched a new campaign against the Pope. The Patriotic Association throughout the country then organized many accusation meetings against the Archbishop of Canton, slandering him, accusing him of treason, banning his return to Canton, thereby, forcing him to remain in Hong Kong. Exhausted by the duty of witnessing to his experiences in prison by writing and preaching, he died at 87 in Connecticut, U.S.A., on June 27, 1995.

In March 1984, Fr. Huang made a detailed report on my case to the chief of the newly-established Religious Affairs Division in Suining and requested him to seize the matter. The chief of the Division explained to him that to establish regular correspondence with foreigners, to receive financial help from abroad, and to have found my fifth brother in Taiwan were all permitted by the government, and that I did not break any law. But Fr. Huang would not hear of it. He even went so far as to denounce my correspondents, accusing me of writing not to any ordinary foreigners but to Fr. Bernard Hwang and Fr. Felix Tang, two Benedictine priests. He called the responsible official's attention to the fact that the Benedictine Monastery was reactionary and had been founded by Fr. Raphael Vinciarelli who had been expelled as an imperialist. After hearing his accusation, the responsible official promised him he would investigate the whole affair and deal with it accordingly.

The crafty plot of Fr. Huang did not stop here. He continued to stir up and influence my sister-in-law. On the morning of April 15, 1984, Palm Sunday, after the Mass, he took her upstairs and related to her that two Protestant ministers in Nanchong had recently been arrested for writing letters abroad. He assumed a countenance of deep concern, feigning worry on my account, and whispered in the ear of my sister-in-law that if anything untoward should happen to me, the consequences could be dire. Not only would I endure sufferings, but the whole family would be implicated!

Hearing all that Fr. Huang had said to her, my sister-in-law was greatly disturbed. Three days later, on Holy Wednesday, when a good opportunity came to her, she discreetly came upstairs and secretly advised me of all the remarks of Fr. Huang. She implored me not to write overseas any more, nor to continue asking for money, and surely not to apply to leave the country. She besought me to listen to her, because, if something went wrong, her family would suffer all the consequences and they would "lose face", which would be an extremely shameful thing, unbearable before others. Moreover, her three daughters and their husbands might be prevented from joining the Communist Party; and this would amount to jeopardizing their future.

As soon as my sister-in-law had finished confiding sincerely in me her fear, I felt my heart bleeding. I was at my wit's end. I did not know what to do anymore. I did not know how to cope with the situation. I had just handed in my petition for a passport to the local Public Security Bureau. It was a critical time for me. Deeply disturbed, I was very worried about how all this would hamper my passport application. At that moment, I could not imagine what the Lord reserved for my future, but I suddenly recalled the words of Psalm 139: "Your eyes have seen my actions. In Your book they are all written; my days were limited before one of them existed." (Ps. 139:16). These words quickly brought me light and comfort, and I immediately felt at ease and justified. I happily offered anew all my being to my good Lord. I handed over everything into His hands and let Him decide for me. I also determined to maintain my efforts in pursuing permission to leave the country.

遊香山公園

采桑子
一九八四年十一月八日
於北京

纜車載我登山頂,
頭上秋光。
雲霧茫茫
不見京都見太陽!

香山霜葉紅如火,
遐邇飄香。
早已秋涼,
未睹妖嬈欲斷腸!

A TRIP TO XIANGSHAN (FRAGRANT HILLS) PARK

To the Tune of Cai Sang Zi
(Song of Picking Mulberries)
Peking, November 8, 1984

The cable car carries me to the top of the mountain,
The sunlight of autumn caresses my head.
Vast clouds and mists fill the sky,
The Capital has disappeared,
Only the sun shines!

The Fragrant Hills are radiant;
Autumn leaves, red as fire,
Have spread their sweet scent far and near.
The chillness of fall has already come;
Were I never again to see their rich color,
My heart would break!

CHAPTER VIII

PETITION FOR EXIT

March 1982

My first six months out of prison were extremely trying. Living in a hostile environment with an uncertain future made my heart deeply troubled and weighed down with anxiety. To get myself out of the tiger's lair and to rejoin my monastic community seemed at this stage unrealistic and unattainable. Thinking of this was somewhat like the Chinese proverbs saying, "drawing cakes on canvas to allay one's hunger," or still "building a castle in the air." Yet, just as I came to the place, depicted in a poem by the well-known poet of the Southern Song Dynasty, Lu You (1125-1210 A.D.), where "the mountains and the rivers end, there where any way out seems impossible," something like a miracle happened. Before my eyes there stretched a wonderful landscape: "A village lost among weeping willows and flowers of all colors." (Lu You).

God's magnificent Providence was content not only to open a channel for me to obtain news and financial help from my monastery abroad, through our old friends, Professor Pansy Lang, a famous Chinese soprano, and her husband, Dr. Michel Xiao, but also to provide me with another means of finding two of my confreres, Fr. Bernard Hwang Kuo-wei and Fr. Felix Tang Tien-shou. From them both I received letters and a donation of five hundred American dollars. This amount equaled 900 Chinese Communist dollars, Renminbi (RMB) or so. With this money I repaid my sister-in-law all my boarding expenses outstanding since my return in the previous July ($12 RMB for each month). I also bought clothes, a desk, books, and some other articles I needed. Then I deposited the remaining cash, about $700 RMB in a bank. In this way, the anxiety about my livelihood was solved, and my external circumstances began to improve.

On March 21, 1982, on one curb of the sidewalk of Great West Street, I set up a table as a public letter writer to be of some service to uneducated people and earn a little income. Thereby, at least, I had an idea of having a job and even being regarded as nominally employed. Many Chinese were illiterate and when they needed letters or statements of self-criticism, application, appeal or complaint written out, they had to ask outside help. This course of action allowed me to escape somewhat from my brother's surveillance and harassment and to get some freedom to read and write. Thus, I was able to recover my equanimity.

It was very likely at the end of the same month that my eldest niece, Maria Beata Zhou Xiaozhen, then a Sister at the Mother House of the Sisters of the Sacred Heart of Mary in Taichung, Taiwan, wrote me a letter through Fr. Bernard Hwang, who had informed her about me. She gave me good news about her parents who were still living. Four months later she replied to my letter dated April 18. This meant that it was completely possible to continue henceforth in correspondence with them. At the end of September of the same year, I also got a letter from my fifth brother Philip Zhou Zhimin. I had seven brothers but no sisters. My second, third, seventh and eighth brothers died all very young, so did the eldest one at age 20. My fourth and fifth brothers and myself, the sixth brother and youngest of the three, survived. My parents had died long before. My brother, Philip, had been living in Taiwan with his whole family since 1949. After having heard from him, I was finally able to keep in touch with him directly.

———————

After a careful analysis of my situation, I was convinced that my petition for leaving the country, which I had been thinking about, would never be granted. My reasons for believing this were as follows. I had been a prisoner for many years, and I had continuously upheld my original ideas against the Religious Reform since my release from prison. Moreover, the incident with Archbishop Dominic Tang was still irritating the Chinese Communist Party, and the attack against the Vatican at that time continued to shake the Patriotic church of China. Consequently, my chances of getting the petition approved seemed slim indeed.

In view of all these facts, I thought of getting enough money to buy a house so that I could get away from my brother John Baptist and live by myself, thus escaping his control and surveillance. This done, I could look to the future more serenely, make long-range plans and act as the occasion demanded.

On September 4, 1982, my brother Philip wrote me a negative reply and refused to send me the money. His opposition to my plan, and especially his severe criticism and blame, surprised and embarrassed me. His response shook me so much that I felt wronged and found it hard to express my pain. But from this I was also determined to pluck up my courage to set out in a straightforward manner to Fr. Bernard and Fr. Felix my desire to leave China and go to Hong Kong to visit relatives and obtain medical care. Since, however, I had very little chance to gain an entry visa from the authorities of Hong Kong, there was no solution left to me except making an application to the United States.

After almost endless correspondence, with the full support of my Benedictine monastery now located in Valyermo, California, channeled through Fr. Bernard and Fr. Felix, and with the encouragement and cooperation of my brother Philip, on January 23, 1984, I made a decisive step and boldly went to the local police station to present to the County Public Security Bureau my petition for a permit to leave China for the United States of America to visit relatives and to seek medical treatment.

Mr. Deng Shanghai, the responsible official of the Second Division in the County Public Security Bureau, in examining my petition for a passport, did not raise an objection, nor try to create difficulties for me. On the contrary, he showed great care to abide by the current policy.

On July 11, 1984, while conducting the first interview regarding my petition, he openly declared, "It will soon be half a year since you handed in your petition. Petitions to go overseas, particularly to go to Hong Kong and Macao, have been so numerous that we cannot process all of them at the same time. We have to deal with each case according to the order in which it is received. Now your turn has come. The government has adopted in recent years an open-door policy giving citizens freedom to come and go, this means that they have the right to go out and come back to the country freely. However, before a case can be evaluated, all the necessary documents must be handed in and the situation of the applicant must be investigated. As soon as all the documents and materials are collected and evaluated, we can make a report on each case and then send it to the higher authorities for a final decision."

On July 12, I went back to the office to hand over to the same responsible official all the necessary documents obtained from abroad and the complementary information, written at his request, about my past history, family situation and social relations. After all his requests were met and all conditions fulfilled, I was allowed five days later to fill out an official application form for a citizen of the People's Republic of China to go abroad. I was given to understand that my application would be at once forwarded to the Provincial Public Security Office for examination and approval.

When my file was being examined at the County Public Security Bureau, the responsible official did not overlook, but paid special attention to the problem of the Reform of the Catholic Church. He solemnly pointed out that problem to me. He regarded this point as a matter so crucial to my application for exit that he insisted on some clarifications before anything could be done. So, he asked me to write down my sincere thoughts and views and some clear-cut explanations on this subject.

In face of such a critical situation, such a severe test, I could neither flee nor dodge, nor do a U-turn, nor accept a compromise, I could only proceed to take the official's challenge head-on. Sticking to my usual position and preserving my original attitude, with earnest words and in a polite tone, I wrote an essay, "My Views on the Party's and Government's Policy regarding Religions and My Attitude towards the Catholic Three Autonomies Reform." I sought to achieve a double goal: to uphold my own principles and yet avoid provoking the other side.

Both before and after writing, I worried for a while that my petition to leave the country might be held up by this affair or even aborted. The next afternoon, however, the official in charge accepted my essay, and looked it over carefully while I waited for his verdict. After the reading, he remained silent without expressing the least reaction. He only asked me to translate from English into Chinese all the names, addresses and essentials of the documents I had received from the United States of America and handed in, and then to attach translations written on strips of paper to the originals. To cut the matter short, he asked me to get four two-inch passport photos of myself and bring them to him as soon as possible. Four days later when I came back with the photos, I was finally given the application form for an exit permit.

This meant, in other words, that so far as the County Public Security Bureau was concerned, my request to leave the country was approved in principle. What remained for me then was only the final examination and ratification by the Provincial Public Security Office in Chengdu. I was brimming over with joy and I could not help thinking of the Chinese proverb: "Heaven protects good people!"

According to my estimation, the reasons for the approval of my petition were the following: Even though I had been imprisoned for many years and still opposed the so-called Reform Movement of the Church after my departure from prison, I did not try to engage in any activity to destroy this movement or in any other unlawful practice. I observed the laws of the country. Furthermore, I was no longer young and my right hand was incapacitated. My relationship with my brother, to say the least, was not the most harmonious. I did not have employment, nor any income. I was unable to support myself. If I stayed longer in China, I would eventually become a public charge, thus putting an additional burden on the government. Moreover, I had a blood brother overseas, who had sent me a letter of official invitation and a written certificate guaranteeing to support me for life.

In addition, there might necessarily be some other reasons why the Communist Government would let me leave the country. In order to reconstruct and expand the economy still in a difficult situation and to build up the program of the Four Modernizations, it was not only anxious to win international understanding, sympathy, support and help, but also eager to obtain foreign capital, science, technology and equipment. Hoping to achieve these goals, it had to carry out a liberation policy that would be more apparent both at home and abroad, by allowing its people to go overseas to visit relatives, to study, or even simply to emigrate, provided they went through the proper legal channels.

Of course, the reason why the Communist Government would let me depart was, to cut a long story short, that I presented all the required letters, documents and in particular, the affidavit of support, which was offered by my American sponsor, Dr. John W. Birsner, and signed by an American notary public, Sharon E. Robison. All my past and present situation had been examined under a microscope; my view points on the government's religious policy, and especially my attitude toward the Three Autonomies Reform Movement of the Catholic Church, had been clearly stated as requested and the whole had been found to be open, firm and above-board.

Consequently, the Communist officials acted according to the current policy, or perhaps it is more accurate to say, that they granted my petition according to expediency. Yet, for my part, I was filled with a joy beyond measure when I received the long-sought passport. What really took me by the greatest surprise was the fact that I had to wait for only two months, such a short interval from the day I handed in all my documents. O Lord, truly I wanted very much to jump and leap with incomparable happiness; but, above all, I wanted very much to engrave in letters of gold Your loving mercy and almighty power, to sing my good fortune at the top of my lungs, and to cry loudly to the whole world: "Hear now, all you who fear God, while I declare what He has done for me. When I appealed to Him in words, praise was on the tip of my tongue ." (Ps. 66:16-17).

別矣，祖國

七絕
一九八四年十一月二十七日
於上海

故國變天廿五冬，
風狂雨橫見蒼松。
陽關一唱心將碎，
天父何時降赤龍？

FAREWELL, MY MOTHERLAND

In the Poetic Style of Qijue
Shanghai, November 27, 1984

O my motherland, your sky has changed
Over thirty-five winters;
Violent wind and bitter rain
Have revealed the strength of a green pine.
In singing to you a song of good-bye,
My heart breaks within me!
When will our Heavenly Father
Tame the Red Dragon?

CHAPTER IX

PASSPORT OBTAINED: DEPARTURE

September 1984

On September 17, 1984, at about nine in the morning, the policeman in charge of supervising the household registration on our street, unexpectedly came to our home to inform me that I should go immediately to the Office of Public Security to pick up my passport. This was exactly two months to the day since I had handed in all the required papers and filled in all the forms. Through my mind, at that moment, ran the joyful and grateful prayer, "The merciful love of the Lord is indeed boundless, and His power truly limitless. May His Name be forever glorified and praised!"

On that very day, therefore, I went to fetch my passport and obtained it with joy and exaltation. I was told, however, that my date of departure had to be delayed to the next month because of National Day, October 1, near at hand. During this holiday, Peking would receive many visitors from within the country and abroad to attend the celebration. All the hotels would be full. To avoid aggravating congestion, the central government had taken preventive measures by sending an official directive to all the provinces and municipalities directly under its jurisdiction, instructing them not to allow ordinary travelers into the capital during the period of the National Holiday.

During the three weeks after I had obtained the passport, I was busily occupied spreading the good news, sending a lot of books ahead of me, and saying good-bye to friends and relatives. When my brother John Baptist heard of my departure, he was much surprised and felt very happy because he would be completely shed of the heavy burden of supporting me. He could henceforward live more quietly, more relaxedly and more happily. As my leaving the country neared, he showed me sincere and warm affection.

Four days before leaving Suining, I went to the Bureau of Public Security as requested to receive the last instructions from the official in charge, Mr. Deng Shanghai. He stressed the following three points: "When you speak to foreigners concerning the construction of our economy and all other matters, be prudent and be sure to tell the truth and not to talk irresponsibly. Of course, we are not afraid that you will talk nonsense! Secondly, do not leak our national secrets. Lastly, though you are allowed to keep your own view and attitude which differ from ours, you ought to make an effort to understand well and not be mistaken about the Party's and Government's consistent religious policy towards the Catholic Church. It aims at getting rid of all foreign interference and assuring the Church to be controlled and administered independently by our own people, by the Chinese themselves."

Neither during his talk nor afterwards did he require me to give my reaction or express my opinion. Still less did he ask me to provide the slightest verbal or written promise to guarantee that I would comply with his instruction. For my part, it was not a question that I would impose barriers on myself, just as "a spring silkworm spinning a cocoon about itself," giving my word about something he did not ask of me. Moreover, even if he had insisted on a promise, my promise would only concern at most the first two points of his instruction regarding the economic construction of the country and regarding national secrets.

The reason was very simple. As a sincere Catholic, I had no intention of giving a false image of Mainland China which had nothing to do with reality. I could only confine myself to the facts and discern the truth by considering things carefully. I was able to distinguish clearly between right and wrong, just as I could "differentiate the water of the Jing River from the water of the Wei River."

As to the question about national secrets, it had absolutely nothing to do with me. First of all, I had never been a Party Member nor an official of the Communist Government. Certainly, I never had any access to their classified documents, nor was I in a situation to make myself acquainted with the contents of their internal reports or secrets. Whatever I knew, I had learned only from public bulletin boards and newspapers, which divulged official information, open to all, including foreigners. Yet, especially, what could I have learned after a quarter of a century in their prison? What everybody knows for a fact can one truly call "secret"? As a matter of fact, my case could not represent a particular danger. On his part, however, the responsible official had to devote himself to fulfill all these governmental formalities and procedures.

His instruction lasted about half an hour. We parted in a friendly way, and we wished each other well, even hoping to meet again. The other officials standing by were also bent on wishing me a happy and pleasant journey.

The longed-for historic moment of my life finally arrived. On the morning of October 7, 1984, before dawn, I said goodbye to my brother's family and left Suining by the first nonstop bus for Chengdu. Thus I set out on the road towards new horizons, towards a bright future, and I began a wonderful journey that would take me across the ocean.

The three-year up-and-down battle waged directly with members of the Patriotic church and indirectly with their supporters, the Chinese Communist Party, was now over with the opposition suffering a crushing defeat. The ingenious plan, devised by the gang headed by Fr. Huang Woze, "was thrown into the eastward-flowing streams" and irrevocably lost; their sweet dream went up in smoke. This defeat would certainly leave an indelible mark on their hearts and add another shameful page to their history. For my part, to this day, I continue to pray that the merciful Lord will grant them pardon and lead them to the road of conversion, to the way of truth!

———————

Once in Chengdu, many events of the past rose before my eyes and conflicting feelings welled in my heart.

Benedictine Priory at Yangshi Street,
My home for eight springs;
Cathedral at Peace Bridge Street,
I worshipped there often.

Shude Lane High School,
As a young oblate, I spent three autumns there;
Humble house at Changshun Street, where
Full of ideals, I fought for two years with the Wolf.

Time passes;
The provincial capital had changed.

Where are those places
Which meant so much to me?

In the Ningxia Street Prison
And the Wensheng Street jail,
Against the icy wind and frost
I had contended for three winters.

In the northern suburban district wilderness,
And near the West Contesting Field,
I struggled for two summers
Against the burning sun and hot weather.

All these images of yesterday
Still vivid today!
All these hidden feelings
No words can tell!

In crowded green bamboos
At the Thatched Hut of Du Fu,
Among the emerald cypress trees
At the Temple of the Marquis Zhuge Liang,
How many visitors are so enchanted
As to forget to go home?

At the Wenshu Monastery within the city,
At the Zhaojue Temple outside the city,
How many pilgrims, the good and the wise,
Burn joss sticks and pay homage?

My old friends and acquaintances
Are scattered or dead;
Why is it so difficult
To meet again the ones still loyal?

The sky of the "city of brocade,"
Dense with great gloomy clouds;
My friends did not ask me to stay,
I had to put up at an inn!

When I compare the past and the present,
And when I look to the future,

How can I stop myself from sighing?
From grieving?

Will I see the city once more?
Hard it is to predict!
Filled with a multitude of parting feelings,
My heart is in agony!

On the tenth of October, at midnight, I arrived in Peking from Chengdu by plane. I did not go to the American Consulate to request a visa until the end of the month, because the six-page document from Dr. John W. Birsner, required for my application and promised to be returned to me by the Suining Public Security Bureau, had not yet been received. Thus, all I could do was wait. No sooner had I received them than I went to the Consulate on Xiushuihe East Street, where I was turned down in a totally unexpected way. The American Vice Consul explained to me and gave me the following written reason: "Based on your interview and the documents you have submitted, you do not appear to have sufficient ties to this country (China) to compel your departure from the United States at the end of your visit." Right away, I sent a letter along with all the relevant information and the visa application form to Fr. Bernard Hwang Kuo-wei in Oregon, asking him to get me out of this hole. My monastery resettled in Valyermo, and Fr. Vincent de Paul Martin, O.S.B., with the assistance of Dr. John W. Birsner, a close friend of the monastery, who as my sponsor, had taken care of my departure, intervened. After a fortnight, I received a phone call from the Consulate and was requested to come at once. Without delay, I hastened there once again, and to my greatest good fortune, I was issued a visa to enter the United States.

During these forty-seven days in Peking, besides the visa business, with a quiet and happy heart, I engaged myself in reading daily newspaper at the street bulletin boards, perusing magazines and books at some public libraries, looking for and buying helpful books at bookstores, going sight-seeing and visiting some scenic spots and historical sites, writing letters at the great hall of the post office near my hotel to my supporters of all these last arduous years, and also continuing to compose new poems. Many thoughts were in the making in my mind, and a multitude of feelings sprang up in my innermost being.

Oh Great Wall, so magnificent!
How strategic a post!
How strong a fortress!
For more than 2,000 years
You have known wind and frost!
Because you are now
A servant of Marxism-Leninism,
Sadness comes with me
When I walk upon your high walls!

Oh Imperial Palace, majestic and brilliant!
You survived the Ming and Qing Dynasties,
Beautiful and strong!
But you are now
In the hands of the partisans of Mao Zedong,
And I sigh to gaze upon you!

Oh vast Tiananmen Square!
When I look up at your gate tower,
And when I gaze on your surroundings,
I see your real master is always the ghost
Of the one lying beside you
In his crystal sarcophagus!

Oh Fragrant Hills, covered with red leaves!
Your temples and pagodas, ridges and peaks
Stand like jade, fair and graceful!
Paying you a visit, I learn:
You have been made the secret palace
Of the Red Chinese Communist Imperial Court
During its early period (February 1949-
*   February 1950)!*

Wandering up and down Wangfujing Street,
I would like to ask the passers-by:
"Where are you going?"
Strolling along Chang'an Avenue,
I want to know:
"Are people happy in their hearts?"

Oh Cathedral, seat of the late Cardinal,
His Eminence Thomas Tien Keng-hsin!
You have been hidden in the noise and clamor.
Because of the difficulty knowing
Where you were,
I did not come to lament over you
From the depth of my heart!

Oh Father Matteo Ricci,
Your renown remains forever in China!
Having heard of your tomb too late,
I let slip a golden opportunity
Of making a pilgrimage to pay my homage to you!

During the seven weeks
I spent in the famous city,
All seems to smile at me.
One shadow only remains:
To have missed the Cathedral and the ancient tomb!

In the midst of pleasant moments,
This is a regret
Which will remain in my heart!
But now while thinking again of the past
On the remote other shore,
I feel merely tired !

逰美國

七絕
一九八四年十一月二十七日
於洛杉磯

大洋彼岸慶飛臨，
美夢成真喜詠吟！
偉大國邦良頗獻：
宏圖壯志滿胸襟！

ARRIVAL IN THE
UNITED STATES OF AMERICA

In the Poetic Style of Qijue
Los Angeles, November 27, 1984

Having flown over the vast ocean,
I happily arrive on the other shore;
My fond dream has become a reality,
With tremendous joy, I compose a poem!
To this great nation
I offer my best wishes:
May your heart brim over
With bright prospects and lofty ideals!

CHAPTER X

SINGING SONGS OF TRIUMPH

November 27, 1984

What an unforgettable and memorable day! It was one of these particularly fine days at the beginning of winter in Peking. The sun was warm. The wind was still mild. The scenery was glowing with beauty and it was enchanting. It was as if the whole city was humming the ancient melody of a farewell song to me. I felt something, however, like a refrain of homesickness, that held me back.

At about eleven that morning, our airliner took off right on time. I sat quietly in the cabin, facing south. Looking down at the capital, I felt an upsurge of emotion. Many thoughts crossed my mind, and all sorts of feelings swept over me. I was leaving my motherland, my magnificent and my beautiful country!

About one and a half hours after departure, our plane landed safely in Shanghai. There the Chinese Customs would make a final check, and I was afraid of a body search. I had with me my two little notebooks filled with private notes, precious documents and recently-composed poems. I would not like to see them confiscated or even used as a pretext of suspending my passport! Fortunately, there was no body search, but only a final check of my papers. In the course of the verification, one of the customs officers pointed out to me that my exit receipt attached to my passport was not valid. I explained that I had been unable to go back to Chengdu to get the necessary one directly from my native provincial department for want of sufficient time and money. Owing to the intervention of another customs officer who championed my case, my "exit receipt" was finally accepted and collected. Thanks be to God! The last barrier of the Bamboo Curtain had just fallen!

> *Good-bye to you, Red Flag!*
> *Good-bye to you, Fetters and Handcuffs!*
> *See you again, Bamboo Curtain!*

See you again, Dark Prison!

As mad dogs,
You yap at both God and man!
As a raging furnace,
You burn jade and stone alike!

Year in, year out,
Tempered and retempered,
Loyalty grew up in the crucible
In the presence of the Lord!

At this moment of parting,
What have I to offer to my friends?
Gratitude or indignation?
They themselves should know!

———————————

Arriving in Tokyo by night was enchanting. The city was lit up with tens of thousands of twinkling lights, far more numerous and bright than the stars I saw in the sky. During the stopover the passengers to Los Angeles were to change airlines. Soon afterwards our new plane took off at night, towards the distant western shore of the New World, piercing through the endless darkness of night to catch the first rays of the rising dawn. As the night died away, the first light of morning appeared on the horizon. The genial sun slowly moved upwards. When it was about to reach its highest position, the lands of the free nation of which I had been dreaming so much came into view. It was almost to the exact hour and day we had left Peking that the Pan Am flight reached the Los Angeles International Airport.

A fellow traveler, Ms. Linda Cleman helped me through the entry formalities, made a phone call for me, and, when having made certain that everything was well in hand, she bade me farewell and took her leave. Three of my Benedictine brothers came in less than two hours to pick me up by car. When I saw them, I did not recognize who they were. It was not myself but Linda who at my request had telephoned Fr. Bernard Hwang and talked with him. Furthermore, in his last letter, received just before my departure from Peking, he informed me that Dr. John W. Birsner would very likely come to welcome me at the airport and be in charge of examining my state of health and seeing to my medical care. As a result, when I saw Fr. Gaetan Loriers moving forward with his silver hair, I took him for Dr. Birsner and called him with that name. At the time, I did not realize that I was faced with my brother from our monastery in Chengdu who had been expelled from China and whom I had not seen for thirty-two years!

Fr. Denis Molaise Meehan, our Irish monk, aged seventy, kindly said to me, "Now you are safe; no trouble will come upon you again!" When I showed him my passport, he put his hand on my head in a friendly way and added, "You will never go back to the Chinese Mainland!"

Br. Dominic Guillen hurried to carry my luggage to the car. He also took care of me throughout the journey when I suddenly began to vomit from carsickness.

Not long after we reached the monastery at Valyermo, our Fr. Prior, John Borgerding, the priests and brothers of the monastery, and also its employees and guests gave me a very hearty welcome. That evening at dinner, our Prior renewed his welcome. The next day at noon he celebrated a holy Mass of Thanksgiving to God, which was followed by a grand dinner with many guests.

Thus, my thirty-three-year holy struggle was ended with the realization of my long-cherished wish and dream of leaving China to rejoin my monastic community. I was beside myself with joy. I had difficulty controlling my emotions. I had a feeling that I was experiencing the same happiness and the same honor received by the Patriarch Joseph in the Old Testament when he was released from prison, overwhelmed with blessings, and appointed prime minister of Egypt. I raised my voice in songs of triumph, in songs of thanksgiving to the Lord: "How wonderful is Your Providence and Your loving-kindness! May Your Name be praised forever and ever! And eternal joy to those in my country and in other places who remain faithful to You under religious persecution and show valor in the midst of rigorous ordeals!"

FIRST NEW YEAR IN THE UNITED STATES OF AMERICA

In the Poetic Style of Qilu
St. Andrew's Priory, January 1, 1985

Welcoming in the New Year
In this place of sunshine,
I devise some bold plans
In this haven of peace.

I want to be assiduous
In my study of English and Scripture,
I wish to dedicate myself body and soul
To a life of fervor and prayer.

I will write the poems kept in my mind,
An offering to my neighbors;
I will record the story of my struggle
To sing the loving-kindness of the Lord.

The warm sun in the blue sky
Is shining on the snow-covered earth.
I am writing a new chapter in my life,
Going forward to greet my future!

Br. Peter as a professed monk in Chengdu Priory, Chengdu, Sichuan, China, November 1950.

Br. Peter (R) with his older brother, Philip; Chengdu, Sichuan, China, fall 1944.

Br. Peter (center) with his parents, his brother John Baptist (R) and his sister-in-law during summer vacation; Suining, Sichuan, China, August 1946.

In August 1960, the Communists bound Br. Peter's arms tightly in bronze cuffs for four weeks. His right hand remains permanently crippled.

This was only one of the Communist Prison officials' many attempts to "reform Br. Peter's obstinate and stubborn will."

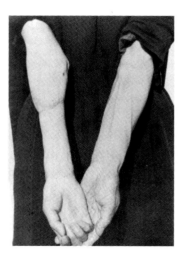

(L-R) Fr. Alberic, Fr. Hildebrand, Fr. Kowacheck, S.V.D., Fr. Eleutherius, Fr. Prior Raphael and Fr. Werner at the gate of the new building; Chengdu Priory, Chengdu, Sichuan, China, late fall 1949.

Br. Peter with Fr. Prior
Raphael and seven fellow
oblate students. Chengdu
Priory; Chengdu, Sichuan,
China, September 1945.

(R-L) Fan Tingsen (five years later a Communist spy), He Guoliang, Fr. Hildebrand Marga, Br. Peter, Mr. McWilliams (a bene-
factor of the Priory and an American offical), Lu Shengping, Fr.
Prior, Liu Huaiyuan, the driver of Mr. McWilliams, Sun Liyong,
Wang Yongfu and Shi Mingkai.

Br. Peter with three
oblate students of Cheng-
du Priory: (L-R) Br.
Peter, He Guoliang, Mao
Yongchang (now in Tai-
wan) and Fr. Felix Tang
Tien-shou (died in Cali-
fornia on April 14, 1994);
Chengdu, Sichuan,
China, January 1945.

Fr. Eleutherius (L) and Fr.
Gaetan in front of the new build-
ing; Chengdu Priory, Chengdu,
Sichuan, China, 1949.

New building of Chengdu Priory completed in the summer of 1949; Chengdu, Sichuan, China.

Entrance to the quiet desert of St. Andrew's Abbey, established in 1956 by the Benedictines of Chengdu Priory, expelled from China; taken by Fr. Gaetan Loriers.

(L-R) Fr. Gaetan Loriers, Fr. Prior John Borgerding, Br. Peter, Supervisor Michael D. Antonovich and Br. Dominic Guillen at the Devil's Punchbowl Nature Center, Peachblossom, CA, April 16, 1988.

Br. Peter and Fr. Bernard Hwang Kuo-wei, who was instrumental after Br. Peter's release from prison in arranging his reunion with his Benedictine family; Valyermo, August 27, 1990.

Br. Peter and Dr. John W. Birsner, his American sponsor, in Santa Barbara, CA, March 23, 1985.

A procession of the Benedictine Monks at Valyermo with some of the Catholic faithful; Palm Sunday, March 24,1991.

The Chapel at St. Andrew's Abbey, Valerymo, CA.

Inside the Abbey Chapel at Valyermo where guests may join in daily Mass and the Divine Office with the Benedictines of St. Andrew's Abbey.

Two years after arriving safely in the United States, Br. Peter visits the Vatican and attends the Mass of Pope John Paul II, October 30, 1986.

Br. Peter Zhou visits the Vatican October 30, 1986, and presents Pope John Paul II with a copy of his manuscript, *Dawn Breaks in the East,* in addition to four poems composed for His Holiness while imprisoned by the communists.

On November 15, 1938, a farewell meeting for Fr. Thaddeus' and Fr. Vincent's departure to Chongqing to take part in the work concerning the War of Resistance against Japan, held at the playground of the monastery-run Zhongyi Primary School at Sishan on the outskirts of the city of Nanchong, Sichuan, China; taken and provided by Fr. Eleutherius Winance.

(Left) 3 novices (the fifth is Fr. Paul Wu Yong) and Fr. Emile Butruille; (center) Fr. Prior Raphael Vinciarelli, Fr. Vincent Martin, Fr. Thaddeus Yang An-yuen and Fr. Wilfrid Weitz; (right) seminarians from the local diocese, studying philosophy or theology in the monastery, the last one with a flag in his hand is Fr. Huang Woze, today the "bishop of Nanchong" appointed by the Communists in July 1989; (front) about 50 boy and girl pupils among whom is Br. Peter, hidden in the last row.

In early March 1952, just expelled by the Chinese Communists from Chengdu in Sichuan Province to Hong Kong, (standing from left to right) Fr. Eleutherius Winance (3rd), Fr. Werner Papeians (4th), Fr. Prior Raephael Vinciarelli (8th) and Fr. Subprior Hildebrand Marga (9th) visit their friends and fellow refugees from the Bamboo Curtain, Fr. Paulinus Li, O.C.S.O., (5/30/1906-7/31/1980) (6th), the first Prior (Fr. Benedict Chao, the third Prior, and Fr. Maur Pei, the actual Prior), and the other Trappists from the Trappist Monastery of Our Lady of Joy, originally in Zhengding County, Hebei Province, then transferred to Xindu County, Sichuan Province, very close to Chengdu, and from the early fifties until now resettled in Lantau Island, Hong Kong.

Br. Peter (seated, second right) with his brother John Baptist (seated, center) and his wife, Mary, and their entire family: three daughters, three sons-in-law, three grandsons (first row) and one granddaughter (second row, first left); taken in Suining County, Sichuan Province, during the Spring Festival, February 1, 1984.

Br. Peter on the Great Wall at Badaling, the outpost of Juyongguan, 75 km. north-west of Peking, October 15, 1984, six weeks before leaving for the United States.

During his first visit to the Priory of Saint-Andre of Clerlande in Ottignies, Belgium, October 21, 1986, Br. Peter with Fr. Prior Martin Neyt, O.S.B., and some monks in the parlor.

Fr. Gaetan Loriers (died of illness on August 27, 1996) and Br. Peter with Mother Prioress Marie-Claire Willocx, O.S.B., (seated), during their visit to the Conventual Priory of Rixensart, Belgium, November 17, 1986.

On November 29, 1986, Marie Alghisi accompanies her parents, Primo and genevieve, her grandpa, Leopold Davreux, Fr. Gaetan Loriers and Br. Peter to visit Fr. Adolf Mignot and the famous Chapelle Sainte-Anne, under his care, built in the 11th century at Val Duchesse, Auderghem, Brussels, Belgium. Here, Marie is listening to the Reverend Father, aged eighty-four, conversing with Br. Peter in his house before showing the chapel; taken by her father.

Suky Lee, Br. Peter's good friend from South Korea and volunteer typist, visits the Lake Tianchi (the Heavenly Lake) on the Changbai Mountains, Jilin Province, China, August 21, 1987.

Br. Peter's good friend, Anne Huang Ziying, an artist (second left), with her husband, Zhou Mingchan, a senior agricultural engineer (right), and their children, (L-R) Zhou Hong, Zhou Kui and Zhou Yan; taken in Wudu County, Gansu Province, China, at the Spring Festival, February 17, 1988. Anne's late brother, John Baptist Huang Zifu (Xingzhu) (May 1924-January 1987), also an artist, was a prisoner in a Chinese Communist jail for a quarter of a century. As a close friend, in early October 1984, he offered five special traditional Chinese paintings to Br. Peter as gifts for the latter's brother in Taiwan and friends in the U.S.A.

Br. Peter (center) with his good friend, Jean DeBettignies, a physical therapist in Santa Barbara, CA, and her father, Jerry DeBettignies, at the back of the Abbey Chapel, Valyermo, June 4, 1989.

Br. Peter's American friend, Jeannine M. Veraldi (R), and his two new Chinese friends from Taiwan, Isabella Chang Chienhsi (L) and her mother, Jane Chang Hou Chiu-ke (center), on the Abbey grounds, Valyermo, CA, March 24, 1991.

Cynthia Clark (R), principal at Soquel High School, Soquel, CA, and editor of Br. Peter's two books, with her children (L-R): Kathryn, Lucas and Anthony; taken in Upland, CA, January 1992.

On August 8, 1993, James Mao Yongchang from Taiwan, Br. Peter's early classmate, visits their original Benedictine Monastery at Sishan in Nanchong, Sichuan, China. This two story building near the gates of the Monastery was built in the summer of 1938 for the first oblate students. There both of them lived all year or at least during the summer and winter vacations for six years (August 1938-July 1944).

Br. Peter (center) with his publishers, Jim Moeller (right) and Jim's brother, Ken Moeller (left), in front of their music-cassette and book booth featuring *Dawn Breaks in the East* during the 36th annual Valyermo Fall Festival, St. Andrew's Abbey, Valyermo, CA, September 25, 1993; taken and provided by Dana Peters-Barber, a photographer from the *Antelope Valley Press*, Palmdale, CA.

Br. Peter (L) with two old Chinese friends from his Benedictine Monastery in Chengdu, China: Professor Pansy Lang Yuxiu, a famous Chinese soprano (R), and her husband, Dr. Michel Xiao Ji (second from left), in the cemetery of St. Andrew's Abbey, Valyermo, CA, April 9, 1994.

Br. Peter's good friends from South Korea, Paul and Christina Kim with their daughters (center, L-R): Jennifer and Amanda; taken in Los Angeles, CA, May 1995.

Br. Peter's good friends, the Chavez family from San Gabriel, CA: Gilbert M. and his wife, Dolores, with their daughter, Deanne (R), their son, Stephen (L), and their little granddaughter, Stephanie; taken after the ceremony of Gilbert's Ordination to the Permanent Diaconate by Roger Cardinal Mahony, Archbishop of Los Angeles, at Blessed Sacrament Church in Hollywood, CA. June 10, 1995.

Br. Peter's good Chinese friend and the inscriber of the Chinese title of his two books, Mimi H. Fleischman (L) with her American husband, Robert, and their daughter, Lisa, Assistant U.S. Attorney; taken in their home in Pasadena, CA, January 1, 1996.

Fr. Francois Dufay, M.E.P., was an inspiration and help to the loyal priests, seminarians, sisters and laymen in Chengdu, Sichuan, since the beginning of the religious persecution before his expulsion by the Chinese Communists on March 31, 1952. This photo was taken during the period of his pastoral service in Singapore, October 1, 1996.

Br. Peter with His Eminence Roger Cardinal Mahony, Fr. Abbot Francis Benedict, O.S.B. (L), and Br. Tim Mayworm, F.S.C. (R), Chairman of the Los Angeles Archdiocesan Council of Religious Brothers, sponsoring a "Brotherhood Recognition Dinner" at the Holy Spirit Retreat Center, Encino, CA, October 13, 1996; provided by Br. Tim Mayworm.

Br. Peter's correspondent since December 1986, Martha Benker-Lecomte with two of her sons: Christian (L) and Pascal (R); Sprimont, Belgium, April 15, 1997.

With the guidance of James Mao Yongchang (the disappearing photographer), Fr. Vincent Martin visits Br. Peter's brother Philip Zhou Zhimin's family in Longtan township, Taoyuen County, Taiwan, May 28, 1997. (L-R) Wang Shuzhao, Br. Peter's sister-in-law, Zhou Zhonglan, his youngest niece, Fr. Vincent and Philip, who died of illness just two weeks later on June 11, 1997.

Br. Peter (second right) with some of his new Chinese Catholic friends from Southern California at the back of the Abbey Guesthouse, St. Andrew's Abbey, Valyermo, CA, July 28, 1997. (L-R) John Su, Mary Chiu, Mary Chu, Sr. Marie Stella Lee, Fr. Gabriel Lui and Sr. Maria Bosco Chay.

Sr. Marianna So, O.C.D., Br. Peter's good friend from South Korea, by the statue of St. Therese of the Child-Jesus, at the Carmelite Monastery in Terre Haute, Indiana, on the day of her solemn profession of vows, August 15, 1997.

Fr. Louis Suchet Amiotte, M.E.P., had made certain contribution to the dioceses of Shanghai and Chengdu during the religious persecution and was expelled by the Chinese Communists on May 5, 1955. Since 1956, he has been serving as the pastor in different parishes in Singapore. This 80th birthday photo was taken on August 23, 1997, at the Church of Our Lady, Star of the Sea.

Shannon MacDonald (second row, fourth left) from Palmdale, CA, Br. Peter's good friend and his interviewer and producer of a cable show regarding his "Story of a Struggle for the Faith" on Continental Cable Vision, Downey, CA, released in June and August 1994. She has also organized the St. Michael's Prayer Group to promote the story of his resolute witness to the Catholic Faith and his indomitable spirit in the severe ordeal to be told everywhere, far and wide.

Her whole family (L-R): (first row) her sister-in-law, Rebecca MacDonald with her little niece, Alexandria, and her uncle, Daniel Bresnahan; (second row) her mother, Janis MacDonald, her grandma, Caroline Bresnahan, her uncle's daughter and her cousin, Christy Higgens, herself and her grandpa, Joseph Bresnahan; (third row) her father, Dean, Real Estate Editor of the *Antelope Valley Press* in Palmdale, California, and her fiancé, Bobby Vidal; Taken by her brother, Mark, at her grandparents' house in Downey, CA, November 27, 1997.

His Eminence Ignatius Cardinal Kung Pinmei, Bishop of Shanghai and Apostolic Administrator of Soochow and Nanking; taken in November 1997 at age 96 in Stamford, Connecticut, U.S.A.

Some of the monks: (L-R) Fr. Phillip, Br. Benedict, Fr. Prior Luke, Fr. Werner, Fr. Joseph, Br. Joseph and Br. Peter; taken by Margie Holman on December 2, 1997, under St. Andrew's Abbey Chapel Bell, to the left pole of which are attached two copper inscriptions, reading as follows:

1. "The French Village of Soleilhas to St. Andrew's Priory of Valyermo, Christmas 1972."

2. "Blessed at Easter 1973. My name is Raphaella. On November 14, 1972, the day that Father Raphael Vinciarelli, O.S.B., founding Prior, was called home to the Lord, I came to call all to prayer. Saint Andrew's Priory, Valyermo."

Br. Peter with workers of the Abbey Ceramic Shop, taken in the sales room on December 2, 1997. (L-R): (front row) Mary Kouf, Carole Young, Sergio Samano and Wenceslao Tovar; (back row) Lucino Garcia, Tim Benedict, manager of the Shop, Patrick Bradley, Sabrina Bradley and Mario Garcia Castro.

Br. Peter with two of the workers of the Abbey Guesthouse: (L-R) Margie Holman and Casey Cook; taken on the guesthouse grounds, Valyermo, December 2, 1997.

Br. Peter with workers of the Abbey Business Office:
(L-R) Marlene Parks, Sr. Theresa, O.S.B., Sue Pressler and Bart Dal Ponte; taken by the side of the Abbey Chapel, St. Andrew's Abbey, December 3, 1997.

The monastic family of St. Andrew's Abbey at Valyermo, CA, U.S.A.; taken on the cloister grounds, January 8, 1998.

(L-R): (Front row) Br. Joseph Iarrobino, Br. Peter Zhou, Fr. Vincent Martin, Fr. Subprior Simon O'Donnell, Fr. Abbot Francis Benedict, Fr. Prior Luke Dysinger, Fr. Eleutherius Winance, Fr. Werner Papeians and Fr. Phillip Edwards;

(back row) Br. Carlos Lopez, Fr. John Bosco Stoner, Fr. Paul Pluth, Br. Michael Weeks, Fr. Joseph Brennan, Br. Dominic Guillen, Br. Benedict Dull Fr. Martin Yslas, Br. Thomas Babusis Fr. Gregory Elmer and Br. James Brennan.

(L-R) Christina Kim, Sr. Pachomia Kim, O.S.B., Fr. Abbot Francis Benedict, Br. Peter, Sr. Daniela Kim, O.S.B., Jim Cooksey and Helen K. Rhoden; taken by Marlene Parks in front of the Abbey Art Shop, January 13, 1998.

The retired and eighty-six old Fr. Abbot President Ambroise Watelet, O.S.B., visits Marie-Therese Thoreau (L) and her daughter, Agnes Thoreau, in Embourg-Chaudfontaine, Belgium, January 18, 1998.

Br. Anselmo Taborda (left) visits Fr. Abbot Paul Standaert, O.S.B., (center) and Fr. Maur Van Doorslaer, O.S.B., (right), designer for the Ceramic Shop of the daughter monastery, St. Andrew's Abbey; taken at the mother house, the Abbey of Saint-Andre, Bruges, Belgium, January 28, 1998.

Br. Peter visits El Camino College, Torrance, CA, February 10, 1998.
(L-R) Richard J. Chacon, Professor of Anthropology and Dr. Gloria Miranda, Dean of the Behavioral and Social Sciences.

As a close comrade-in-arms from January 1952 to November 1955 during the Chinese Communist religious persecution in Chengdu, Lucia Shu Dejun along with her husband, Teddy Ling Desung, and their good friend Joan Lustbader visits Br. Peter on April 19, 1998; taken on the Abbey grounds by Joan.

(L-R) Dennis Brennan, Br. James' father, Fr. Vincent Martin, Br. Peter, Nancy Chen, her son, Richard, her mother and her husband, Paul Chen, by the Abbey Chapel's Bell, Valyermo, May 17, 1998; taken by Patti Brennan, Br. James' mother.

Frederique Barloy with her husband, Oliver, and their children (L-R): Laurie, Marie and John, on summer vacation in the countryside, France, August 10, 1998. Frederique is the French translator of Br. Peter's biography, *Dawn Breaks in the East.* Her translation will be published by the Editions Religieuses Pierre Tequi in Paris probably before the Christmas of 1999.

On November 15, 1998, Fr. Eleutherius Winance (fourth left), Br. Peter (third left) and the visiting Chinese priest, Fr. Joseph Yang (fifth left) receive some Chinese and Korean visitors: (L-R) Shirley and Tim Song, Alice Bian Fengxia, Joyce Zhang Jieyi, Mike Li Yi and Zhang Jingcheng (the disappearing photographer); taken on the Abbey grounds, Valyermo.

Since 1991, as a usual practice, Br. Peter (left) is welcomed to the family Christmas gathering of his good friends from the Philippines. Jaime (right) and Audrey Abrera (second left); their children (L-R): Jainee, Janine and Joseph; Burbank, CA, December 25, 1998.

On December 25, 1998, in the afternoon, under the guidance of Jaime and Audrey Abrera, Br. Peter (center) visits their fellow countrymen, the Hizon family in Sun Valley, CA. (R-L): Joey, Nora, their son, Joseph, and their daughter, Jennifer.

PART II

MUSIC IN THE AIR

PROLOGUE

Good Jesus, "You changed my mourning into dancing, You removed my sackcloth and clothed me with gladness." (Ps. 30:12). It is only because of Your loving-kindness and help that I can undertake to recall and narrate the story of my struggle. Lord, omniscient God, You scrutinize and know everything, as in the Chinese idiom, "one knows what is at his fingertips." You know better than I, myself, that this narrative of my thirty-three year struggle is totally sincere and truthful. There is no exaggeration, nor any invention. I have tried my best to make my thoughts, feelings and impressions of those years reappear here as they really were.

I feel that I have the obligation to share with all the world the merciful love and great power which You have shown in my life, a life of a poor sinner, thus to lead back to You people who do not know You and do not believe in You, and also to strengthen and help Your believers to know You better and to love You more. If this brings glory to You, to Your Father, and to the Holy Spirit, I will be greatly honored and supremely glad.

I want to say with Your great Apostle St. Paul: "But by God's favor I am what I am." (I Cor. 15:10). Truly, it is by Your mercy and goodness that I was able to maintain that tense, arduous and endless struggle for so long a time and until the final victory. You have been my personal guide and my staunch supporter. As St. Alphonsus Liguori, Doctor of Your Church, said, "God can save others without you, but He cannot save you without your cooperation," I have placed all my trust in You and wanted to give You all my cooperation.

Both to complete my narrative and to give my readers more intimate access to my heart, I would like to add a last reflection as the conclusion. This final touch, I hope and believe, will give, as the Chinese proverb says, "the finishing stroke which draws the eyes to the dragon painted on the wall!"

CHAPTER XI

THE KEY TO VICTORY

Lord, You are the origin of all things. You create us, feed us, and fortify us. We cannot be separated from You for one single moment. We must rely on You in order to live and exist. It is absolutely certain that our visible body and temporal life, without a doubt, depends entirely on You. As for our invisible soul and supernatural life, it is still more evident, true and indisputable as an unalterable principle.

You are the source from which we receive our life. In time of conflict, You are the strength on which we rely in battle. This source, this strength, is lavished on us without ceasing in many ways so that we may fear no shortage of anything, but have a superabundance, whether it is in our daily life, in our work or in our struggles. Yes, really, Your great help accompanies us always and everywhere!

Good Jesus Christ, You are the true strength in my struggle and the key to my victory. It was nothing else than my reliance on You that in the fight for the true faith I could suffer setbacks without being discouraged and win without falling into pride; and that I could always find the strength to exert myself to move forward courageously, to go on the offensive and to triumph over the adversary. This lofty ideal and this dogged determination that You bestowed on me are vividly described in the tenth of the thirteen poems entitled "Reading *'The Shan Hai Jing (Mountains and Seas Classic)'*" by the famous poet, Tao Yuanming (365-427 A.D.). The poet praised the unyielding will and indomitable fighting spirit shown, continuously and even after their tragic death, by Jing Wei and Xing Tian, mythological personages in classical Chinese literature.

> *"The mythical bird, Jing Wei,*
> *Carries in its beak*
> *Small twigs and little pebbles,*
> *Trying to fill up the Eastern Sea!*

> *The valiant, Xing Tian,*
> *Brandishes his shield in one hand*
> *And broad axe in the other*
> *To keep his great ideals always before him!"*

1. Prayer Attracts Divine Grace

Lord, in the course of Your pilgrimage on earth, You left us a divine model of prayer. In the Garden of Gethsemani, on the eve of Your death when You prayed to Your Father, You admonished us, with a heavy heart and solemn words, through St. Peter, the Apostle: "Be on guard, and pray that you may not undergo the test. The spirit is willing but nature is weak." (Mt. 26:41).

Certainly, prayer in our supernatural and spiritual life is not an accessory which we can use or not according to our convenience. For life it is an absolute necessity which cannot be neglected and its value cannot be underestimated. It is the channel by which we can always come near to You more closely, and by which You infuse Your grace into us and fill us with Your inexhaustible blessings to fortify us and to make us worthy to receive food and strength necessary for our supernatural life. If it is true in our daily living, how much more is it so in time of our spiritual warfare.

At three different times I spent months and years in solitary confinement. Each time there was a marvelous opportunity for meditation and a happy, priceless occasion for fully tasting the sweetness of prayer.

Even though my daily prayer often became routine, like mechanically reading a text without giving all my attention, in Your infinite goodness, Lord, You still, through this channel of prayer, poured out upon my soul an unceasing shower of graces to enable me to live and to fight for You. You treated me as You promised in the Gospel, "Ask, and you will receive. Seek, and you will find. Knock, and it will be opened to you." (Mt. 7:7).

2. Liturgical Calendar Is a Guide

Lord, You are the center and ideal of our life. We cannot live without You even for a moment. And we should often draw our inspiration from the exemplary human life which You led in our midst and for us. To help us, Your Church gives us her liturgical calendar with the principal feasts of Your Birth and Your Resurrection as the center, surrounded with all the feasts consecrated to Your Holy Mother, to all the Angels and to all the Saints.

The liturgical calendar plays an irreplaceable role in the daily life of a Catholic. It traces the landmarks on our long journey to eternal life. Its importance can be brought to light by the saying, full of wisdom, spread among the early Chinese Catholics and handed down from generation to generation: "Three days without consulting the liturgical calendar will result in ruining a great part of one's soul!"

Indeed, it was very fortunate for me that from my youngest years I understood the meaning of the liturgical year. It had been engraved on my mind. I remembered very well that the Solemnity of Christmas fell on December 25, and I knew also that the Solemnity of Easter was movable and came on the first Sunday after the full moon that followed the vernal equinox on March 21. Besides, I had been strongly impressed by the great Feasts in honor of Your Holy Mother and in honor of Your other Saints.

When I was in prison, at the end of the year, I always managed to buy the calendar for the coming year. I calculated the exact days of the Resurrection and the dates of all the other movable feasts according to the new calendar. I noted all these feast days, together with the other fixed feast days, so that I could follow You as before, day by day, and thus share happiness and sorrow with You throughout the year. In this way, all my life was rhythmic, in step with Your Holy Mother and the whole Church, and this allowed my living faith and my fighting will to stand out, and to be reinforced.

3. Bible and Philosophy Enlighten the Mind

You bestowed upon me my holy vocation as a favor. Then I had the opportunity to study the Bible, Church history and philosophy. My studies continued right up to the eve of the terrible political storm. I was fortunate enough to acquire some knowledge of metaphysics and to understand the teachings You gave to us through Sacred Scripture and the Church.

You are the Ultimate Existence, Highest Wisdom, the First Cause, the Prime Mover, Absolute Truth, Infinite Goodness, Boundless Mercy and Invincible Power. From all eternity, You dispose and arrange all things in order. This basic principle of philosophy has been deeply ingrained in my mind. It allows me to recognize and understand objects and events of life.

If You had wanted me to die in prison or under torture, how could I have escaped my destiny, even had I gone down on my knees in surrender to the Communist officials? In the same way, if You had willed that I not die under the harsh treatment, how could the prison officials have taken away my life? They could do nothing more than what You had planned for me. As it was, they finally had to watch me walk out of prison, as the Chinese idiom runs, "with frowning brows and cold eyes" and let me pass through the Bamboo Curtain with my head high and chest up.

You have very clearly taught me in the Psalmist's words: "In Your hands is my destiny." (Ps. 31:16). And I did not forget Your exhortation in the Gospel: "Seek first His kingship over you, His way of holiness, and all these things will be given you besides." (Mt. 6:33).

When I was in prison, I understood that what You call "holiness" or "justice" is nothing else than the "fidelity" I owe You. I had only to preserve this fidelity to You and to live it as perfectly as possible. Then You would one day reward me with a double harvest both material and spiritual. And You would make, according to the words of the Chinese philosopher Mengzi (372-289 B.C.), "clouds gather to pour forth a bountiful rain" over my withered body and mind, and bring them forth into the new life of the Resurrection with You.

These eternal truths and basic principles explain the true meaning of life. Rooted in the deepest part of my mind and heart, they made my perceptions more sharp, my will more daring and energetic and my spirit full of vigor and vitality. In the most harsh and painful days, they brought me overflowing comfort and kept me in joy, faith and hope. When some of the Communist officials and fellow prisoners taunted me by saying to me repeatedly a word, written long ago in the Psalms: "Where is your God?" (Ps. 42:4), O Lord, inevitably I was compelled to have only "my tears as my food." Yet, my mind remained entirely self-possessed, continuing to recite the Psalms, to compose my poems and to sing Your praises with Gregorian chants.

Like the exiles of Jerusalem, "By the rivers of Babylon we sat and wept, when we remembered Zion." (Ps. 137:1), I could not refrain from asking myself, "How could we sing a song of the Lord in a foreign land?" (Ps. 137:4), in a country where God is excluded and where I myself was detained in captivity? Yet, even in that sorrowful moment, I still kept my zeal as before. Despite being thrown into a solitary cell and completely isolated from the rest of the world, with my crippled hand and with the accompaniment of the clanking fetters on my feet, I found the strength to write to You an Act of Faith in more than ten thousand words and to sing for You a *Song of Life* in my own peculiar style. In doing all this, I gave no thought to life or death, blessing or curse.

Yes, Lord, You have truly shaped my intellect and my will with the Faith, the study of the philosophy of the Church and the teachings of the Scriptures. Thus, was I able to discern the truth, distinguish between good and evil, brave the winds and the waves, and take my destiny in hand to push ahead towards the eternal shore, singing songs of battle until the final victory was won.

4. Writing Encourages the Will

At the outset, I did not know the domain of poetry and prose. Still less could I claim to have a special gift. However, Lord, You wished me to learn while I wrote, letting me feel my way forward. It never occurred to me that with Your hidden inspiration and help, despite my fragile pen and withered hand, what I conceived and wrote would grow and increase little by little in volume, as water is stored up drop by drop to make a pool. Moreover, You actually turned my compositions, not only those already on paper, but also those in my head, into a powerful weapon, capable of resisting the adversary and of defending the truth throughout my struggle. Yes, my writings certainly played their role in wiping out insults and winning glory for You. In the time of difficult struggle, they proved decisive for me and produced an influence upon others not to be underestimated.

In the beginning of November 1951, when the streets of Chengdu began to be overrun with the noise of battle drums, at a public accusation meeting of the local neighborhood, I read boldly my strong declaration I had prepared for the defense on behalf of You and Your Church. In August 1952, I wrote an open letter addressed to the clergy and laity of the Church in China. Afterwards I drafted the manuscript, *From Paradise to Purgatory*. Simultaneously, I wrote a certain number of letters to comfort, encourage and support friends who were, like me, fighting for the true faith. In December 1956, to correct the mistake I had made in writing a "confession" at the very start of my detention, I delivered to the authorities of the Second Detention House of Chengdu a copy of my *Summary of My Thoughts* which was written with the purpose of re-establishing the truth. One year later, I wrote again a lengthy *Memorandum*. During my first two-year solitary confinement, with fetters on my feet, I handed to the First Provincial Prison of Nanchong a Nine-Point Declaration as my irrevocable profession of faith. Then I sang for You my composition, *The Song of Life*.

Since the midsummer of 1966, I had the courage to enter the sacred garden of classical Chinese poetry. I began, at that time, to sing to the wind and serenade the moon with my own poems. Instead of reining in my poetic inspiration, I released the bridle and let it keep on running wild like a runaway horse, or like water from a burst dike rushing out uncontrollably. Though clumsy, undisciplined and few in number in the beginning, my poems grew swiftly to an eventual 2,600 after sixteen years of effort.

I realized that all I wrote and thought of ought not to be aimed at others only, but also at myself; nor to be designed to make others react only, but also to urge myself to action. Rather, all my writings, especially my declarations and many of my poems, were intended to be a signal of alarm and a stimulus both for others and for myself, particularly in my moments of doubt. They were like a mirror to help me reflect on them within and examine my conscience, obliging me not to deviate from the way of Your Commandments, and giving me the impression, as in the Chinese expression, of "approaching the brink of the abyss" or "walking on thin ice." Indeed, Lord, my essays and poems brought me closer to You, enhanced my vigilance from morning to night, and fortified my constantly striving mind. They increased in me the strength to fight and strengthened my belief in certain victory. Yet, a Chinese sage in the Zhou Dynasty (1122-256 B.C.) left us an unforgettable saying: "The way for a man to achieve glory is first of all by moral integrity; secondly, by meritorious service and devotion; and last of all, by writing." St. Paul, the Apostle, did he not say the same thing when he wrote: "If I speak with human tongues and angelic as well, but do not have love, I am a noisy gong, a clanging cymbal." (I Cor. 13:1).

5. Warnings Kept in the Heart

Lord, by Your own brilliant example in generously and bravely sacrificing Your life, you gave me the strength both to fight and to suffer for You. I remembered the innumerable martyrs of the past, "through blazing fire or boiling oil", "one stepping into the breach as another fell," for You. Their heroic deeds have always encouraged and supported me under torture, exhorting me to bear witness to You and giving me "the image of death as assurance of a joyful return home."

Besides all these excellent models, which astonished the ancient world and is the admiration of the modern generations, and which moved me to the depths of my soul, You also showed me some pitiable and distressing contemporary examples. Thus, You taught me to keep constantly a sober head in the struggle, never to lower my guard, and to remain watchful and prudent all the times, as the Chinese dictum runs, "with head pillowed on a spear, waiting for day to break." Eventually, You aroused within me the desire of throwing myself into the battle "to capture the enemy's flag and to put his general to flight." In the meanwhile, You, Lord, gave rise to my lofty project of composing poems of praise for You right in the midst of the clamor of the enemy.

CHAPTER XII

WHY ONE WINS?

Lord, You are unique, the origin of life and the "I AM." Everything we have and everything we are comes from You. This is perfectly expressed by St. John at the very beginning of his Gospel:

"In the beginning was the Word;
the Word was in God's presence,
and the Word was God.
He was present to God in the beginning.
Through Him all things came into being,
And apart from Him nothing came to be." (Jn.1:1-3)

At the same time, You also taught us Yourself, saying:

"I am the vine, you are the branches.
He who lives in Me and I in him,
will produce abundantly,
for apart from Me you can do nothing." (Jn.15:5)

Not only my life depends on You, O Lord, but also all the details of my existence. Yes, it was by reliance on You alone that I was able to hold out so firmly and so long, and finally surmount this painful and unusual trial. It was through Your favor that I was able to relinquish battle dress for the monastic habit, attend daily Mass, receive Holy Communion, and say the Divine Office on schedule. It is truly through Your loving-kindness that I can enjoy now the tender spring sunlight of Southern California and the peace of my clean room. I owe all this to You. There is no question that in my victory over the forces of darkness Your merciful love was the guiding principle and decisive factor.

In Your infinite love for mankind, You chose to give the Blessed Virgin Mary to us as a mother so that she could distribute to us the infinite merit of Your Redemption most generously. From the very beginning of my struggle on Your behalf, I had the privilege of testifying in public to the Legion of Mary and of affirming the legitimate and sacred nature of this organization, which was named after her and entirely dedicated to her veneration. While in prison, I recited the Rosary every day. Besides the usual five mysteries, I also recited all fifteen mysteries as regularly as I could in place of the Divine Office. Each day upon rising and upon retiring, I presented to her three "Hail Mary's." Every Saturday and during May and October, I offered extra prayers to venerate her Immaculate Heart, glorious life and Holy Rosary.

During my first solitary confinement, while I was composing my *Song of Life,* I devoted to her a fifth of its nine parts, namely, 9 paragraphs, 199 stanzas and 796 lines. Since I started to write poetry, I have offered her about 150 laudatory poems. I have also composed nearly forty poems to praise the exalted virtues and the heroic deeds of St. Joseph, Your earthly father and her chaste husband. On every Wednesday and during every March when I was in prison, I recited with still more fervor the prayer devoted to his seven sorrows and seven joys. These prayers and the others addressed to Your special saints and my holy patrons helped me enjoy Your consolation and encouragement while "going forth weeping, carrying the seed to be sown," and taste Your joy and happiness while leaving the battlefield and "coming back rejoicing, carrying my sheaves" of a good harvest. (Ps. 126:6).

I know with assurance that one of the main reasons for my victory over Communist persecution was the support of the Church given me through the Benedictine order, the Congregation of the Annunciation, the Mother Abbey in Belgium and the two monasteries to which I belonged: St. Benedict's Priory in Chengdu and St. Andrew's Abbey in Valyermo. When I was eight years old, my father asked me to accompany him to the local church. He presented me to Fr. Prior Gabriel Roux and asked that I might be admitted as an oblate student at the Benedictine monastery in Nanchong about seventy miles away from our city of Suining. It was in the early winter of 1934, just at the time when Fr. Gabriel was going to Chengdu from Nanchong via Suining, accompanied by Fr. Theodore Neve, the Abbot of the Abbey of Saint-Andre in Bruges, Belgium. The latter had come that autumn to Sichuan Province to visit his foundation, the Licheng Monastery. This daughter house had been built on the mountainside of Sishan (Western Mountain) on the outskirts of the city of Nanchong in 1929. The kind faces of these two superiors of the monastery left a deep impression engraved in my young heart, bringing me a bit of warmth in the depth of a cold winter's day.

Two years later when I was ten, I remember frequenting the chapel and competing with my brother Philip to serve at the Masses celebrated by three monk-priests from the Monastery of Licheng. These were Fr. Eleutherius Winance, Fr. Vincent de Paul Martin and Fr. Wilfrid Weitz. They came to Suining to learn Chinese and lived in a two-story building outside the North Gate with a wall which divided their backyard from that of my parents' house. Sometimes in the afternoon I visited them alone with the simplicity of a little schoolboy of ten years and was always given fruit and shown kindness.

In the month of August 1938, You, Lord, granted me at the age of twelve admittance to the monastery as an oblate student. From that time on, I strove to be gradually nurtured in the spirit of the monastic universe which surrounded me so that I could finally live up to Your expectation. Fr. Raphael Vinciarelli, the third prior of the monastery, carefully educated me for more than thirteen years. His regular homilies and heart-to-heart talks molded my intellect little by little. On October 15, 1949, he admitted me into the novitiate, and in the following year on the same day allowed me to profess triennial monastic vows. On the eve of persecution, he prepared and formed me for the coming conflict. All the Fathers of the monastery instructed me in many ways and directed me in how to acquit myself as a good monk. They left an indelible mark on my mind and unforgettable, happy memories in my heart.

From the time the religious persecution began in Chengdu, O Lord, You never forgot me. In 1952 and 1955, after their expulsion from the country, our Fr. Prior Vinciarelli and Fr. Gaetan Loriers continued from abroad to answer my letters, to offer me advice and encouragement, and to send me religious books. During this difficult period, their letters along with those from other priests and sisters inside and outside Mainland China were for me a great support.

For what other reason does one win, Lord? In my case, there is another reason, that I was born into a Catholic family, and I received a good education during my earliest youth from my parents, Paul Zhou Zinan and Mary Zhou Wangshi, who were both pious believers. They also generously offered me to

You and allowed me to respond to Your sacred call and follow You from my boyhood.

During Advent of 1951, when I had just begun to fight for You, I returned home to visit my father who was ill. At the end of April, the following year, when I was driven out of the monastery and found myself without shelter, I moved back to Suining to live under his roof. During my sixteen months at home, he never stopped lavishing on me his loving care and spared me free time for reading and writing. Though the circumstances hindered him from openly supporting what I had said and done against the "Catholic Reform Movement of the Three Autonomies," he did not fail to show me his tacit approval and gave me his protection as much as possible. In the first summer after my arrest, I wrote to him from prison and he himself answered my letter. Six years later, I wrote to him from prison a second time, not knowing that he had already passed away in 1958 at the age of 73.

It is precisely because You have chosen me, Lord, because You have accepted me, and because You have taught me to love You that I am able here and now to hold this pen in my crippled hand and to bear witness to Your magnificent love which I have experienced over and over for more than thirty-three years.

———————————

Even though the prison officials regarded me as a diehard and a thorn in their flesh, they never took the extreme step of getting rid of me. Why? They could not find sufficient excuse to kill me. Moreover, it was much more important for them to destroy my ideals!

Obedient to Your Commandments and Your teachings, O Lord, I kept the ordinary regulations of the prison as well as possible. I also devoted myself to the forced labor to the best of my ability as soon as I had no other alternative but to submit to it. I was simply content with preserving my own proper ideology which they considered as utopian and reactionary. Nevertheless, my attitude could not justify my condemnation to death.

From the Communist viewpoint, they might have felt that since I was not that old and had some education, then if I recanted, I could be of some use to them. I did not try to oppose the discipline; and at hard labor, I did what I could. The only thing they had against me was the persistence in my religious faith and my different ideology. When over a long period of time all their efforts and cruelties did not produce the desired result, they had only one way left--to let me live my life in my corner. Reluctantly, they were much obliged to let me live, to admit my particular convictions and to let me "set up," in the Chinese idiom, "a separate flag" in prison.

They remained faithful to the words of the command of their great master Mao Zedong, "All the obstinate cannot be obstinate forever!" Accordingly, they thought that by using both "carrot and stick," and both relaxation and pressure, as the years went by, the torments would become unbearable in the end, and my resistance would wear down and finally collapse. Then I would find myself at an impasse and have to barter away my honor for their protection.

They told me repeatedly that they were above all dialecticians of historical materialism and that they were accordingly judging me from a certain progressive outlook of historical dialectical materialism, instead of the reactionary static outlook of idealistic metaphysics. They would never admit that as a piece of iron plank, I could never be changed, nor would I ever join their revolutionary ranks. Consequently, they regarded my future conversion to their side as relatively certain, as though they had had a well-thought-out plan.

Strangely, though the prison officials were materialistic atheists, they attached primary importance to an invisible and spiritual ideology. They put great emphasis on reforming the thoughts of others, on breaking their resistance, on bankrupting their moral integrity, and on enslaving their spirit. To attain such goals, they would use any means. These means could take a terrible toll on their victims.

Not succeeding, like a silkworm, in nibbling away my faithfulness, nor like a whale, in swallowing my loyalty, they were not in a hurry to take the last drastic step of my physical destruction. Perhaps they reasoned that one day I would accept their reform and become their slave. This would have given them an ideal subject for propaganda and an excellent occasion to pour more Marxist poison into the hearts and souls of more people.

The truth, however, meant that the realization of their plans did not depend on them, but on You alone, Lord. It was You, Lord, who directed and commanded all things. Thus, all their dreams and false hopes would be doomed to disappear like a mirage; while I myself, with my weak appearance and withered hand, would one day fly out of the dark prison and beyond the Bamboo Curtain to rest peacefully in the depth of a rich and green forest.

The course of history continued to change and with it the plight of the Communist Party in China worsened. The death of Mao Zedong plunged the country into darkness. Hua Guofeng was not able to be acclaimed new leader of the Party and the country until he had taken a preemptive measure to round up his political enemies, the Gang of Four, in one fell swoop. Yet, his policy was still dominated by the ideology of the class struggle; thus, the Mainland remained in the same economic crisis, and the political climate of fear was so rampant that, as a Chinese saying goes, "one would turn pale at the mention of a tiger" (his policy).

Under the extreme leftist policy regarding religion and the Church adopted by the Communist Party during the Great Cultural Revolution, even the Chinese Catholic Patriotic Association, an anti-Catholic administrative tool under the control of the Party, became paralyzed and dysfunctional in the summer of 1966 up to the first years following Mao Zedong's death. If this state-created organization, which had been intended to replace Roman Catholicism in China, did not disappear entirely, it existed in name only. In reality, it was dead. Of the few churches that had remained open almost all were closed. Even some priests of this organization who had from the start or long ago followed the Party's lead, waving flags and lending their voice for the Party always in the first line, did not, ironically enough, escape this tragic storm. They were placed in an extremely awkward position and some of them even were chained and thrown into prison. This certainly darkened the image of the Communist Party both within the country and overseas. They found themselves at center stage with their name disgraced and their reputation dishonored.

In order to remedy this disastrous situation and also to win international sympathy and support in developing China's economy and implementing the plan of the construction of the Four Modernizations, the new Communist leader, Deng Xiaoping, felt obliged to initiate a more open policy. In March 1978, the first session of the Fifth National People's Congress hypocritically legislated and passed the new constitution which sanctimoniously reaffirmed and guaranteed religious freedom to all citizens. In May 1980, the Communists ordered the surviving members of the Patriotic church, a contingent of old and weak people, to call the Third Representative Assembly of the Chinese Catholic Patriotic Association in Peking. They instructed those members to imitate the Church in Taiwan by forming the Chinese Catholic Religious Affairs Commission and the Chinese Bishops' Conference. They also gradually re-opened the doors of a number of churches and began to treat the clergy and laity who were imprisoned, with leniency, and to release some from prison.

The Communists should have taken into account the fact that after thirty years of oppression, and after the expulsion of all the foreign bishops, priests and nuns, most of the indigenous loyal clergy, sisters and lay Catholics had almost all been imprisoned, or scattered, or liquidated outright, or died little by little in prison for their faith, or eventually were forced to lay down their arms and surrender. They discovered that the lot of the true believers among the survivors was no longer a threat. Therefore, they did not feel the need to maintain their pressure toward the Catholic Church which they regarded as basically destroyed once and for all. It was under these circumstances that the leaders of my reform-through-labor camp, conscious of their own past mistakes and considering the present situation, took a decision to put me on the list of victims whose cases had been unjust, false or wrong and needed to be redressed. The wheels of my eventual release were thus put in motion.

———————

Good Jesus, I thank You for having heard my prayer and having filled me with such abundant grace that I determined to fight on Your behalf to victory or to death. Finally, the stubborn Communists were conquered and victory was won. This victory filled me with gratitude. It was not won overnight, but by Your providential wisdom; it was born because of Your abhorrence of Communist arrogance and deception, and because of Your sorrow at the desertion and compromise of many believers at the beginning and / or in the middle of the struggle. This shows that You strongly willed to preserve a remnant of Your faithful servants, in the words of Mengzi (372-289 B.C.), an ancient Chinese philosopher, "unshaken by temptations of riches and honor, undaunted by poverty and unsubdued by force." Through my victory, You indicate that it is not impossible to resist the arctic darkness of a deep night on Your behalf and to wait for the song of the cock and the first rays of dawn. With Your help alone this can be accomplished and crowned with sure success and final triumph, as proven by the living examples of His Eminence Cardinal Ignatius Kung Pin-mei (Gong Pinmei), S.J., Bishop of Shanghai since July 15, 1950, still strong at his present age 98; of His Excellency Dominic Tang Yee-ming (Deng Yiming), S.J., Archbishop of Canton (5/13/1908-6/27/1995) who left his memoirs behind *"How Inscrutable His Ways: Memoirs 1951-1981";* of His Excellency Peter Joseph Fan Xueyan, Bishop of Baoding (12/12/1907-4/13/1992); of His Excellency James Su Zhimin, Bishop of Baoding; of His Excellency Jia Zhiguo, Bishop of Zhengding; of his Excellency Thomas Zeng Jingmu, Bishop of Yujiang; and of many others. The battle for the Lord at present is continuing in the heroic deeds of a very large number of bishops, priests, sisters and laymen who remain loyal today in Communist China and particularly in the dioceses of Baoding and Zhengding located in the Province of Hebei.

CHAPTER XIII

SINCERE WISHES

Lord, during the darkest depths of the war years filled, as the Chinese idiom says, "with the roar of guns and the smoke of gunpowder," when the Chinese Communists were storming Your Church, I prayed to You full of confidence saying, "... with Your aid I storm the barbican, and by the help of my God I leap over a wall." (Ps. 18:30). Truly, "You girded me with strength for war; You subdued my adversaries beneath me." (Ps. 18:40). It was no one else but You, O Lord, who not only allowed me to be thrown into jail and become a lowly prisoner for You over a quarter of a century, but also helped me frequently to gain laurels in the most terrifyingly adverse and dangerous circumstances and in the most lonely and difficult months and years of isolation. Finally, You restored my freedom.

I personally experienced the wonderful power You manifested through my weakness during the last few decades. While I felt impelled to write songs of praise to You, I seemed to hear in secret Your words of encouragement. On one occasion when some of the Pharisees asked You to rebuke those of Your disciples who were rejoicing and praising "God loudly for the display of power they had seen" (Lk.19:37), You replied, "If they were to keep silence, I tell you the very stones would cry out." (Lk. 19:40). But now I am drawing the history of my struggle to a close; I realize that the extent of Your power cannot be revealed in a few lines and that my words fail to express all I wish to say.

The Chinese Communist ruling clique and all their followers have caused great harm and sufferings not only on Your Church and believers, but also on the thoughts, minds and bodies of all the Chinese people. There is no need for doubt; their sins are truly both many and serious. They have directly and indirectly slaughtered countless numbers of people not only on the battlefields during those years of the so-called revolutionary war, but also by executions, torture, beatings, imprisonment, "criticism and struggle," and even the forced suicides of despairing victims during the various and unending political campaigns of their dictatorship. How many people have become their victims? Will anyone ever know? Fifty or a hundred million? Only You, O Lord, know the exact number!

At the present time, the Communist regime's murderous actions are most especially manifested on the generations yet to be born and still yet to be conceived. Under the pretext of controlling the population and improving the standard of living of the Chinese people by means of propaganda, persuasion, education, coercion, rewards and penalties, the Communist Government exerts a constant pressure on the people to put the policy of "one-child per couple" into practice. It requires all fertile married couples to practice birth control, namely, contraception, and forces them to use abortion when contraception fails. How many little ones have been already killed in silence, in their mothers' wombs? And how many little ones have even been deprived of their right to be conceived? I do not know the faces of the Communist officials, great or small, important or unimportant, who have performed these things and have been responsible for these crimes; nor can I picture them as they really are. But, at least, I can pray for them and implore You, O God, to forgive their sins and change their hearts.

Truly, the hour has come for the Chinese Communist rulers to review and re-evaluate the ideological system and the tyrannical dictatorship they believe in and exercise. They should at long last admit that because of their opposition to God, religion and the dignity of man, in such a fundamental way, their system is a gross error. They must acknowledge that because of the oppression of men's minds and spirits, hearts and bodies, their dictatorship is inhumane, unpopular, rejected by the people and therefore doomed to collapse. The should be able to see, with a little objectivity, the upheaval which has taken place in the Communist world during the recent past.

Practically, all the Communist dictatorial regimes of the countries in Eastern Europe have been swept onto the rubbish heap of history, and the liberated people there are building new, democratic and free countries on the ruins of Communism. The Soviet Union has collapsed like a house of cards, and after suffering seventy years of slavery, the Soviet people have begun enjoying the freedom of religion. Today, the Chinese Communists in power have been driven into a corner, besieged on all sides. They should yield to the facts and agree to learn a bitter lesson from the current world situation which grows increasingly unfavorable to them.

They must stop clinging to their irrational ideology of the "Four Basic Principles": "Socialist Road, People's Democratic Dictatorship, Communist Party's Leadership and Marxism-Leninism-Mao Zedong Thought." They should take into account my recommendations and my sincerest wishes to alter their attitude toward the Catholic Church and her faithful.

I most firmly believe that first of all, the Chinese Communists must stop persecuting the Church and must release unconditionally all imprisoned bishops, priests, sisters and laymen. They should cease sowing division and forcing the separation of Catholics from their religious leader, the Holy Father, the Pope. It is necessary for them to restore the confiscated churches, chapels and other Church property. My second wish is the dissolution of the "Chinese Catholic Patriotic Association" and all similar anti-Catholic organizations, established and controlled by the Communist Government. They must allow the members of these organizations to return to the welcoming bosom of the true Church, they must stop spreading subversion among the faithful or pursuing their efforts to destroy and uproot the presence of the Church in China, and they must avoid also all interference in her affairs and activities. My third wish is the recognition of the authority of the Holy Father and the Vatican over the Church in China, just as in the case with all the other countries of the world. My fourth wish is that they should truly and effectively implement religious freedom and worship not only in theory, but in name and in fact, in spirit and in truth. My fifth wish is that the Gospel should be freely proclaimed in all the counties and all the provinces of China, and that all Chinese people have the freedom to accept and believe in the Good News. My final wish is that the Chinese Communists forsake the darkness for the light and gain their own salvation by accepting Christ and His Mystical Body, the Catholic Church. O Lord, loving and almighty Jesus, please lead them together with all their followers to walk the bright road of conversion trodden by St. Paul, Your Apostle!

Lord Jesus, under Your direction and with Your support, the account of my struggle, *Dawn Breaks in the East,* can be at last considered finished. I offer it to the Blessed Virgin Mary and to You, Lord, with reverence and respect. And I entreat You to allow it not only to show the witness of my own personal struggle and of the graces I have received from You, but also to mani-

fest the witness of the high ideals and common feelings of all
Your soldiers in our time who have fought and still fight Communism to this day for You.

Those unforgettable years
Today I recall
With great excitement,
With deep gratitude.

The impressions of the past,
Engraved on my memory,
Came vividly before my eyes,
With made me reflect again and again.

In the police station
I held firmly to the truth;
At the public meeting
I presented my convictions passionately.

Having walked courageously into prison,
I strenuously corrected my early mistakes.
I endured tortures without flinching,
And remained faithful during criticism.

My three exiles to solitary confinement
Made me smell the fragrance of my monastic cell;
My prison term twice increased
Quickened my steps towards the victory.

At home my articles burst forth,
Like the spirit of running water;
In jail my poems were heaped up
With ideals towering like high mountains.

Neither did I walk out of prison
With my body bent;
Nor leave my country
With my head bowed.

With Your providential Wisdom, O Lord,
All of this opened the way to me;
And with Your great Power
All of this succeeded.

In the weakness of Your soldier,
You have displayed a miracle,
A miracle--silent,
But striking and brilliant!

Thank You, Lord Jesus, for evermore
For Your boundless kindness!
Please help all people of all nations
Obtain Your salvation!

BIOGRAPHICAL NOTES

*(This information was originally inserted in the "Application Form for
leaving the country for citizens of the People's Republic of China,"
which was filled in and submitted to the Public Security Bureau of
Suining County in the province of Sichuan on July 17, 1984.)*

1926 - 1932	I was born and grew up in the county town of Neijiang, Sichuan Province.
1932 - 1933	I moved with my mother to her mother's house in Tianlinchang, Anyue County. For six months I studied the prayer book in a Catholic primary school.
1934 - 1938	I moved again with my mother to Suining County and lived with my father. I received over a year of religious education. I then studied in a public elementary school for two and a half years.
1938 - 1944	I was admitted to the Catholic Benedictine Monastery at Sishan in Nanchong County in August 1938. I studied for three years in the Zhongyi Primary School, established by the monastery. After that I entered the provincial high school of the county and finished the first three years.
1944 - 1952	I moved with the monastery to 172 Yangshi Street in Chengdu. Having finished the last three years of study in Shude High School, I pursued the study of foreign languages, philosophy and some other courses in the monastery for four years. After a one-year novitiate, I professed my triennial vows and began my life as a Benedictine monk.
1952 – 1953	With the closure of the monastery, I returned home to my family in Suining. I helped my father in his small business to sell and repair eyeglasses.
1953 - 1955	I went back to Chengdu and lived at 184 Changshun Middle Street. I entered into partnership to open a grocery.
1955 - 1981	My opposition to the Communists' Catholic Reform Movement of the "Three-Autonomies" led to my arrest and my imprisonment. I was sentenced originally to 20 years in prison, but later five years were added. Having served my 25 years, I was released.
1981 - 1984	After leaving prison, I returned to Suining and lived in the house of my fourth brother Zhou Bengu. I set up at the side of the street the stall of a public letter writer.

PART III

FIRST COLLECTION OF POEMS

1963-1981

PREFACE

This is the first collection of my poetry, truly very small, which contains only a sample of 19 of my poems composed in prison. These poems were first collected in September 1991, and then revised in October of the same year by Ms. Joan Chen of New York. The English translation was completed in December by Ms. Cynthia Clark with the help of Ms. Sharon Ho, Professor of Chinese Studies at Pomona College in Claremont, California.

Later, the second collection appeared in September 1995 by Serenity, the same publishing house, under the title, *The Mountain Pierces The Blue Sky.* More that fifty of the 171 poems published there were composed in jail.

OFFICIAL ZHU OPENS
MY CELL

To the Tune of Ru Meng Ling
(Like a Dream)
In Solitary Confinement at the Nanchong Prison
August 1963

The chamberpot so full to overflowing,
And my cell smells foul as the abode of the dead.
Door opens, I am called out.
To Chu's questions, I remain unmoved.

Unmoved,
Unmoved,
No matter how the waves will roar!

A BUDDHIST MONK YIELDS, WHEN BEING HANDCUFFED

To the Tune of Ru Meng Ling
(Like a Dream)
Nanchong Prison, September 1966

In the chill night,
Under the fading moonlight,
In the course of the "struggle meeting,"
The Buddhist monk stoops.
He had meant to be heroic,
But under the handcuffing, so violent,
He sheds bitter tears.

Shedding tears,
Shedding tears,
To beg the Communists' forgiveness,
Who would not do so?

PRAISE TO ST. STEPHEN, FIRST MARTYR

In the Poetic Style of Qilu
Nanchong Prison, December 26, 1967

Long Church history stained with brightly-
colored blood,
Records this deacon's name in very first chapter.
Taking pains to wait on the tables
without complaint,
He preached the truth with courage exceptional.
Tolerating the stubborn stone to harm his body,
He besought the merciful King to forgive his enemy's sin.
Heavenly sky opened— Son of Man appeared,
All martyrs, in endless succession,
St. Stephen's path have followed.

ODE TO ST. JOHN, APOSTLE

In the Poetic Style of Qilu
Nanchong Prison, December 27,1967

Chaste flowers profusely bloom and yield fragrance;
Flowers and sincere love for the Lord
Accompanied Him to His untimely execution site.
At the lake you had insight to recognize your Master;
On the King's chest you reposed, a virtuous minister.
You, the disciple, received the privilege to serve His Virgin
*   Mother;*
As the eagle flying the high sky,
With your wonderful pen you touched the heavenly mysteries.
Your Wisdom, Longevity, Loyalty, and Chastity
*   deserve admiration,*
Your writings for the ages have nurtured
*   righteous men.*

EPIPHANY

In the Poetic Style of Qilu
Nanchong Prison, January 6, 1968

When Jesus was born in the City of David,
A strange star appears in the eastern sky.
The Magi's vision opens, gazing at the star,
And the sages coming to worship Him earnestly.
Gold, Myrrh, Frankincense—offerings for the Babe;
King, Man, God— all in one newly born.
These three kings may all the world follow,
Knowing salvation and singing praises to the Redeemer!

PRAISE TO OUR LADY OF SORROWS

In the Poetic Style of Qilu
Nanchong Prison, September 15, 1968

News never heard before—One physically lives
But the heart is in death's agony.
Acclaiming you, their Empress, martyrs are happy.
Seeing your Baby circumcised, you tasted bitterness;
Hearing Simeon's saddening prophecy, you worried.
Cruel crucifixion witnessed; you shed tears like rain,
The sharp sword pierced your heart,
Painful as though burning in fire.
A mother's sorrows overflow towards the ocean,
How profoundly you love the King of all peoples!

A PRISON SEARCH ON NEW YEAR'S EVE

To the Tune of Huan Xi Sha
(Yarn Washed in the Stream)
Peng'an Labor-Reform Camp
December 30, 1971

At year's end, the usual prison search.
Prisoner Chen arrived to check my clothes box,
My old overcoat! He touched, pressed,
His chest filled with suspicion.

Chen wanted scissors for a thorough search!
But Official Pu refused, and on that very spot
Saved me from the emergency!
My Nine-Point Declaration luckily preserved,
My thanks to Heaven!

(Note: A copy of my Nine-Point Declaration written in solitary confinement and submitted to the authorities of the Nanchong Prison on January 6, 1964, was hidden in the right shoulder of my old overcoat. Chen Zuobin, a chief prisoner of my group, had just been appointed one of the inspectors and Official Pu was in charge of the platoon.)

LAMENT OVER THE MANUSCRIPT OF MY "NINE-POINT DECLARATION"

To the Tune of Lang Tao Sha
(Waves Washing Sands)
Peng'an Labor-Reform Camp
January 5, 1972

With frequent prison searches executed strictly,
I found it hard to keep my treasured manuscript intact, safe;
Just six days ago it survived a narrow escape.

Now torn into many pieces, thrown into the toilet,
The pages destroyed by my own hands,
I suffer grief beyond description.

I should have been the first to perish,
Why should you die an untimely death?
My funeral odes unfinished; my tears keep falling!

My vow to the death before you is to carry out
Your spirit,
Your language!
I wish you rest in peace!

JINPING PRIMARY SCHOOL

To The Tune of Lang Tao Sha
(Waves Washing Sands)
Peng'an Labor-Reform Camp
January 14, 1974

To the primary school of Jinpingchang,
To repaint walls of the classrooms,
To leave our prison quarters we are ordered.
In the town, people's houses all like before. . .
Very poor—primitive and depressing.

Mao Zedong's portrait in military attire
Hangs on the front walls of the classrooms,
Several sheets of his quotations posted alongside.
Poisonous elements injected into the youth
       from childhood,
The thought makes me angry and sad.

CONSTRUCTING
THE FORGE

To the Tune of Cai Sang Zi
(Song of Picking Mulberries)
Peng'an Labor-Reform Camp
August 30, 1974

In building the forge all kinds of labors done urgently,
All day long we have been busy.
The labor very demanding; the time very long;
In just three days, I suffer numerous hardships.

One hand disabled; my body weak;
Shoulders with no strength at all:
It is hard to carry the cross.
Without complaints, without hurting,
In the footsteps of Jesus Christ,
I follow courageously!

NEW YEAR'S DAY

To the Tune of Huan Xi Sha
(Yarn Washed in the Stream)
Peng'an Labor-Reform Camp
January 1, 1975

Twenty-five cold winters pass swiftly
Like flowing water,
But the face of China remains red.
Under the cloudy sky on the chilly earth,
I pass this New Year's Day.

All these years, these endless years,
My physical body has been placed in jail.
When will my innocence be restored?
Will there be a spring
To offer my life for the Lord?

RECONSTRUCTION OF THE PRISON WALL

In the Poetic Style of Wulu
Peng'an Labor-Reform Camp
January 12, 1975

We rebuild an old prison wall,
And the Lord's Day is as busy for us as any other.
Our bodies tremble with the cold freezing winter,
The enshrouding fog hangs low over the building site.

Where is truth hiding?
In what direction will the sun rise?
I raise my head to pray to the Heavenly Father:
"May You drive away the fogs,
And save people from stupidity and craziness!"

MAO ZEDONG'S PORTRAIT

To the Tune of Ru Meng Ling
(Like a Dream)
Peng'an Labor-Reform Camp
May 12, 1975

Picking up stones on the mountain of Jinping,
Passing through the little town,
I look all around.
In almost every old house
Mao's portrait hangs on the wall.

Mao's portrait,
Mao's portrait,
His insanity has brought disaster
To the country and people!

FEELINGS ON THE "OCTOBER 1, NATIONAL DAY"

To the Tune of Xi Jiang Yue
(Moon over the Western River)
Peng'an Labor-Reform Camp
October 1, 1975

Endless bitter rains, desolate winds,
Behind the iron window,
Who is joyful in the cold cell?
Sighing in grief, I interrogate Heaven:
"Why is it that the people are still in distress?"

Every year I harbor hope,
Yet each year my hope vanishes like cloud and smoke.
May, in the coming autumn,
I not have to welcome October First.
Once again, to the Lord, I present my dear wish!

MY TWENTY YEAR CAPTIVITY

To the Tune of Jian Zi Mulan Hua
(The Magnolia)
Peng'an Labor-Reform Camp
November 7, 1975

Time passes swiftly,
For the Lord I have been years imprisoned.
Fighting in the north and south,
I have survived all troubles to come to Jinping.

When will I be martyred?
When will I walk out of prison to sing victory?
With delight I obey Heaven's order,
And again don military attire
To fight against the Red Spirit!

A GRACIOUS REFUSAL
TO FELLOW PRISONER, YAN JINLONG

To the Tune of Qing Ping Yue
(The Qing Ping Song)
Peng'an Labor-Reform Camp
November 13, 1975

I left the prison to carry sheaves of straw
In the company of gracious Mr. Yan.
Often discreetly expressing his good will,
Today he again approaches,
Trying to persuade me:

"In the meeting, if you could only say some nice thing,
Definitely your suffering will pass,
And the sun after the rain will shine over you!"

Politely declining his sincere advice,
I answered:
"It is really impossible for me to flatter the Communists
In order to seek peace!"

OFFICIAL WANG
ADVISES ME TO WRITE AN APPEAL

To the Tune of Pusa Man
(Beautiful Barbarians)
Peng'an Labor-Reform Camp
October 7, 1980

"If the legal case of increasing punishment
Can be appealed,
Perhaps the court would correct the error.
Yet, if you want to depart from prison
As soon as possible,
Resort to gentle words
When you make your appeal."

I have been summoned for investigation tonight;
The official has offered me this judicious advice.
With my ambition unharmed,
With my head unbowed,
I follow his earnest advice
As naturally as a river follows its course!

MY LETTER TO
MR. VINCENT YUAN NENGDING,
SR. ASSUMPTION JIANG QIFANG
AND SR. ANNA LEI JINGYUAN
RETURNED

To the Tune of Xi Jiang Yue
(Moon Over the Western River)
Peng'an Labor-Reform Camp
October 14, 1980

The letter—no one accepted it;
On the envelope the reason is made clear:
"Sr. Assumption and Sr. Anna Lei—
Whereabouts Unknown;
Mr. Vincent Yuan—Deceased!"

I have lost all books,
Lost all things before.
It is impossible to move back to Chengdu,
An old place now.
How many loyal and chaste persons
Luckily are still alive today?
I scratch my head,
Raising this question to Heaven--
Without answer!

(Note: All three of my old friends fought bravely for the Faith.
Sr. Assumption Jiang, the bravest one, was imprisoned and died
in a labor-reform camp in Sichuan Province in the 1970's. Sr.
Anna Lei passed away of illness in Chengdu, April 3, 1989.)

NEW YEAR WISHES

To the Tune of Yi Qin E
(Remembering the Beauty of Qin)
Peng'an Labor-Reform Camp
January 1, 1981

Roc's wings spread out,
Pushing through the clouds,
The fog,
Reaching to heaven.

Reaching to heaven,
Returning to paradise,
I am filled with great joy!

Winter clouds, severely cold,
I denounce them in strong words;
Spring light, glowingly warm,
I sing its praises with a loyal heart.

Singing praises with a loyal heart,
To the salvation of souls,
To the glorification of God
I offer all the rest of my days!

(Note: In Eastern legends, the Roc is a fabulous bird with great strength and enormous stature. Because of its flight so fast, so high and so long, it is a symbol of a bright future.)

APPENDIX I

THE DECLARATION OF NOVEMBER 4, 1951

At the neighborhood assembly of the
Yangshi Street Police Station in Chengdu

Note: After the loss of the original manuscript, this declaration
was rewritten on November 19, 1951, at the request of Fr.
Prior Raphael Vinciarelli, O.S.B., and then sent to Hong
Kong by Fr. Hildebrand Marga, O.S.B., and Fr. Paul Wu
Yong, O.S.B. At first, in May 1952, Fr. Prior Raphael in
Hong Kong translated it into French and gave it a title, a
subtitle, a preface and a postscript. After that, Fr. Gaetan
Loriers, O.S.B., translated the French into English. In the
spring of 1985, several months after my rejoining the
monastery at Valyermo, Br. Dominic Guillen, O.S.B., and
Fr. Gaetan delivered these translations to me, and I did
some changes and restored the missing paragraph. I
made a retranslation of the Chinese text. Accordingly,
this version is the same as the one which appeared in
Hong Kong in 1952 and as the following ones which
appeared in other places.

RELIGIOUS PERSECUTION IN CHINA

Profession of faith of a young Chinese Benedictine Monk

Up to the end of October 1951, the Chinese Benedictines
and their associates were able to stay clear of the schismatic
movement of the "Three Autonomies." Since they did not join
themselves to the "commission of reform," the attack against our
monks began. There followed a struggle which lasted for ten
days. The Communists wanted them to attend public meetings
of the commission of the "Three Autonomies." However, they
failed. The Communists ended up compelling them to take part
in the mass assemblies. These assemblies, which often gathered
together several hundred persons, were completely directed
against the Catholic Church.

One morning, the monks and their associates came and
asked their superior: "How should we answer? We are all being

called together this morning to denounce the Legion of Mary."
The superior replied: "Today they ask you to denounce the
Blessed Virgin Mary and tomorrow they will ask you to
denounce Jesus Christ." Then, they all went to confession and
came back saying: "Now we are ready; we are not afraid."

On the evening of November 4, there was a great public
meeting. The youngest monk, Br. Peter, aged 25, who had finished his first year of philosophy, was questioned in his turn by
the Communists. He knew that he would have to explain himself, sooner or later, once and for all. He had written out his profession of faith. He read it in a calm voice before this assembly
of several hundred persons, among whom there were also some
Catholics. The meeting was presided over by Communist officials.

Here is a faithful translation of his speech. In order to
understand well the concrete situation, the reader, who has not
experienced Communist religious persecution in China, must
realize that this persecution is very real and that the Communists
know, in a devilish way, how to alternate persuasion and force.
When indoctrination, which can last several months or more,
does not succeed in "brainwashing," to wit, "forcing acceptance
of their ideas," they have recourse to forced labor or prison and
torture. The Christians, who bravely resist the Communist persecution of religion, know that they risk being thrown into
prison, perhaps even dying there, as has happened in numerous
cases. They have the psychology and the strength of martyrs
and it is only in this light that their words take all their true
meaning.

Hong Kong, May 17, 1952

Comrades, Fellow Citizens and Fellow Catholics,

Before speaking of the question which we will discuss this
evening, I would like to make clear to you my identity. My
name is Zhou Bangjiu from Suining County in the North of
Sichuan Province. My family has been Catholic for several generations. For my part, I was baptized into the Catholic Church
in infancy. My father has a small business dealing in eyeglasses,
and my elder brother is a weaver. At the age of twelve, I entered
the Benedictine Monastery at Sishan, located outside the city of
Nanchong, with the goal of becoming a priest to preach the
Gospel of Christ. After my three years of primary school at Sis-

han, I spent the first three years of middle school at the provincial school of the same city. Coming to Chengdu in the summer of 1944, I finished the final three years of middle school at Shude Middle School. In the fall of 1947, after receiving my high school diploma, I returned here to the monastery to study Chinese literature, to take courses in Latin, English, French and higher mathematics, and at the same time, to receive the various teachings of Catholic doctrine: history, liturgy, Scripture and philosophy. I spent four years pursuing these studies.

I am deeply grateful to God for His great grace and infinitely merciful Providence, for having breathed into me the light of the truth of Jesus Christ, His unique Son, and for having made me understand in a profound way the true meaning of life. Today, with full knowledge of the facts and after mature deliberation, I am ready to assume my duty and my responsibility of being a witness to the truth of Jesus and to the purity of His Church, even though if you do not understand me, I risk becoming the target of your insults and criticisms.

To speak plainly, I cannot lightly follow the opinion of the masses in problems concerning religion, especially the Catholic religion. Regarding religious questions, such as "What is religion?", "What is the Catholic Church?" and "What are the dogma, laws, history and organization of the Catholic Church?", I venture to say that I certainly have more knowledge and a deeper understanding than you. Furthermore, I do my utmost, without ceasing, to conform my whole life to this high ideal. Therefore, with reference to our discussion, in all frankness, here is the position I uphold.

1.   On the subject of the "Three Autonomies Reform Movement". I cannot in any way participate in it. First, because this movement has never received, either before or after its inauguration, the approval of the one and only visible head of the Catholic Church, the Pope of Rome. Next, because in its present stage of development, this movement directly leads to separation from the Pope of Rome.
If you say that other Christians are already taking part in this reform movement, that is within the competency of the individual liberty of every one, and they are responsible for their own acts.
Are those who participate in this Reform Movement schis-

matics? Have they apostatized? I beg you to excuse me. I am not in a position to resolve these questions. Here, I only wish to express my personal position, and that is all.

2.   With regard to the Legion of Mary. I have never belonged to it. Since it is not an essential part of the Church, I might admit that the People's Government could dissolve it. However, I do not agree when this purely religious association is called "reactionary." The simple reason is that this organization has been recognized by the Pope, and the Pope would not allow the formation of a false religious association for political purposes with the design of opposing a country or a government.

If it is true that spies, special agents, or brigands have been found in the Legion of Mary, they are merely sham members. The Government of the People then has the right to punish them according to common law. Solely for this reason, however, one cannot consider the Legion of Mary as a "reactionary organization."

I know that my opinions are completely contrary to those of the "people". There is a real divergence between my point of view and yours. Since our views and our values are different, logic wants that we are naturally led to different, or even contrary conclusions.

The same result would occur, if we measure temperature with different thermometers. Suppose I use the Celsius thermometer and you use the Fahrenheit thermometer. If I measure the atmospheric temperature at 10 degrees Centigrade, you would have 50 degrees Fahrenheit on your thermometer. I do not claim that you are incorrect. In the same way, you cannot assert that I am wrong. Simply, our measuring instruments are different. Although the standards may differ by which men judge truth and falsehood, right and wrong, good and evil, and men's words and deeds in human society, truth is one and remains always the same. Consequently, even if this example, taken from nature, is far from satisfactory, it is no less clear and unalterable that different instruments of measure produce different results.

Therefore, as to the question which concerns us tonight, I do not wish to persuade you to uphold the same belief as mine, though one of us must be wrong necessarily. Since my values are unknown to you, you may have no choice but to keep your own position and reach your own conclusions.

In other words, inasmuch as my ideas on these religious questions do not coincide with yours, nor with the decrees of the People's Government, then, as a citizen of the People's Republic of China, I must submit to your judgment and to the punishment imposed by the People's Government. This judgement and this punishment, according to your point of view, are truly just, consistent and even necessary. As for me, I will not harbor any resentment or any hatred; I desire only to accept all with joy and enthusiasm. If it is the holy will of God to have so disposed of my life from all eternity, then how can I refuse to drink this cup of bitterness? Moreover, if I desire to be a true disciple of Jesus, I must follow in His footsteps by carrying my cross and climbing Mount Calvary so that I may glorify His Holy Father and at the earliest possible moment find my rest in Him.

Whether you understand me or not matters little; as long as God, who searches the minds and hearts of men, understands me. That is enough for me, and it is the only thing that counts.

You will probably find my beliefs strange and incomprehensible. If you please, you may say bluntly that my thoughts are "backward and reactionary." If you sincerely believe that belief in the existence of God is "backward and reactionary" thinking, then my thinking truly is "backward and reactionary". Furthermore, I have made up my mind to remain "backward and reactionary" for eternity. If you say that I am intoxicated with "slavish education," and if you claim that the education of our holy religion is a "slavish education," then, I regret not having received an education still more profoundly "slavish." If you say that I have too much veneration for "foreigners" and that I put too much trust in them to the point of allowing myself to be deceived by them, then, you must know that there is for me no other "foreigner" of whom you speak than Jesus Christ, a Jew and the founder of the Catholic religion. In Him I not only believe, but also I adore Him, and I wish to live totally by Him and for Him. If you say that I have been poisoned by the "imperialist" to such a high degree as to use language so shocking to your ears and so contrary to your opinions, even to the point of wishing to become his "running dog," then, you must know that this "imperialist" is no other than He, the Jew, Jesus Christ, whom no one can conquer. At present, my only regret is that I have not yet reached the total likeness to Christ, nor known the complete transformation to a true "running dog" for Christ.

Consequently, I feel unworthy and ashamed to bear the glorious title you give me.

Because of what I have said, I would ask you not to take me for a fanatic, nor for a miserable one who has been poisoned, nor even for a man who is drowning and calling for help. Let us speak calmly and frankly. My head is completely calm and clear, my soul is impregnated with the truth of Jesus and with His inexhaustible goodness. To sum up, I know who Jesus Christ is; I fully understand where man comes from and where he goes after death. This gives me a more profound knowledge of the meaning of human life.

Therefore, do not worry about me. Do not try to offer a hand of sympathy to save me from what are my chains of truth. I only ask you to do with me whatever you like, according to the common judgment of the people. I deliver my body to you, but I keep my soul for the good God, for Him, who has created me, nourished me, redeemed me and loved me.

My talk has been long and disorganized. This evening I have wasted your precious time; please excuse me.

That is all.

When Br. Peter finished his profession of faith, the assembly did not dare to show its feelings. However, one Communist woman sitting at the chairman's table simply said: "I admire your attitude, but what a pity that it is not for the truth!"

On leaving the meeting, a non-Christian gentleman said in a low voice to one of our Catholic workers: "This young man has spoken very well, really very well, very well,... He dares to resist the Government! But what a shame...he is so young!"

Finally, the chief of police called together our monks and their associates one day and said: "You are all so young; you dare to resist the Government and you have no arms... You resist only with spiritual arms!"

The monks were then left alone, at least until the time of the expulsion of all the foreign monks.

APPENDIX II

THE APPEAL OF MARCH 8, 1981

To the Peng'an County People's Court for the review of my sentence to an additional five-year imprisonment

To obtain the rescission of your wrong decision of September 1977 concerning the extension of my sentence, I submitted to you two appeals in October and December of last year. On the first day of this month, I learned from Mr. Deng, Chief of the Section of Discipline and Education in our camp, that it was because your Court would like to have time to reexamine carefully my whole case that I had not received any response from your Court even after this long delay. In spite of harboring some regrets about such action by your Court, I think it necessary to state briefly but clearly my position and viewpoint. I want to point out the facts of the matter with the help of the following four aspects. I hope your Court will conscientiously examine my case in a positive and realistic spirit, not bringing hostility, misunderstanding or prejudice against the Catholic religion, and in this way, return a just verdict as soon as possible.

(1) Concerning the so-called question, "Admitting my crimes":

I was arrested and sentenced only because I had resolutely defended the Holy Catholic Faith, which was gravely undermined by the "Three Autonomies Reform Movement." The Vatican is the supreme organization of the Church and the Pope in Rome is the highest authority. This is one of the foundations of the creed of the Catholic religion. Yet, under the cloak of the eloquent slogans "Self-government, self-support and self-propagation" and "opposition to Imperialism and Love of the Motherland," the "Three Autonomies Reform Movement" forced us to sever our relationship with the Vatican and the Pope. The Church's canon law has stipulated long ago in explicit terms our duty to respect our religious elders and our absolute avoidance of wanton attack and slander against them. With regard to the negligence of some religious elders, it also directs us to ask the authorities of the Church to deal with these men seriously, but through the appropriate channels provided for by the ecclesiastical rules. However, the "Three Autonomies Reform Movement" urged us to fight, accuse, insult and calumniate all those elders who were in reality good and competent. Isn't this a brazen violation of and a public provocation to Catholic dogmas and laws? How can it be viewed as due manifestation of respect for and protection of religious freedom? How can a resolute struggle against such a "Three Autonomies Reform" be taken as a "criminal offense" aimed at overthrowing the proletarian dictatorship? On the contrary, it is an absolutely just and lawful action in defense of our religion. It is a sacred, lofty and inshirkable duty. This is a responsibility for me and for every other Catholic who treasures his own faith.

The "Letter to All the Catholic Clergy and Laity in China" that I previously wrote was based on the dogmas and canons of the Church. It was an objective analysis both of the current situation of the Church in China and of the damage caused her by the "Three Autonomies Reform." It was written with the purpose of persuading the People's Government to change its policies in regard to the Church so that she could enjoy proper unity, freedom and honor. This was in no way an "anti-revolutionary activity in the garb of religion."

I did not belong to the Legion of Mary. Despite this, I knew full well that it was a purely religious organization for fervent Catholics. It had been set up many years ago with the purpose of honoring our Holy Mother Blessed Mary, advancing Catholic spiritual life and faith, and evangelization. Moreover, it had been approved by the highest authorities of the Church. Up to this day, I still hold that in the early winter of 1951 at the mass assembly in my original residence in Chengdu, my speech concerning the legality and purity of the Legion of Mary was totally correct and was the voice of a Catholic with good judgment.

As a loyal Catholic, I can do nothing but show my allegiance to the faith, not tolerating even a hint of betrayal. And that is why, with good reason, I will never regard as "crimes" what I said and did in the past in defense of the Church. As a result of these actions, I have over many years endured all kinds of suffering and hardship. I have been jailed, sentenced to long-term imprisonment, criticized and struggled against innumerable times, scolded, beaten, cursed and insulted. Several times I have been handcuffed, shackled, placed in solitary confinement, penalized with small and big demerits, received two extensions of my sentence, and had my right hand crippled... Despite all this, if necessary, I am ready to follow my countless brothers and sisters who have been martyred for their faith throughout the past 1,900 years. If this happens, I shall be able to write, with my blood, additional pages in the brilliant and glorious history of our beloved Church, and make my meager contribution to the spread of the truth and to the salvation of all humankind.

(2) Concerning the so-called question, "Accepting transformation":

Being a faithful Catholic, I must insist on the Catholic position, and in no way accept that of Marxism-Leninism which is atheistic. For more than twenty years I have taken a personal course and placed myself outside the prison activities, such as "political studies," "speaking at sessions," "mid-year review," "annual summary appraisal," "reciting *The Quotations of Chairman Mao,"* and "purchasing *The Selected Works of Mao Zedong.* This attitude is quite fair and reasonable, and should be understood, respected and allowed in a country where religious freedom is guaranteed. Regrettably, in my case, this behavior became a cause of attack and grounds for two additional sentences. I hope that your Court will carefully reflect and judge whether what has been done to me in prison is right or wrong, compatible or incompatible, with the spirit of "rule by law," so often mentioned in recent years.

As far as I myself am concerned, there is no reason to deny that love for the Catholic faith is ten thousand times more important than love for my own life. I am willing and ready to pay the highest price and make the greatest sacrifice for this loyalty.

(3) Concerning the so-called question, "The first extension of my sentence":

One day in the summer of 1966, in the First Provincial Prison of Nanchong, I refuted the defamatory remarks which Ni Huashan, an inmate of my group, had launched in my face to slander the Catholic Church and her high dignitaries. About two weeks later, Official Lin, in charge of discipline and education in our company, organized a public meeting of our small group to criticize me. This continued for four days, and during the course of these sessions I rebutted point by point their various attacks and calumnies. In addition, I composed a poem and recited it at the meeting to show my feelings of boundless reverence and gratitude for Jesus Christ, Our Saviour. Unfortunately, this was

perceived as an "attacking speech" and a "reactionary poem." In
September of that same year the poem served as the main basis
of a five-year prolongation of my sentence.

When the Catholic Church, her clergy and myself were
obliged to suffer serious and groundless attacks, why should I
not have the right to refute and defend? How could a little poem
that evidently talked only about my ideals be willfully distorted
as a slander on the Communist Party? To facilitate the work of
the Honorable Court and to help it to make a correct and just
evaluation, I would like to present a copy of this poem which I
still remember very well:

"Almighty Son of God, good Jesus,
You descended to earth as a slave to save mankind.
Worshipping the Lord, honoring Your parents,
You set a holy model for us;
Bestowing Your benevolence, preaching Your doctrine,
You transformed our narrow and blind hearts.

Oh, Master, You died on the Cross
To ratify the New Covenant;
I, Your disciple, accept the Good News,
Walking the Way with confidence.
Thankful for Your loving-kindness,
Defending Your honor,
Only to be imprisoned, insulted-
Now I am ready to lay down my life for You!"

(4) Concerning the so-called question, "The second extension of
my sentence handed down in September 1977":

In my first appeal, submitted to your Court last October, I had
already explained clearly how the extension of my penalty, suffered three and a half years ago, had resulted directly from my
refusal to purchase and study the fifth volume of *The Selected
Works of Mao Zedong.* I need not repeat it here. In order to
protest strongly, I rejected the written judgment, as I had done at
the time of my first added penalty. This time it was because of
several fellow prisoners of my small group, at the officials' beck
and call, suddenly seizing me by the hand that my fingerprints
were forcibly put on the original written judgment. This, of
course, never meant that I had agreed with the wrong verdict.

I remember that in the beginning of 1976, the disciplinary
official of our company, Mr. Jiang, and one of the responsible
officials of our camp, Mr. Song, mentioned to me the following

two events during their interrogation.

The first event happened at the outset of 1971. During the time of that annual summary evaluation in the First Provincial Prison of Nanchong, I wrote fifty words in eight sentences without rhyme to express my steadfastness in faith and loyalty to Jesus Christ. But my words were misrepresented as a "reactionary poem." Were they "reactionary" or not? Were they "hostile" or not? Your Court by itself can surely draw its own proper conclusion as long as it examines carefully and deliberate attentively on the documents referring to the extension of my sentence prepared that year by Official Jiang.

The second event took place in the fall of 1972. My responses to Ren Gongbi, a prisoner of my group, had been regarded as provocative to him. After careful reflection, I came to realize that this prisoner, acting at the order of Official Pu of our platoon, had come to me with a hidden intention of inquiring of me privately about some matters connected with the Church and thus of getting my responses so that he could accuse me and lead to an increase of my punishment. This was a trap laid to frame me. My words were intentionally misconstrued as "agitation." This kind of action is scarcely consonant with the open and above-board methods always advocated by the Communist Party and the People's Government. How can a judgment reached in these conditions be fair, just, rational and legal? Moreover, it was a very obvious error, known to all, that following the failure to force a Catholic to purchase and study *The Selected Works of Mao Zedong,* an added penalty was inflicted upon such a faithful believer. Is it very useful now to persevere in this error? Is this a way of manifesting the spirit of "rule by law"? This truly perplexes me.

During these recent years much has been said about the policy of redressing all unjust, false and wrongful cases as soon as possible and about applying this policy to all the victims who have a right to expect some thing. For this reason, though I had not intended to write my first appeal last October, I submitted to the explicit advice of the responsible official here involved. Since my twenty-five year imprisonment had already expired and had become a matter of the past, I would not have mentioned the two previous cases again. It was only because I had recently learned that your Court was going to reconsider and re-evaluate "thoroughly" my "whole case" that I felt obliged to refer briefly to the past events.

Indeed, there are some things that seem incomprehensible to me. Why after failure in forcing him to change his behavior, were all means exhausted to find every possible excuse to extend again and again the term of imprisonment of a loyal Catholic, unshakably faithful to his sacred faith, who would never under any circumstances "admit his crimes," or "accept reformation"? For more than two years now the Constitution and the new criminal laws have been issued and put into effect. At the same time, according to newspaper reports, some of the central leaders in Peking have never stopped repeating: "Freedom of religion is guaranteed for the people", "There are no ideological prisoners in China", "Everyone is equal before the laws", "A court's judgment should be based on facts and made in the light of the law", "All the unjust, false and wrongful cases must be amended", etc. Why are the two appeals submitted during the last five months by a Catholic, who has already been imprisoned for twenty-five years, and whose additional sentence was evidently wrong from all possible angles, being shelved indefinitely and ignored? An attempt is still going on to seek excuses for perpetuating the wrong judgment inflicted upon him three years ago.

A quarter of a century in prison is but a very short time, a moment in the long river of history of both the human race and the Church. It cannot be reckoned a great cost to pay in defending and upholding everlasting truth. However, on the basis of the present policies of the Communist Party: "seeking truth from facts", "acting in accordance with the law", and "correcting all mistakes", truly it is time to end this kind of injustice.

Consequently, I sincerely hope your Court will act quickly to correct this case of wrong judgment. Please do not hesitate, shirk, or delay. Please do not keep an innocent victim of many, many years in the same suffering state. On the contrary, I beg you earnestly to reach a new verdict as soon as possible and to rescind the original one.

Forgive me if what I have said offends you. With all sincerity, I submit this appeal to you, to the respectful Peng'an County People's Court, and earnestly look forward to your instructions and your decision.

Appealing: Zhou Bangjiu
From the second company of the Jinping Labor-Reform Camp, March 8, 1981.

APPENDIX III

THREE POEMS

BALLAD TO JINGSHAN PARK

To the Tune of Lang Tao Sha
(Waves Washing Sands)
Peking, China; November 6, 1984

Having ascended the Ten Thousand Springs Pavilion
(Wanchunting),
I look down at the capital city
With joy in body and in mind.
Forbidden City, unfolding before my eyes,
You should not be pleased with yourself:
Gone away are the Ming and the Qing Dynasties!

The Beihai (North Lake) stretching out on the right,
With water sparkling and crystal-clear;
The Zhongnanhai (1) seems cold and deserted.
Red Imperial Palace,
What will your end be?
You must not repeat the history of Zhongzhen! (2)

---

(1) The Zhongnanhai, situated at the front side of Jingshan Park, in the front of the Beihai and on the right of the Imperial Palace (the Forbidden City), is the Red Imperial Palace of the supreme authorities of the Chinese Communist Party and Government, a forbidden and top-secret area.

(2) Zhongzhen was the last Emperor of the Ming Dynasty. He died by hanging himself on a locust-tree in Jingshan Park on March 19, 1644, when Li Zicheng, leading his insurgent troops, stormed into Peking.

MY BEST WISHES OF HAPPINESS TO YOU, JIANG YUN, MY DEAR GRANDNIECE, ON THE OCCASION OF YOUR MARRIAGE TO CHEN WENDONG

In the Poetic Style of Siyan Shi
St. Andrew's Abbey, California, USA
December 8, 1995

Perfectly suited to each other,
You both have flown side by side;
May the search for truth and good
Be your common ideal!

CONGRATULATIONS

To His Eminence Ignatius Cardinal Kung Pin-mei, Bishop of
Shanghai, on the occasion of the celebration of his 97th
Birthday at his reunion with His Eminence, the new
Cardinal Paul S. Shan, S.J., Archbishop of
Kaohsiung, Taiwan, Republic of China.

To the Tune of Zhegu Tian
(The Sky of Partridges)
St. Andrew's Abbey
July 3, 1998

Your thirty years in the great furnace
Are like so many blessings upon you.
Because of your ardent loyalty,
You have come to the United States
To enjoy your advanced age.
Honored with a Cardinal's hat,
Your example shines in the world,
As a lamp set forth in the house.

Welcoming your dear friend,
Filled with joy,
You pray together with him,
In the union of one voice,
For the humble transformation of Peking.
If only the Holy Spirit would descend
Upon the Chinese Mainland
So that the whole country may celebrate
    your centenary
In Shanghai, your native city!